FONDA ON FILM

FONDA ON FILM

THE POLITICAL MOVIES OF JANE FONDA

NELSON PRESSLEY

Published by Chicago Review Press Incorporated
814 North Franklin Street
Chicago, Illinois 60610
ISBN 978-1-55652-257-4

Library of Congress Control Number: 2026930242

Cover design: Jonathan Hahn
Cover images: (from top) *The Electric Horseman*, Moviestore Collection Ltd. / Alamy Stock Photo; *Coming Home*, RGR Collection / Alamy Stock Photo; *9 to 5*, Moviestore Collection Ltd. / Alamy Stock Photo; *The China Syndrome*, Pictorial Press Ltd. / Alamy Stock Photo

Typesetting: Nord Compo

Printed in the United States of America

CONTENTS

PROLOGUE

There were glimmerings of emergent feminism. I think Jane Fonda saw to that. She never played a secondary part to the male leads. Every part was . . . it evolved from something less to something more.

—Julie Christie, in the 2003 documentary *A Decade Under the Influence*

Late March 1979: a high school kid in Newark, Delaware, is startled to be seventy miles downwind of Three Mile Island, the Harrisburg, Pennsylvania, nuclear plant where an "accident" is triggering a national panic and galvanizing the anti-nuke movement.

Of course the threat feels real. The kid's generation had grown up with duck-and-cover drills during America's midcentury Atomic Age, scrunching down in school hallways, heads between knees. Theirs was the era of stockpiled annihilation, the frigid comfort of "mutually assured destruction."

Deadly radiation cloud drifting their way? Sure. They'd been waiting. In the college town of Newark, plenty of people packed and fled.

Plus, the kid had just been spooked by the movie *The China Syndrome*, a nuclear power exposé that worked exactly like a horror film. Jack Lemmon plays a conservative power plant engineer, Michael Douglas is a liberal TV cameraman, and Jane Fonda is a lively but lightweight features reporter keen to graduate into hard news. The picture, with its realistic-looking nuclear facility growling and looming like a monster, sounded alarms about the loose regulation of nukes.

Then *bam*: Three Mile Island, validating the movie less than two weeks after its release. The picture's argument was clinched in the dazzling closing scene, improvised by Fonda and performed in a single unflinching take. It felt exactly like breaking news.

Barely a month later the student got on a bus to the No Nukes rally in Washington, DC. Consumer advocate Ralph Nader, California governor / nascent presidential candidate Jerry Brown, New York congresswoman Bella Abzug, musicians Joni Mitchell and Jackson Browne: the country was engaged and the headliners were there, led by movie star Jane Fonda. A pressing issue was being hashed out in the great American public square. The Harrisburg chaos ignited it. *The China Syndrome* had called it. A template was stamped upon the student's consciousness about the civic potential when art and activism overlap.

And he—I—thought: Impressive. Jane Fonda is *on it*.

Fonda and husband Tom Hayden at the May 1979 No Nukes rally in Washington, DC. *ZUMA Press Inc. / Alamy*

This project is about how, for a sliver of time, Jane Fonda melded movies and activism as effectively as any screen actor ever has. Acclaimed as she is, Fonda gets too little due for the short, sharp sequence of films that bloomed in the mid-1970s with the war-based *Julia* and *Coming Home* and persisted through the early 1980s with her economics and workplace movies, the forgotten *Rollover* and the undying *9 to 5*. She's been too famous for too long for too many other things.

Right on cue: when I started this project in 2019, Fonda delivered an autumn surprise, moving to Washington and leading weekly rallies on the US Capitol's East Lawn. She donned a flame-red coat and banged the climate crisis drum on what she called Fire Drill Fridays, a name drawn from Naomi Klein's book *On Fire: The (Burning) Case for a Green New Deal.* All that fall, Fonda made headline-grabbing political theater of getting arrested.

Fonda sparked Fire Drill Fridays as the issue hit a tipping point. *Climate emergency* was named Word of the Year by Oxford Dictionaries. *Time* magazine dubbed sixteen-year-old Swedish climate activist Greta Thunberg—the inspiration for Fonda's four-month move to Washington—as its Person of the Year. In Australia, 2019 closed with the biggest evacuations in the country's history as blazes and smoke from over a hundred wildfires overwhelmed Victoria and New South Wales, punctuating the hottest, driest season on record.

Almost exactly a year after Fonda's final Capitol Hill rally wrapped, her structured, instructional civil disobedience was obliterated by the wild incivility of the January 6, 2021, insurrection. Many of the 1960s–70s movies I was revisiting—Fonda's and others'—were eerily in tune with the spigot of berserk headlines as Trump flumed down a newer, deeper Nixonian gully. Hanoi Jane's wacky era was back with a vengeance. As those breezes blew between the decades, I kept the window open.

But this twenty-first-century resurgence of Activist Jane, right in the thick of Trump's long bull-goose-loony act, challenged my original goal: to keep the movies front and center.*

* One solution: relegating a lot of the madcap political echoes to footnotes.

Fonda did not invent the consciousness-raising movie, of course. But her twisty path remains unique. It began at the end of old Hollywood in the 1960s and didn't really take flight until after the ballyhooed 1967–77 "New Hollywood" era, when a battery of maverick male moviemakers—Francis Ford Coppola, Martin Scorsese, Warren Beatty, Alan Pakula, Peter Bogdanovich, Hal Ashby, and more, the *Easy Riders, Raging Bulls* of Peter Biskind's 1998 cornerstone New Hollywood history—steadied a town in chaos. The studio system had collapsed, and new, movie-ignorant corporate conglomerates were desperate for creative direction.

That New Hollywood was not Fonda—she didn't direct, didn't write. But, on top of acting at platinum heights (two Best Actress Oscars in the 1970s), she formed a production company, named it IPC Films after the Indochina Peace Campaign she'd created with soon-to-be husband Tom Hayden, and developed politically informed, of-the-moment stories. She was influenced by the New Hollywood auteurs and, earlier, by the old Hollywood that had made an icon of her father, Henry Fonda. She also was marked indelibly by her 1960s moviemaking in France. The connections flow left and right. The journey is a learning sequence.

This, then, is about a lot of movies—Fonda and non-Fonda films—and about how her most exemplary work was formed by her increasingly rugged on-the-ground politics. On both fronts, acting and activism, it's the story of earning her stripes with the public, from *F.T.A.* ("Fuck the Army") to *9 to 5*.

1

SHE USED TO BE A MOVIE STAR, OR IT'S THE PICTURES THAT GOT SMALL

Movies take time. And we don't have time.

—Jane Fonda, during a 2019 Fire Drill Fridays "Teach-In Thursday"

By the time Patricia Bosworth published her Jane Fonda biography in 2011, she had known Fonda since the 1960s when they were both rising actors, a pursuit Bosworth soon quit for journalism. That familiarity put Bosworth in a reasonable position to make this sweeping claim: "She's a genuine American icon who *won't be remembered for her movies* but rather for her outsize serial lives" (italics added).

Forgetting Fonda's movies would be a shame, for in her Hollywood prime Fonda melded radical activism and A-list moviemaking as virtually no actor has ever managed. "The most politically outspoken star in Hollywood history," film critic J. Hoberman declared in a 2001 retrospective. It's a title of dubious value, a double-edged sword cutting hard both ways. Being this kind of figurehead comes at a price.

One rainy November afternoon in 2019, a Washington tourist—an older man, part of a group from the Midwest passing between the Capitol and the Supreme Court—filmed the arrest of actor Diane Lane and other Fire Drill Friday activists. Fonda watched from the sidewalk; she had already been arrested three times and spent a night in jail. One more arrest risked incarceration for a month or ninety days.

"And over there in the red coat," the tourist narrated into his phone. "That's Hanoi Jane."

Ah, *Hanoi Jane.*

It has gone on for decades, Fonda's apology tour for her infamous 1972 photo perched on a North Vietnamese antiaircraft position, and for recording radio messages urging US forces in Vietnam to reconsider their mission. Still, even bogged down with the heaviest political baggage in Hollywood history, few movie stars have ever enjoyed as much artistic success.

"You'll never catch me now," Katharine Hepburn told Fonda after Hepburn picked up her fourth Best Actress Oscar for *On Golden Pond.* They would have been tied had Hepburn lost and Fonda won a third Oscar for her supporting role in the same movie, which she coproduced and spearheaded as a project for her father. Hepburn, Meryl Streep, Bette Davis, and Greer Garson are the only women with more Best Actress Oscar nominations than Fonda. That makes her one of the most formidable Hollywood stars of all time.

Yet *she won't be remembered for her movies.*

"This is a stupid fucking actress," fabled American journalist and Vietnam reporter David Halberstam volunteered to Bosworth before his death in 2007. A full-blown Jane-hating subculture has thrived for decades. She's been targeted by such artifacts as urinal stickers, and reviled at the US Naval Academy by ritualized bedtime cries of "Good night, Jane Fonda!" with a group response of "Good night, bitch!"

That Hanoi Jane blowback is one of two headwinds she's sailed straight into for decades. The other is the knee-jerk critique whenever stars speak up as citizens. "No one voted for you. Shut up and dribble," Fox News host Laura Ingraham said of NBA superstar LeBron James in 2018, after James and fellow NBA star Kevin Durant released a video critical of Donald Trump.

Comedian Ricky Gervais rebooted the attitude as he hosted the Golden Globes in the thick of election year 2020. "You're in no position to lecture the public about anything," Gervais scolded the celebrity audience during his opening monologue. "You know nothing about the world. Most of you spent less time in school than Greta Thunberg." Columnist Megan McArdle agreed the next day: "The people on that stage are already better looking than most mere mortals, and richer, and more famous, and better loved. But somehow that isn't enough; they also want credit for being more moral than everyone else."

"Actors, you see, are not trained to take responsibility for what they say," film historian David Thomson declared in *The Whole Equation.* "That's why politics eats them up." And former *New Yorker* editor Tina Brown sniffed in a 2005 *Washington Post* column, "I love looking at Angelina Jolie (and I believe that she cares), but on Africa I'd rather hear from Paul Theroux."

Album / Alamy

Even Tom Hayden—a leading 1960s political radical (author of the Port Huron Statement and one of the Chicago Seven) who became a California state senator, and who was Fonda's husband from 1973 to 1990—displayed striking hostility to his ex-wife's lifelong enterprise during a 2008 interview with author Steven Ross. "By playing to celebrity you undermine democracy by turning citizens into fans," Hayden theorized.*

The antipolitical backlash was tidily captured as Francis Davis interviewed legendary *New Yorker* film critic Pauline Kael at the end of Kael's career. Like the old MGM honcho Louis B. Mayer, they wrinkled their noses at *messages*, taking a special swipe at Fonda's 1978 Vietnam picture *Coming Home* and knocking what they dubbed the "cinema of good intentions."

> DAVIS: It's as though we want movies to be good for us, to be medicinal in some way—
>
> KAEL: Yes, isn't it awful?
>
> DAVIS: Instead of just being pleasurable.

But Fonda gets it. "Whether we like it or not," she wrote in *What Can I Do?*, her 2020 Fire Drill Fridays journal, "our society is very celebrity focused, and having a famous person publicly join a movement helps bring the press out and expand the reach of the message."

The bigger problem is that people tend not to think about her 1970s movies *at all*, due to the glare from her spectacular shape-shifting stardom.

In a 2011 profile, *New Yorker* writer Hilton Als introduced her as "the actress, philanthropist, feminist, political activist, model, Christian,

* A counterargument: Plato's trepidations about artists notwithstanding, it's in fact a civic good when celebrity artists thoughtfully incorporate politics into movies, plays, music, books, etc.; see Shakespeare and Arthur Miller, Anna Deavere Smith and Lin-Manuel Miranda. It's less good when American democracy, intoxicated by how even warped celebrity can monopolize public attention and invigorate antipathies, devolves into mindless frothing fandom; see Trump. Hayden was right—but facing the wrong way.

blogger, fitness advocate, licensing magnate, and memoirist"—understandably fractionalizing "actress" as one-tenth of a mushroomed identity. It's a writer's way of throwing up his hands, recognizing there's no way to embrace the whole megillah.

And it's true: JaneLand is almost unmappably vast.

Its first flags were planted by a well-born Hollywood kid, a magazine cover girl, and a screen ingenue debuting at age twenty-three in *Tall Story*, a 1960 romantic comedy costarring Anthony Perkins. By 1962 she was the subject of D. A. Pennebaker's documentary, simply titled *Jane*, which studied the emerging personality during a Broadway flop. Her 1960s output included everything from flip, swinging romances to expat movies she made in French. In 1972 she won her first Oscar for *Klute*, then skipped Hollywood for an activist fact-finding tour. She toted a camera through Vietnam to make her own documentary, *Introduction to the Enemy*.

By the 1990s she completely dropped out of acting for fifteen years to be Mrs. Ted Turner.* While married to the media mogul and Atlanta Braves owner, Fonda was seen doing the tomahawk chant and chop at Braves games, a belittling gesture she quickly gave up. The Turner phase was "a wildly contradictory part of her third act in our public imagination," Haley Mlotek reflected in 2018.

Grace and Frankie, her sitcom with Lily Tomlin, ended its 2015–22 run as Netflix's longest-running series to date. In 2023 Fonda starred in no less than three movies. "Even at the height of my career—whenever that was, I guess in the '70s—I never had three movies in one year," she told the *Hollywood Reporter*.

In 2024 she made headlines at age eighty-six for her eye-grabbing outfit at Cannes: "Rocks red lipstick and sparkling jumpsuit," noted *Page Six*. Los Angeles County declared April 30 "Jane Fonda Day" in honor of her activism, only to change the date when South Vietnamese Americans complained that April 30 was Black April day, marking the fall of Saigon—*not*, this constituency argued, a fit day to fete Hanoi Jane.

* During the January 2, 2020, Teach-In Thursday hosted by Fonda on Facebook Live, a question about the media's climate coverage comes from "Ted in Montana." After the panelists reply, Fonda pivots toward the iPhone camera and asks, "Ted of Montana—did I used to be married to you?"

Colossal malleability, never-ending controversy: that inevitably becomes the story. "Most Americans over the age of fifty associate Jane Fonda's name with the war," Mary Hershberger wrote in 2005's *Jane Fonda's War: A Political Biography of an Antiwar Icon.* Hershberger documented how that public awareness is built on anti-Fonda efforts that exploit the Internet's easy amplification of fakery, and how anti-Jane-ism became part of a propaganda campaign that transcends movies. "Jane Fonda's name has become intimately bound up with a myth intended to intimidate democratic opposition to U.S. military ventures," Hershberger wrote.

Hershberger also noted the fascinating flip side: "In 1973, after she went to Hanoi, the Gallup poll first listed her as one of the most admired women in America, a position that she held for years."

That's right—it was *after* the stigma of "Hanoi Jane" that Fonda achieved the only Hollywood power that matters: economic leverage. She not only survived the flap, she took control, and did it by acting *as an activist*, fulfilling in her own way Pauline Kael's famous prediction in her 1969 *New Yorker* review of *They Shoot Horses, Don't They?*

Kael, an expansive, slashing, lyrical critic, was over the moon about Fonda's performance in the gloomy late-1960s zeitgeist movie about a grueling Great Depression dance marathon. "Jane Fonda stands a good chance of personifying American tensions and dominating our movies in the seventies," Kael wrote, "as Bette Davis did in the thirties." Kael envisioned more riveting performances of devastating characters like the movie's suicidal Gloria: "The strongest role an American actress has had on the screen this year," Kael declared, adding that "Jane Fonda goes all the way with it."

For the next decade, Fonda *did* personify American tensions onscreen. Her producing arm was IPC Films, the initials plainly drawn from her antiwar organization Indochina Peace Campaign. By 1982, the *New York Times* acknowledged the power of IPC Films' output: "Since 1977, IPC—alone or in combination with other independent film companies—has produced five movies: 'Coming Home,' 'The China Syndrome,' '9 to 5,' 'Rollover' and 'On Golden Pond,'" Aljean Harmetz wrote. "'Rollover' was a critical and box-office dud. The various kinds of successes the other four movies have had is extraordinary."

The China Syndrome and *The Electric Horseman* (not an IPC film, but Fonda costarred with Robert Redford, and it was on brand) were among the five best-attended movies of 1979. *9 to 5* was the second-biggest movie of 1980, after *The Empire Strikes Back. On Golden Pond* was the second most popular movie of 1981, trailing only *Raiders of the Lost Ark* and doubling the gross of that year's James Bond movie, *For Your Eyes Only*. Fonda's IPC role was to develop projects, but not always to play the leading role: "She will star in 'The Dollmaker,'" Harmetz wrote of the pending 1984 TV movie, "and it will be, she says, her first 'challenge' as an actress since 'Coming Home.'"

History has been eroding these on-screen achievements since Richard Dyer heaped attention on Fonda in his influential 1979 book about celebrity, *Stars*. Susan Lacy's 2018 HBO documentary *Jane Fonda in Five Acts* is less interested in her films than her emergence into selfhood. The "acts" are titled "Henry" (father), "Vadim" (first husband), "Tom" (second husband), "Ted" (third husband), and "Jane."

No one did more to obscure her hard-won 1970s activist movie triumphs than Fonda herself. The eclipse was inadvertent but thorough as she adrenalized the 1980s home video craze with her hit workout tapes, and you can't overstate how omnipresent this obsession was. One of Eddie Murphy's countless funny lines in Walter Hill's 1982 action comedy *48 Hrs.* is a Fonda joke: Murphy's character, just out of prison for the first time in three years, is mesmerized by a video. A lithe woman in a tight leotard and long brunette hair swings her limbs flexibly, suggestively.

"TV has *changed*," Murphy murmurs.

TV changed. Jane changed. The '80s turned materialistic, corporate, toned. The great movies Fonda sweated into being nearly evaporated in history's mists.

Two decades later, Fonda wrote very little about her movies in *My Life So Far*, her 2005 memoir; she had so much more going on. The book recalls this conversation with Katharine Hepburn:

> "What does this mean to you?" she asked, pulling on my cheek.
>
> "What do you mean?"
>
> "Your image. What do you want your image to be?" She gave my cheek another little tug. "This is your package. We all

> have our package, what presents us to the world. What do you want your package to say about you?"
>
> "I have no idea," I answered.

Hepburn had her image. "I, on the other hand, was a hodgepodge, still searching for who I was, lacking self-consciousness about my persona, and this bothered her."

Putting together a video for Fonda's sixtieth birthday, her daughter Vanessa suggested that a fitting image of her mother would be a chameleon crawling across the screen.

Yet all is not quite forgotten. In a 2005 *Guardian* interview, producer David Puttnam (*Chariots of Fire, The Killing Fields*) told Fonda, "I and the people I was working with in the '70s and '80s were learning an enormous amount by what you were doing and achieving, and the way you were living your life, and the way you were using the metaphor of cinema to make points which badly needed to be made." And in her review of *Jane Fonda in Five Acts*, critic Nell Minow sounded surprised and intrigued by the occasional glimpses of Fonda's movies. "Fonda's work as an actor deserves its own appreciation," she suggested.

Indeed, *all* of her work as an actor deserves that look—especially that brief, shining time when she hitched her peculiarly crafted talent to hard-learned politics and willed a surprising string of films onto screens.

To begin . . .

2

A NEW STAR IN OLD HOLLYWOOD

Jane • Tall Story • Walk on the Wild Side • The Chapman Report • Period of Adjustment • In the Cool of the Day • Sunday in New York

Fonda is a different type altogether.

—Richard Dyer, 1979

STORY OFTEN TOLD: SHE IS the daughter of a mother who slit her own throat when Jane was twelve.

"For all its privilege and beauty, her childhood was almost Dickensian in its sadness," novelist and Fonda fan Ann Patchett wrote in her disappointed book review of Fonda's 2005 memoir *My Life So Far*. (Patchett added, "I wish the book contained more discussion of her life as an actress . . . her career gets fewer pages than it deserves.") Jane grew up jealous of her younger brother, Peter, and her older half sister, Pan. She was uncomfortable with her body, and felt so physically overscrutinized as she entered the acting profession, yet so driven to "confess" and be truthful in the burgeoning age of Method acting, that she "performed" bulimia in an Actors Studio class; she also impulsively smashed a glass during the final audition for the studio. She modeled early and was the Pentagon's Miss Army Recruiting in 1959 (commonly reported as 1962, but Fonda's memoir gives the earlier date, which is more plausible).

And her father was Henry Fonda.

In John Ford's 1939 film *Young Mr. Lincoln*, Henry Fonda is an arresting physical ringer for the sixteenth president—high cheekbones, lanky frame, loping gait, slow talk; *Henry Fonda for President* is the title of the three-hour 2024 documentary on the actor. A year after *Young Mr. Lincoln*, again for Ford, he starred in the film version of John Steinbeck's *The Grapes of Wrath*. The cinematography by Gregg Toland, whose deep-focus *Citizen Kane* work with Orson Welles followed in 1941, is as full of black spaces as an Edward Hopper painting. Actors are shown in silhouette or in shadows, heads frequently bowed toward the earth. Toland's gorgeous darkness and Ford's eye for hard, starved faces give the picture a durable grittiness, even as the reality it portrays was still palpable for audiences first watching this now-legendary picture. The disaster of the Depression-era Dust Bowl was even less distant to *Grapes of Wrath* viewers in 1940 than Vietnam was to still-raw audiences when Jane's *Coming Home* came out in 1978.

Henry Fonda's Tom Joad has a sharp, angry edge. He scans the American waste with the disgust and frustration of a decent but helpless man. "One guy with a million acres, and a hundred thousand farmers starving," Henry Fonda spits. And then: "As long as I'm an outlaw anyways, maybe I can do something. Maybe I can just find out something, just scrounge around and maybe find out what it is that's wrong, and see if ain't something can be done about it."

It's a formidable credo. Watching Henry Fonda speak these lines—fierce, committed—it's possible now to hear it predicting his daughter Jane's path. *As long as I'm an outlaw anyways, maybe I can do something . . .*

In 1947 Henry Fonda was one of 116 Hollywood signees of a letter protesting the House Un-American Activities Committee's hysterical inquisition targeting supposed Communists in the film industry.* In retaliation, was he then "graylisted" by studio executives? Patricia Bosworth notes that after putting his name on the line, Henry Fonda didn't appear in a Hollywood film for another seven years—the gap between *Fort Apache* in 1948 and *Mister Roberts* in 1955.

* This resistance group called itself the Committee for the First Amendment. In October 2025 Jane Fonda headlined hundreds of Hollywood signees reviving the committee.

After her headline-grabbing Hanoi trip in 1972, Jane Fonda barely flickered on Hollywood screens again until 1977.

"I couldn't get a job," Jane Fonda said in 1974. "I can't say I was blacklisted, but I was graylisted. I was disillusioned by the exploitive quality of the few offers I was getting and by the cowardice of people who didn't disagree with my stand against the Vietnam War but who didn't dare give me a job. I was seriously toying with leaving the business."

Jane (1962), Part 1

The emerging documentarian D. A. Pennebaker was one of five filmmakers credited on *Jane*, a bleak fifty-three-minute portrait—practically a teardown—of the young celebrity actress onstage; it was Pennebaker who filmed Fonda.

Actor's Daughter Gets Lead in Her 3rd Appearance Here, read the *New York Times* subheadline announcing Broadway's upcoming comedy *The Fun Couple*. The March 1962 article noted how busy Jane was already in Hollywood, with the slight comedy *Tall Story* behind her (the collegiate Fonda in romantic pursuit of egghead and basketball star Anthony Perkins), the southern gothic prostitute drama *Walk on the Wild Side* in cinemas (starring Barbara Stanwyck as a brutal madam), and coming soon enough to be mentioned in the item, *The Chapman Report* (based on Irving Wallace's sexology-focused novel, with an all-star cast including Glynis Johns, Shelley Winters, and Claire Bloom under the direction of George Cukor). When *The Fun Couple* opened on Broadway seven months later, another of Jane's movies was playing down the block, the film version of Tennessee Williams's honeymoon play *Period of Adjustment*. Young Jane was bursting all over the scene.

But *Jane* is a portrait of a flop. The documentarians trailed her with cameras as she rehearsed the play, and it stank of failure out of town in Wilmington and Baltimore. In Philadelphia, Fonda's acting guru Lee Strasburg popped backstage to skewer its shortcomings. In New York, *The Fun Couple* previewed October 25, opened October 26, and closed after the October 27 show.

Who, as a young performer, was this new sensation, Jane Fonda? Whatever its motivations, *Jane* asked a good question—though the slim documentary did not answer it. The rest of this chapter considers the sudden star, exploring what Fonda's first six Hollywood pictures looked like, and how the business began molding her as she absorbed lessons galore . . .

Tall Story (1960)

During the opening credits the Warner Bros. shield logo actually turns into a cartoon heart, and then the image dissolves into Fonda mooning over a photo of Anthony Perkins. She's a tall girl, she explains to the first two professors she meets, so she's chosen a school known to have a good basketball program where she can meet a tall man. Naturally, she signs up as a cheerleader.

Fonda's debut Hollywood moment is as a yelping coed nervously swerving her bike across campus until she crashes into the professors played by Marc Connelly (in real life an Algonquin Round Table writer and a Pulitzer winner for *The Green Pastures*) and longtime character

Fonda with Anthony Perkins (left) and Marc Connelly in *Tall Story*. *Moviestore Collection Ltd. / Alamy*

actor Ray Walston (about to enter TV lore with the 1963 debut of *My Favorite Martian*). When Fonda cackles merrily at a quip by Connelly, Walston—a stern ethics professor—scoffs. "Was it that funny?"

"Of course not," Fonda's cheerful June replies. "I'm buttering him up."

The professors' heads spin in the face of her charm and determination. Perky Jane admits she's at college "for the same reason that every girl, if she's honest with herself, comes to college: to get married."

Plainly, "pre-feminist" is a gentle term to describe this and much of what Fonda would be tapped to do in the '60s. Late in the '70s, calling her own shots, having lived through a lot of history and acted in projects ranging from embarrassing to profound, her stories inevitably would be different—crafted with a will from a deeper well of experience.

Tall Story's nonsense plot expands to include a Cold War visit by the basketball team from space-race rival Russia and an illegal gambling scheme to get star player / part-time campus taxi driver Perkins to throw the big game. Everything falls into the lap of the hyper-principled Walston, sputtering as he gives Perkins an oral exam in the locker room so Perkins can restore his athletic eligibility (Perkins blew a test on purpose) and beat the Russians in the nick of time.

Dewy Fonda and stammering Perkins are skittish and appealing together, and producer-director Joshua Logan watches them bumble fetchingly in long close-ups. Both stars, tremulous and alert, hold the camera, with Perkins gulping as a shy, science-minded athlete and Fonda's eyes brimming with romantic anxiety. Luckily, Fonda and Perkins also keep a sense of humor, settling all the way into the breathless, palpitating logic of their puppy-love scenes while never winking at the sappy material or compromising the essential sweetness.

Inventive though the actors are, the close-ups become a trap. The frame is bland. Logan, working as he often did from Broadway material, has a stage-bound eye except in his closing shot, in which the filmmaker directly echoes the sexualized *North by Northwest* finale of a speeding trailer plowing into a tunnel.

Logan was a longtime friend and colleague of Henry Fonda's, director of *Mister Roberts* on Broadway and portions of the movie adaptation. He was well known for such stage and screen hits as *Picnic* and *South Pacific*. Logan was Jane's godfather, and he had her under contract to launch her career. It was none other than Logan who, as Jane underwent screen tests, suggested she break her jaw to reshape her face. ("She resisted his suggestion," the *New York Times* confirmed in 2009.)

Logan also directed Jane's 1960 Broadway debut, as a rape victim in *There Was a Little Girl.* From Brooks Atkinson's *New York Times* review: "Her acting style is her own. As the wretched heroine of an unsavory melodrama, she gives an alert, many-sided performance that is professionally mature and suggests that she has found a career that suits her." Atkinson added that Henry Fonda, also on Broadway at the time, might want to fish his daughter out of the mess of a play.

Though Logan made bad work of both Fonda debuts—he suffered a breakdown while working on *There Was a Little Girl*—you can't say that in *Tall Story* she wasn't surrounded by pros. The movie's story is from the 1957 Howard Nemerov novel *The Homecoming Game*, adapted for the stage in 1959 by Broadway royalty Howard Lindsay and Russel Crouse (*Anything Goes*, Pulitzer winners for *State of the Union*). The screenplay was adapted by Lindsay and Crouse and Julius Epstein (*Casablanca*). The cast includes Tom Laughlin—later the writer-director-star of the cult hit *Billy Jack*—as the married friend who sells his trailer to Perkins and Fonda; Laughlin's randy character gets the final punch line about having found a justice of the peace to marry lovebirds Fonda and Perkins not a moment too soon. Somewhere in the background as a basketball player is an uncredited Robert Redford.

In *My Life So Far* Fonda called the *Tall Story* experience a "Kafkaesque nightmare" that triggered body shame and bulimia and squashed her appetite for acting. It doesn't show. But as evidence of Logan's slipshod command and taste for romantic tripe, he treats Perkins and Jane like Nelson Eddy and Jeanette MacDonald: they actually warble a love duet.

"A tall ear of comedy corn," the *New York Times* judged in a dismissive review, adding of Fonda, "The pretty newcomer shows charm and promise in her film debut. If Miss Fonda seems to be looking a bit askance, now and then, who can blame her?"

"I had to play the part of a ridiculous woman," Fonda says in French film star Delphine Seyrig's documentary *Be Pretty and Shut Up*, filmed in 1975–76. Fonda, fluent in French, asks Seyrig, "How do you say 'cheerleader'?"

Seyrig: "It doesn't exist in French."

Walk on the Wild Side (1962)

The setting is early-1930s Texas, where Fonda, a roadside tramp in baggy pants, plays hard-boiled Kitty Tristram, an impetuous young runaway discovered in a culvert by denim-clad drifter Laurence Harvey. She's a strapping, baby-faced figure from Paducah with an accent as broad as Kentucky and her messy braided hair going every which way. The face is smudged, the eyes and teeth are blindingly white. She's a ruffian, beautifully made up.

This is a juicy, pulpy black-and-white picture from director Edward Dmytryk, veteran of films noir and high dramas *Murder, My Sweet*, *Crossfire*, *The Caine Mutiny*, and *Raintree County*. An exuberantly louche tone is set with the socko opening credits fashioned by Saul Bass (of *The Man with the Golden Arm*, *North by Northwest*, *Psycho*, *West Side Story*, and no end of flashy Hollywood openings): the camera tracks a sleek black cat sauntering down an alley while composer Elmer Bernstein's jazz orchestra blasts a gritty tune. The black cat is tossed onto a white cat, which it promptly trounces, and there's your sassy prelude.

Hopping a boxcar, Fonda's Kitty sneers at Harvey's Dove as a "greenhorn." Her companion, a twig of straw between his teeth, looks like he couldn't care less.

Off the train and into the depot, Kitty brushes her hair and flaunts a tight dress. "I'm a big-league kid from a big-league town," she says, patting her rump at Dove. He's a Bible-driven boy. Mischievous young Kitty throws herself all over him.

Dove is on a mission to find his old flame in New Orleans. Hearing the gal's name, "Hallie," Kitty flares with jealousy. Fonda's hand balls up into the shape of a claw.

Fonda gets big scenes of low cunning once Kitty and Dove reach a roadside café run by Anne Baxter as a Mexican Texan named Teresina. Fonda's bratty Kitty feigns a bellyache, then steals a fancy rosary from Teresina's bedroom. Dove, disgusted, ditches Kitty, with snarls all around.

Fonda angrily smashes her hair over her face. She exits at minute twenty-five, concluding a massively pouty, flouncy performance.

She disappears for nearly an hour as Dove works for the saintly Teresina. He gradually tracks down Hallie in a whorehouse; Hallie is played by refined model/actress Capucine as a captive Holly Golightly. (*Breakfast at Tiffany's* hit screens mere months before this, and Elizabeth Taylor had claimed her *BUtterfield 8* Oscar barely a year prior. In a decade, Fonda would win her first Oscar as the prostitute in *Klute*. "Fallen women" were thick on the mid-twentieth-century Hollywood ground.)

"You don't know what I know," Hallie says with a shrug to one of her brothel colleagues. "What's the worst that could happen? You die."

Hallie is the platinum attraction in the sleazy "Dollhouse" run with an iron fist by Barbara Stanwyck, an imperious presence; Dmytryk repeatedly frames Stanwyck's steely madam in a powerful, arrogant profile pose. Shades of *Sunset Boulevard*: Stanwyck's assistant, manically devoted and legless—a wicked, cruel metaphor—is her ex-husband.

Walk on the Wild Side is noir staggering into Tennessee Williams territory, suffused with illicit desire, isolated and vulnerable women, abusive men, and lo, a sacrificial lamb (Dove). Dmytryk turns all his burners way up, driving the great, sinister Elmer Bernstein theme music into your ears, saturating the action with atmosphere. Bernstein's theme is on Hallie's radio, and then performed live in the Dollhouse salon, where it's given a sinuous beat by a New Orleans jazz band.

How devilish is Dmytryk's sense of fun? When holy Dove can't find Hallie and feels sorry for himself back at Teresina's, he sulks at the counter, obviously a little drunk, next to a sign for—wait for it—a Poor Boy sandwich. Likewise, right before Dove gets to the whorehouse—which this innocent doesn't recognize for what it is until his second time in—he passes a pedestrian on the sidewalk with a sandwich board over his shoulders declaring, Beware the Wrath to Come. If only Bible-clutching Dove could read the writing on the wall.

Set design is by the eventually legendary production designer and 1970s Paramount production head Richard Sylbert, whose other 1962 work included *The Manchurian Candidate*, also starring Harvey. Sylbert leaves no spaces blank inside Teresina's small but organized café or Hallie's art-filled room (Hallie is a fallen artist) or ruthless Stanwyck's seedy Dollhouse. The look is cramped, menacing, psychologically thick. It compels acting of a certain size. Fonda rises to it.

Fonda's Kitty resurfaces for good at the eighty-four-minute mark, sneering, "Hallelujah! Look who I see, if it isn't the Reverend Dove Linkhorn." She's a glamorously dressed new "doll" in the whorehouse, bailed out of jail by the spider Stanwyck, glad for the "work," a grifter who's finally found a home. Fonda brandishes her body again, leaning way back over the bar. When she squinches her face with meanness, she's almost convincing as a minor.

The savage Stanwyck puts the squeeze on the classy Hallie, forbidding her from leaving, and demands that Dove get out of town. Stanwyck's leverage: Fonda's Kitty. Stanwyck threatens with two-fisted menace that unless Dove disappears, the local police will bust Dove for transporting an underage girl (Kitty) across state lines. Dmytryk goes to baroque depths as henchmen hold Dove down so the legless husband, frothing with hellish, twisted vengeance, can thrash him.

Kitty, on a balcony, looks on in horror.

And that is an early glimpse of what will become Jane Fonda's gaze of moral recognition: the moment when she sees evil in the world, is transformed by it, and begins to fight.

Fonda, pivotal to Dmytryk's big finish, begins to show a bit of genuine acting range as Kitty's loyalty shifts through the climactic evening. The reversal is complete: Kitty discovers empathy for Dove. She expresses genuine reassurance to Hallie, then uses her flair for deception to flirt dangerously with the Dollhouse thug Oliver. She creates the diversion that catapults Dove and Hallie together one last time.

By the showdown back at Teresina's café, Capucine looks as lost as Ingrid Bergman in *Casablanca*, and she sounds like Bogart when Oliver points a gun at her. "Go ahead," she says. "Do me a favor."

The film ends with the cat from the opening credits sauntering over tabloid headlines—DOLLHOUSE CROWD CONVICTED; STATE STAR WITNESS; KITTY TRISTRAM REMANDED TO JUVENILE AUTHORITIES. The slinky jazz blows to its big finish.

For a young actress, Dmytryk's picture is a superb exercise in genre driven all the way to the wall, and Kitty gets a solid story arc. Fonda bears down, leans into the style, and creates a character who thrives in the hothouse . . . and who wises up.

The Chapman Report (1962)

Still more fevered sexuality, this time in a drama inspired by the work of sex researcher Albert Kinsey, directed by George Cukor from the swiftly adapted 1960 Irving Wallace novel. In a Swamp of Erotica, read the *New York Times* headline for their review of the book, with the critic calling it "merely titillating and frequently salacious" while also noting that the movie rights were snapped up before the novel's publication. Cukor's picture boasts a quartet of stars from the powerhouse days of the Actors Studio: Fonda, Shelley Winters, Claire Bloom, and Glynis Johns.

"Cukor loves to watch his actors lose control," Dan Callahan wrote in a 2004 survey of the director's work. Lose it they do: *The Chapman Report* is a gothic testament to the discontents of America on the cusp of a sexual revolution, with neurotic, frustrated women staggering around darkened rooms.

Sex is unfortunately kept "under the table," "suppressed" and "indecent," contends the scientific Dr. George Chapman (Andrew Duggan), arriving in a tony suburb with his investigators amid so much hoopla that he is interviewed at the airport by breathless journalists. Fonda's role: a frigid young widow with a daddy fixation. Highlighting her character's arrested development, her late husband was named Boy.

As Chapman recruits volunteers at a ladies' club with a wall of books behind him, Fonda's fashionable stiff white skirt suit commands the center of the frame. The costumes are by Orry-Kelly, already a three-time Oscar winner for the sexually keyed-up *An American in Paris*, *Les Girls*, and *Some Like It Hot*, and he's tailor-made for Cukor's percolating extravaganza. Orry-Kelly locks up Fonda in fancy *Don't touch me!* chastity couture, while, on the other hand, his dark, simple, filmy clothing for Bloom's self-destructive nymphomaniac alcoholic practically falls right off.

A rival doctor sounds a moralistic warning: What about love? The clinical approach to sexuality—the researchers' unusual questions and sex-positive (in modern parlance) mission—will wreck the subjects' daily function, contends Dr. Jonas (Henry Daniell). "You set off a chain reaction, then let them go," he scolds. Unintended tragic consequences, Jonas warns, can be expected.

That plays out all around, and certainly with Fonda's character, Kathleen Barclay, who is desperate to be "normal." For her anonymous interview (the questions are asked from behind a partition), she wears a demure white dress with a stunning wide-brimmed hat, a protective canopy that makes her look like a giant orchid—Orry-Kelly in full bloom. Cukor goes for long, unblinking takes during the interviews, watching his great actors get as nervous as cats, their eyes darting, faces crumbling, until they break down fully. Fonda slowly, duly flips out before our eyes in a scene anchored by a medium close-up that lasts two full minutes.

Fonda's Kathleen fields the questions, confirming that she attended the Sorbonne, and politely recalling that there was no petting as a teen but a little kissing (we see a small smile). The interviewer asks about her resisting advances; her face darkens. She answers immediately, cautiously, that resisting was due to her sense of "right and wrong," in line with the teachings of school, church, home.

Questioned about her marriage to the late Boy, a test pilot, Fonda lights a cigarette.

Another question. Physical relations?

"Let me think," she says, buying time, exhaling smoke through her nostrils.

The scene crosscuts to shots of the interviewer, Paul (Efrem Zimbalist Jr.), gaining tempo as Kathleen gets defensive. Fonda tries to perform "normalcy," but her Kathleen is rattled because she doesn't know the "normal" answers, hasn't had a "normal" experience. She drops her bag and fumbles with the mess to avoid answering. The camera lingers on Fonda again as she guesses. She asks, "Isn't that normal?"—then wails into the interviewer's silence, "I can't!"

She presses herself into the room's shadows. The sudden music hits a sinister chord.

Fonda, her hair wound tight as thread on a spool, goes through it all again when Paul comes to her house with the wallet she left behind. She's indignant at the intrusion. She fails at being cool. She fully hugs a wall yet again and tearfully blurts, "Don't look at me like that! I'm not one of your pathological cases! Boy and I had a wonderful life together!"

The sensitive young sexology interviewer will, of course, fall in love with this basket case. His protective attentions sort her out.

The purple picture is intriguing in its performances and much of its calculated mise-en-scène, but it's disappointing in its stereotyped characters and simplistic diagnoses. The gloomiest case is Claire Bloom's doomed turn as a divorcée who took to sex at an early age and now pays society's price. In an early scene, Bloom is strikingly animalistic, hiding a liquor bottle under the bed as she lures in a water delivery guy, whose costume includes the pointed end of a pencil jutting from his shirt pocket.

When a hipster jazz musician (Corey Allen) saunters to her front door and begins leering, she can't resist him. "I don't like this kind of talk!" she shrieks as he comes on hard.

"You look awful hungry, honey," he replies.

Indeed, her character is conceived as the era's idea of a wildcat, and Bloom moves woozily, her body jostling like she's on one of Tennessee Williams's sweaty streetcars. Bloom goes to the musician's jazz club, quivering in a dark corner behind her sunglasses as she watches him play his clarinet (Freudian typo, with apologies to Bloom: Clairinet). Further plunging into Tennessee Williams terrain, the encounter leads to a poker game with his friends, and rape.

The musician dumps Bloom on the street outside her house. Fonda's Kathleen gently shepherds her inside. In her Chapman interview after the gang assault, Bloom prowls the room, finding all the shadows.

Less fraught, Winters plays a pouty wife and mother escaping her dull life by pursuing an affair with a philandering theater director who's never going to leave his wife; in the end she returns to her husband and their windowless den. Winters gets sustained scrutiny during her interview too, as the emotional dam cracks and she answers questions about her "tolerable" Saturday-night relations with her husband and her current infidelity. Her performance oozes a Winters specialty: unvarnished unhappiness.

The friskiest case, and the comic relief, is a poetry-mad Johns as the happily married, adored wife of an effete David Niven type (John Dehner, fussing with flower arrangements). They are a pair of art-loving romantics. Dismayed that she has nothing but contentment to report, she decides to explore a more robust physicality by pursuing a beer-swilling golden-boy football player in tight, tiny bathing trunks. "What a magnificent animal!" she coos.

The scenery is a riot. Johns lolls on the sand, reading aloud into a recorder the love poem "Cynara" ("I have been faithful to thee, Cynara! in my fashion") with seventeen phallic oil derricks behind her on a beach suddenly overrun with strapping football-playing men. She hires one of them as a model and gets him to strip, waxing about "the grace of your body and the freedom of your limbs." The ambient sound throbs with the rhythmic pumping of the wells. Once he gets the idea, he pounces.

But it's too much for her, this actually fleshy business—not *tasteful.* Despite the clues of the derricks, she wasn't ready for sex to be crude. She runs back home to her unmuscled hubby.

The moral? The suicide of Bloom's divorcée is offered as a lesson. "I don't want to be alone," Fonda's Kathleen says, moving close to Paul as they analyze Bloom's tragic case. The three surviving women end happily married. If you're in *love*, the picture says, "real love," hang-ups vanish and happiness is possible.

"The one and only cure," the skeptical Dr. Jonas pronounces near the end of the film. Like *Walk on the Wild Side*, the movie is heavy-handed with dangerous jazz music and creepy lighting whenever the repressed sexual discussions or encounters get tense.

Yet it's another useful opportunity for the emerging Fonda, getting significant screen time yet not burdened with carrying the picture, projecting composure while limning extreme vulnerability—a full twist away from her *Wild Side* role. She holds her own as part of an estimable ensemble, exercising her craft with another sure-handed veteran Hollywood director.

Period of Adjustment (1962)

Like *The Chapman Report*, this film was released in October, a black-and-white, 80-proof pour of straight-up sexual dysfunction, 1950s-style, from a Tennessee Williams Christmas play—the one with the line "The human heart would never pass the drunk test."

Wiliams's Broadway flop ended the fabled collaboration between the dramatist and Elia Kazan, who had been riding high together on

A Streetcar Named Desire and *Cat on a Hot Tin Roof.* But Kazan backed away from staging *Period of Adjustment* to work on a different immersion into youthful sexual anxiety, William Inge's *Splendor in the Grass*, a movie starring a reticent Warren Beatty and a hormone-fueled Natalie Wood and with a striking appearance by Barbara Loden as Beatty's free-spirited sister.* George Roy Hill (*Butch Cassidy and the Sundance Kid, The Sting*) directed *Period* on Broadway and on-screen, making his feature film debut. Like *Tall Story*, the movie announces itself as a cartoon right off the bat with a comic montage about Fonda as a night nurse to hospitalized Jim Hutton. She swiftly marries him. But she is shocked by the hunger of his wedding kiss.

The comedy is broad and low as Hutton's huffy, penny-pinching George (a Korean War vet with shaky hands) buys a hearse for their car and, as the newlyweds stop at a diner, panders to a gallery of leering men. Fonda's hapless Isabel gets soaked by a gushing downspout as they check into the run-down Old Man River Motel, where a slow trombone elbows us in the ribs with a familiar tune: *Be it ever so humble, there's no place like home.* Fonda, called L'il Bit by Hutton, looks like a drowned cat. This disastrous, slapstick honeymoon scene, only discussed in the stage version, is woefully visualized on-screen.

Isobel Lennart adapted the 1960 play, toning down some of Williams's aggressive dialogue and stage directions on carnal attraction; among other details, the movie avoids Williams's instructions to position L'il Bit in front of the fireplace while she's wearing a sheer nightie. The tone of what Williams called a "serious comedy" is like a southern parody, maybe worst of all in Fonda's broad accent and honking. (Williams labeled it as such on the title page of the published script, yet he also told the *New York Times* in 1960 that *Period* is "a comedy, set in Memphis of today, but we are not calling it that because there is a danger of the actors gagging it up.") As a miserable virgin, Fonda acts like a frantic goose. She's a clanging southern belle, at her

* In an underappreciated yet groundbreaking case of an actress making her own movie from soup to nuts, in 1970 Loden would write, direct, and star in *Wanda*, a cheap, 16 mm, grainy color, loosely scripted, and amateur-filled indie film featuring a disaffected main character drifting into American nothingness.

worst bawling incoherently on the phone to her dad. She's identified as a Texan, and when she bellows her husband's name, Williams's spelling is garish: "JAWGE!" Fonda gets two syllables out of it, and three warbled Grand Ole Opry notes. Likewise, "yes" is spelled "yaias," and this partially explains Fonda's performance. She's trying to get the exotic words right. But it stretches her into caricature.

"It is a relatively recent convention," Molly Haskell would write a decade later in her foundational survey *From Reverence to Rape*, "that southerners—particularly southern women—have to be shown as cretins and played by actresses with phony, honey-dripping, 'dumb-female' accents." That describes Fonda's character to a T.

The film then moves to the setting where the entirety of the play takes place: Christmas Eve at the Memphis home of Hutton's war buddy Ralph—built, with Williams's mischievous sense of poetry, on a sinkhole. Williams shows two married couples on the rocks: Fonda and Hutton's newlyweds, plus Ralph Bates (Anthony Franciosa) and his wife (Lois Nettleton, described as homely, and quite compelling in her terrible understanding of how Ralph sees her). The Bateses have split after Ralph finally quit working for his domineering father-in-law (John McGiver). Both couples are, in Williams's benevolent refrain, going through a "period of adjustment."

Blanche DuBois would recognize the playwright's remedy: Kindness. Patience.

It's Fonda's character who marvels at the raw courage it takes for any two strange humans to try to coexist. Most of Williams's grittier stuff is reserved for the end of the movie adaptation, but onstage the theme was consistent: Ralph confesses to a bit of impotence because his wife doesn't turn him on: "Poor ole Dotty. She's got so she always wants it and when I can't give it to her I feel guilty, guilty . . ." He proceeds to lecture George on his "sexual violence." Lennart trimmed all this frank Williams material when adapting it for the screen.

The talk about the wedding night is also more detailed and blunt onstage. You can feel the hopes and frustrations, the sordid ugliness. But unlike better Williams adaptations and the aching *Splendor in the Grass*, this movie is too eager to be cute. It allows Williams and his carnal subject to be only a little earthy.

Fonda throws all her energy into the performance, yelling "I did not touch yore big ol' lecherous body!" at the top of her lungs, hobbling around in heels and a tight skirt and blouse, ogled from behind by all the men, blowing her blonde wig's loose tendril out of her face. It's arguably her pushiest movie, overleaping even *Tall Story*, and—though it seems no fault of hers—her least-bearable performance.

In the Cool of the Day (1963)

Fonda toggles back to *Chapman* mode for more moody neurosis in an uneasy blend of Greek and French tragedy, directed largely as a travelogue, in color, by journeyman TV director Robert Stevens. Producer John Houseman actually took the project in part to spend time in Greece.

Peter Finch plays Murray, a man fated to lose loved ones. His wife, Angela Lansbury, is bitter and disfigured due to a car accident that killed their young son: the couple fought while Finch was driving. Fonda is the alluring Christine, Finch's new lover, condemned to frail health and a deathbed demise in the mode of Dumas fils's tubercular Camille.

"She's moved further and further away," Christine's husband, Sam (Arthur Hill), murmurs of his estranged wife in the opening scene's friendly but glum confessional, plunging us right into the turgid dilemma. "She seemed to come to the end. . . . Like an animal in a trap. . . . How do you deal with this kind of pain?"

The film was adapted by Meade Roberts from the 1960 Susan Ertz novel; Roberts had just cowritten the movie versions of Tennessee Williams's *Orpheus Descending* (adapted as *The Fugitive Kind*) and *Summer and Smoke* and next would handle William Inge's *The Stripper*. *Cool of the Day* is bookish, *literary*, saturated with classical atmosphere: Finch is in New York on a vague publishing mission. The story becomes a tragic quest when Finch—an actor whose persona is next door to Richard Burton's (voices of poets, faces of ruin)—agrees to investigate what ails his friend's estranged wife. Quickly, he falls for her.

Fonda enters as a slinky femme fatale in a tight black silk dress. She's heavily made up in a Cleopatra hairdo—sharp bangs, straight shoulder-length hair—with cocoa-dusted eyelids, big fake lashes, and large reddened lips. Her costumes, as in *Chapman* and the soon-to-come *Sunday in New York*, are by Orry-Kelly, and by the time she appears in a black turban and black gown with puffy sleeves that bulge her forearms like Popeye's, the poor character seems locked up (again) by the haute couture. Houseman, in his 1983 memoir *Final Dress*, attributes Christine's remarkable but misguided look to Fonda and the studio. He likewise sketches Fonda's lover/mentor at the time, actor and director Andreas Voutsinas, as an intrusive on-set acting coach.

When she first meets Murray, Christine expresses a passion for Greece, where Finch's character lived for two years. "Is this the way it really looks?" she asks, examining Greek drawings, settling on the floor, at his knees, like a supplicant. Her "mystery" deepens, though, as she won't even tell her ailing father-in-law where she is staying.

What can revive this delicate being? Again, poor young Jane, the actress positioned as an *orchid*: usefully exotic, singularly alert, alluringly lovely, alarmingly breakable . . .

"Sometimes I think Sam loves me better ill than well," Christine confides to Murray. Fonda and Finch play their early New York scenes very low key, chatting believably. The musical score's violins underline the tasteful yearning.

"I'd lead my own life," she tells him one evening in Central Park. "It might be short, but it would be a life."

With echoes of Henrik Ibsen's Nora (still a decade away in Fonda's career), Christine tells Murray that if she goes back to Sam, "for both our sakes it has to be on my terms, as his wife, not his child." She is tired of being coddled. She had lung operations twice as a teenager, has twice had pneumonia, and has been instructed to be "quiet" for five to ten years.

Christine seems well adjusted, at least at first, next to Murray's embittered, housebound wife, played by Lansbury, who sings "Over the Rainbow" to herself and relentlessly lashes out at her husband. (Soon she will sarcastically refer to the elegant Christine as "her ladyship.") On the banks of the Thames, Murray tells Christine the whole story: he was guilty of the accident that killed their son, so now he endures his punishing fate. He will suffer through Lansbury's bitchy living death.

Working hard for its tragic stripes, the movie slings itself to Greece, where lively Fonda scrambles with Finch up the rubble to the Parthenon while the drudge Lansbury waits halfway down the hill. They reflect at Delphi's famed temple, where oracles of yore delivered warnings. Sure enough, taxi drivers note with portent that the rain is "no good." Inevitably, Finch tempts fate. His command: *Drive on!*

Inside her wildly upscale clothing, Fonda's performance is all soft edges. Her Christine is sweet and kind, even reaching out to Lansbury's sourpuss; it was she who persuaded Lansbury to join the trek to Greece. (The trek does not include Christine's estranged husband Sam, conveniently stuck at work in New York.) Lansbury gloomily checks out of the marriage and scoots toward a louche American seducing her in a hotel bar. Then Finch and Fonda, the innocents, dance on a ferry with Greek peasants, the ultimate Zorba-like expression of *life!!*

But Christine's chance at happiness is dashed with the appearance of her stifling mother, played with sophisticated control by Constance Cummings. Terrified by this maternal monster, Christine knocks over a glass of red wine (omen alert!). Mother's monstrous diagnosis of daughter: she is *unable to love.*

Finch's Murray disproves that in bed.

"I was afraid it might be true, that I was incapable of loving," Fonda's Christine says postcoitally, content and proud. "It isn't true, is it!"

But Christine is too fragile for this Freudian world. Mother's mere meddling is deadly. Christine declines. Hospitalization. The end.

It's tempting to mark this as Fonda's first grown-up performance. Despite the Camille-ish weakening, staggering through a hotel hallway, coughing and sweating, wheezing on her deathbed with all the makeup finally gone, Fonda's face is expressively alive even as breath and words fail. Her good-hearted character treads respectfully around Finch and Lansbury: she can do genuine nobility. And Finch, a dramatic heavyweight of the old school, his ashtray voice full of intellectual nuance and dramatic portent, is a good adult acting partner for her. Christine is calm with him, and Fonda plays the underappreciated maturity with easy sophistication. She is often displayed as an objet d'art (note the chic, ancient-looking gold bracelet around her biceps, among other flourishes), and that, too, is a skill. Fonda is relaxed as a model, comfortable with glamour. It's no mean feat to be this rarefied yet grounded and sensitive. The character she creates is inquisitive, humble, and entirely sympathetic.

Still, in 2018, appearing on Andy Cohen's *Watch What Happens Live* with Lily Tomlin as the *Grace and Frankie* stars answered callers' questions, Fonda was asked which picture she might wish to remove from her oeuvre. Without hesitation—though with no chance to explain on the breathless chat show—she replied, "*In the Cool of the Day*."

With its costume excesses and maudlin fatalism, and the apparent involvement of Fonda's domineering boyfriend Andreas Voutsinas—whose influence, as we'll see, she was eager to forget—*Cool of the Day* is maybe a minor embarrassment.

But the correct answer is *Period of Adjustment*.

Sunday in New York (1963)

Nervous sex comedy, anyone? "It is my firm conviction that I'm the only twenty-two-year-old virgin alive," Fonda laments as Eileen.

Eileen is headed to Manhattan from Albany to see her brother Cliff Robertson, a swinging airline pilot. (As a genre, the jet-set sex farce was in its heyday, reaching cruising altitude with the trend's best title, French writer Marc Camoletti's 1960 Parisian hit / 1962 West End smash / 1965 movie *Boeing Boeing*.) When his flight is grounded, he has a free rainy Sunday afternoon, so he dials up a redhead (Jo Morrow) who answers in bed and purrs. Mel Tormé sings the mellow Peter Nero–Carroll Coates title tune through the opening credits, and Nero plays piano in a club scene and scores the movie (which too often punctuates antic high points with peppy orchestral exclamation marks!). The jazzy opening montage, with everyone pouring into New York, cuts between Rod Taylor on a train smiling at someone's playful kid, Fonda also on a train putting up with a leering businessman, and Robertson grinning as he fantasizes about Morrow while deftly landing his jet.

Filmed in color, the comedy introduces Fonda in an all-American palette, with red lips, white skirt and vest, and a blue-and-white striped blouse. Eileen has a pressing question for her brother: "Is a girl that's been going around with a fellow a reasonable length of time supposed to go to bed with him or not?"

She doesn't know that Robertson is a bounder. Robertson hides his "experience" as he gives Fonda his version of the *Chapman* quiz. When you go out, he asks, is there kissing?

Depends on the fella, she replies, and for the first time on-screen, Fonda begins to *sound* like herself. Eileen sharply critiques the double standards about love and sex, and Fonda gets to knock the ideas around in a decently scripted romantic comedy. (The source material is a 1961 Broadway play by longtime stage and screen scribe Norman Krasna, and it has bounce, even if it's directed on-screen with no particular flair—addled characters pacing and racing around an apartment—by Peter Tewksbury, of TV's *Father Knows Best* and *My Three Sons*.)

Fonda's "meet cute" happens on a city bus with Rod Taylor's sportswriter/music critic, as Taylor's suit jacket gets hooked by her boutonniere pin. What feels like her first true *Jane Fonda* moment in the movie comes in a restaurant by the Rockefeller Plaza skating rink. Taylor tells her an edited but still smutty joke—his idea of flirting.

She blows cigarette smoke at him.

Fonda and Taylor get caught in the rain. Warming up in her brother's apartment, she tries to put seductive moves on Taylor. Fonda is funny portraying Eileen's naïveté; wide-eyed Eileen doesn't know anything about sex beyond where the movies' love scenes fade to black. She's a virgin, so on principle, Taylor resists her. She is outraged: How is that fair? The mise-en-scène ripples with the new sexual freedom as Eileen casually leafs through one of her brother's magazines—*Playboy*, of course. She gets to the centerfold and drops it with a gasp.

Krasna's bedroom farce gets tangled as Fonda and Taylor rope Robertson into a bunch of pretend. Fonda's rich, athletic beau from Albany, Russ (Robert Culp, in a role played on Broadway by Robert Redford), impulsively arrives to propose. But Fonda and Taylor have just been soaked by the rain, and now they're in bathrobes—not a good look for a 1963 virgin in front of a conservative would-be fiancé. How can anxious, still-"innocent" Eileen save face?

Follow along on your scorecard:

Rod Taylor has to *pretend* to be Fonda's *brother*.

Robertson, her *actual* brother, pretends to be a *friend*.

Fonda and Rod Taylor spend a *Sunday in New York.*
Courtesy Everett Collection

As the explanations swirl, Robertson and Culp both end up punching Taylor, defending her "honor" and swinging for laughs. But at the end of the day's shenanigans and dialogues, it's the easygoing, understanding Taylor who wins Fonda's heart.

Earnest Doris Day goes through the same mistaken-identity shtick with winking Rock Hudson in *Pillow Talk* and *Lover, Come Back*, and again in a different way with Rod Taylor in *The Glass Bottom Boat.* Fonda would reprise the business in 1966's *Any Wednesday*, a dumber movie with a character that's less explicable. The good news of *Sunday in New York* is how Fonda the actor begins building a viable screen persona. The wives the young performer has played, eager or petrified, give way to a smart, curious participant in the emerging dialogue on sexual equality. The double standards bug her. She's ready to argue. She's a natural in a Manhattan apartment. She's quick and funny.

In four years and eight more movies Fonda will get to do this all over again, only without the sexual agenda and with Robert Redford in Neil Simon's *Barefoot in the Park*. She will become a very big Hollywood star.

Jane (1962), Part 2

Now let's look back to the D. A. Pennebaker documentary about Fonda's onstage role in *The Fun Couple*. Fonda "hates that movie," Broadway gossip columnist Michael Riedel reported an unnamed source saying in 2008, as Fonda was preparing for a Broadway return in Moisés Kaufman's Beethoven-inspired drama *33 Variations*.* "It was a time in her life she wants to forget."

Indeed, *The Fun Couple* and its director—Fonda's boyfriend, Andreas Voutsinas, frequently seen in the documentary throwing "artistic" tantrums—rate only a sentence in Fonda's 2005 memoir, at the very end of a chapter as she quickly turns the page toward French director and future husband Roger Vadim. *Jane* often observes Fonda kissing Voutsinas. But in her book, he's not even in the index.

Pennebaker made his name five years later with another black-and-white cinema verité backstage chronicle, *Don't Look Back*, about a Bob Dylan who is as bristling and confident as Jane, in *Jane*, is flinching and uncertain.

"The fact that we had [access to] Jane Fonda was interesting," Pennebaker said in a 2005 interview. "Because you had a real actress, you saw her. But she was over-acting!"

Jane chronicles her straining efforts to prove that Henry Fonda's daughter has the goods to make it onstage. But her rudderlessness is stunning, given what we know more than sixty years later of the unbreakable Jane. *The Fun Couple* draws a bruising pan in the documentary from the *New York Herald Tribune*'s Walter Kerr, emerging (since Brooks Atkinson had just retired from the *New York Times*) as

* In *33 Variations*, Fonda played a musicologist whose terminal case of Lou Gehrig's disease prompts an obsession with late-life Beethoven's obsession with an ordinary waltz. Her last appearance on Broadway had been in 1963, in Eugene O'Neill's *Strange Interlude*.

the lion of Broadway critics. For the cameras, Kerr calls it one of the worst shows he's ever seen. "If I had to make a list of five, this would be on it," Kerr says frankly.

Young Fonda is seen reading the review aloud in the wee hours after opening night, alone with Voutsinas. She laughs reading some of it. Then, her voice turning steely, she checks herself: "I don't know why I'm laughing."

Anger begins to blaze just a little, with the knowledge that hers was the only real name on the line; playwrights Neil Jansen and John Haase, working from Haase's novel, are not even identified in the movie. Her anger is growth. She states the lesson twice: the material she accepts has to be better.

But 1960s actresses had scant access to levers of power, and Fonda was years from determining what she was really all about.

3

ON THE GROUND

Winter Soldier

What in the world is the matter with Jane Fonda?

—Richard Nixon, 1971

They arrested Jane Fonda, nothing changes. I remember thirty, forty years ago they arrested her. She's always got the handcuffs on, oh man. She's waving to everybody with the handcuffs. I can't believe it.

—Donald Trump, 2019

On the streets, this is how she does it.*

In April 2006, Fonda says, by no means for the first time, that she won't speak out publicly against the US war in Iraq, fearing that her voice brings "too much baggage." On January 27, 2007, Fonda reverses field and appears at a major antiwar rally in Washington, DC. It's the first time she has raised her voice against any US military action in thirty-four years.

Antiwar protestors radiate carnival adrenaline as they stream out of Union Station. Placards abound: Will Work for Peace. No Dying,

* Details from the 2007 antiwar rally and the 2019–20 Fire Drill Fridays events come from the author's reporting, unless otherwise noted.

No Lying. Out of Iraq. Impeach Bush. No, with three words cascading next to it—

War
NO Empire
Occupation

The rally takes place between Third and Fourth Streets NW, with the US Capitol as backdrop. An Abe Lincoln on stilts totters through the crowd. As celebrities gather by the stage, tall Tim Robbins is a cinch to spot.

"Let me hear you scream!" Jesse Jackson repeats, wrapping up his five minutes.

A theme emerges: The November 2006 election ten weeks earlier was an antiwar referendum. Nonetheless, President George W. Bush instead ordered the deployment of tens of thousands of additional American troops to Iraq, euphemistically referring to the escalation as a "surge."

"When we voted, it was a directive to bring our troops home *now!*" declares Rev. Graylan Scott Hagler.

Kevin Martin announces himself as an activist and a father: "I take personal responsibility to stop these policies," he says. Turning toward the Capitol, he yells, "You have a mandate for peace! Do your jobs!"

The crowd chants: "No! More! War!"

A group called the Raging Grannies mocks Bush to the tune of "99 Bottles of Beer on the Wall." "*He's got an urge to surge*," the Grannies sing.

Massachusetts sixth grader Moriah Arnold says, "There's no excuse for thinking we're better than someone else. . . . Because of our actions, the rest of the world sees us as a bully and a liar." Near the stage as she speaks is a man in a Fuck Bush T-shirt.

More speakers: Dennis Kucinich, Ohio congressman and presidential candidate, who has been "bring 'em home" antiwar as long as anyone. Ellie Smeal of the National Organization for Women (NOW). Eve Ensler of *The Vagina Monologues*. A representative from the AFL-CIO, offering the support of Big Labor. An anti-Israel activist roaring, "Four years is enough in Iraq! Forty years is way, way, way more than enough in

Palestine!" Democratic congressmen Albert Wynn (D-Maryland) and Jerrold Nadler (D–New York), waving but not speaking. John Conyers Jr. (D-Michigan) quoting *New York Times* columnist Maureen Dowd's ridicule of Bush and asserting, "We can fire him!"

The crowd spontaneously begins to chant, "Impeach Bush!" For the first time, there's a real zing in the air.

Maxine Waters (D-California) thunders against Secretary of State Condoleezza Rice: "Condi ain't nothing but another neocon, and she doesn't represent me!" An Iraqi citizen testifies that Sunni and Shia Muslims have coexisted for centuries without US peacemakers and should be allowed to continue that way.

The stage floods with US vets against the war. Military families speak, including the parents of twenty-eight-year-old army lieutenant Ehren Watada, the first soldier to decline deployment to Iraq. A veteran sniper says, "Men and women are coming home, and they're pissed off." He served in good faith and returned disillusioned. This original, personal testimony lands powerfully.

It's the anti-Vietnam playbook all over again.

It's exactly what Fonda was up to in the 1970s with her tours to off-base GI coffeehouses, her involvement with Vietnam Veterans Against the War, and the Winter Soldier Investigation that took place in a Detroit Howard Johnson's, January 31–February 2, 1971.

Winter Soldier (1972)

Winter Soldier is no-frills documentary/cinema verité filmmaking, shot on found and borrowed grainy black-and-white stock. It was made by an anonymous collective of eighteen filmmakers that included Barbara Kopple, who would win Oscars for her labor documentaries *Harlan County U.S.A.* (1976) and *American Dream* (1990). The collective chose anonymity "so who the filmmakers are would not be part of this at all," Kopple says on the *Winter Soldier* DVD.

Their film documents the Winter Soldier Investigation, capturing vets at a dais, in a conference room, in front of an audience and cameras, telling their stories. At the top of the film a narrator quotes Thomas Paine: "These are the times that try men's souls. The summer soldier and the sunshine patriot will, in this crisis, shrink from the service of his country; but he that stands it now deserves the love and thanks of man and woman."

The soldiers describe the atrocities they witnessed and often perpetrated, to their gnawing anxiety and shame; the testimonies are offered as a way of understanding their near-incomprehensible actions. In Vietnam, civilians were mutilated and murdered. Villages were strafed. Prisoners were blindfolded and tossed from planes, which is why prisoners were to be tallied only when the planes landed, not when taking off. "Progress" was measured not by land secured but by body counts.

Future Massachusetts senator and presidential candidate John Kerry is seen briefly. Months later, Kerry would preface his famous April 23, 1971, statement to the Senate Foreign Relations Committee ("How do you ask a man to be the last man to die in Vietnam? How do you ask a man to be the last man to die for a mistake?") with reference to the Winter Soldier Investigation; April 23 was the week of Operation Dewey Canyon III, when veterans against the war gathered at the US Capitol and threw their medals over a fence.* During an early scene before the formal testimonies, amid casual hubbub, Kerry, identified in the credits as one of the "Winter Soldiers," asks a fellow vet, "What brings you here? What makes you want to testify?" The vet's response: "I didn't like being an animal, and I didn't like seeing everybody else turned into animals, either. . . . Until you grasp it, you're not going to end that war, because it's too distant."

* Kerry made a furious public reappearance January 8, 2020, condemning the Trump-ordered assassination of Iranian general Qassim Suleimani. Fallout included a jittery Iraq harmlessly firing missiles into a US base in Iraq and apparently at the same time mistakenly shooting down a Ukrainian airliner, killing 176. Within days the House of Representatives adopted a measure to limit Trump's ability to use further military force against Iran. "I can't explain the chaos of his presidency as it lurches from crisis to crisis, real or imagined," Kerry wrote in the *New York Times*. Kerry, Barack Obama's secretary of state, had helped negotiate the 2015 Iranian nuclear deal that Trump rescinded in 2018. On MSNBC's *The Last Word*, Kerry said of Trump's Iranian escalation, "It's the most dangerous thing I've seen since the war that I fought in, which was lied about and presented such a crisis to our nation."

A Black man in a lobby explains to a White soldier, who listens with near-trembling intensity, that Blacks are ambivalent about the weekend because it ignores the racism that enabled the war in the first place. A Native American makes a similar point from the podium: in Vietnam, he became a perpetrator of the racist violence that as a kid he suffered due to America's film and TV culture of cowboys (White civilizers) and Indians (non-White savages).

The filmmakers increasingly dwell on close-ups of notably cogent veteran Scott Camil. Other men detail boot camp humiliations, systematic desensitization, and violent excesses normalized "in country," all cultivating a barbaric survival/killer mindset. Often they are outraged, or overwhelmed by emotion. Camil is a cooler head. Yet as the documentary unfolds, he grows more reflective, a patriot recanting his actions.

Camil became one of the Gainesville Eight, Vietnam vets (all but one) accused by the government of plotting to sabotage the 1972 Republican National Convention in Miami. "It did not take the jury long to decide that it believed the Government's case was a sorry piece of goods," the *New York Times* reported of the defendants' acquittal. Graham Nash wrote a ballad about Camil called "Oh! Camil (The Winter Soldier)."

The message is persistent: if only Nixon and the misled country would follow suit, the long, pointless national nightmare could end.

To say all this out loud is cathartic, but the men are a mess. The filmmakers—credited only as Winterfilm and Vietnam Veterans Against the War—show how these soldiers got that way. *Winter Soldier*, the film and the investigation it documents, is focused activism: stop the war.

Fonda is nowhere in it. Her name is not on it. But she was behind it.

"Preparing for the Winter Soldier investigation required fast fundraising," she wrote in London's *Guardian* newspaper in 2005, "and I hit the road running, raising most of the money through a six-week speaking tour that took me to 54 college campuses across the country, and during which police arrested me for 'drug smuggling' (vitamins, actually)."

Winter Soldier was buried. It debuted January 1972 at Manhattan's Whitney Museum of American Art, but couldn't get distributed, couldn't get on TV. Fonda wrote about it in 2005 because the picture was finally being revived, at least a little, with a run at the Film Society of Lincoln Center and a handful of other venues. It was bloody timely.

"Its distributors say that the war in Iraq has made the Vietnam-era film as powerful as when it was new, and its filmmakers are calling it eerily prescient of national embarrassments like the torture at Abu Ghraib," the *New York Times* noted, chronicling the picture's history in an article headlined FILM ECHOES THE PRESENT IN ATROCITIES OF THE PAST. "Seldom has a film seen by so few caused so much consternation for so many years."

So: Washington, DC, 2007, more than two years after the Abu Ghraib scandal, begins America's disenchantment with the military mission and conduct in Iraq. The antiwar déjà vu must be rolling over Fonda like a wave—and here she is, in a miniskirt and thigh-high leather boots that most of the crowd can't see behind the podium. What they see are her green-tinted sunglasses, beige turtleneck, and camel coat. She thanks the crowd for being willing to go through it all again.

Fonda protests the Iraq War at the January 2007 rally in Washington, DC. *Abaca Press / Alamy*

This is what she says:

> I'm really here because I want to thank you all, to thank you from the bottom of my heart for being here today. So many of you, and so many of today's speakers, including my fellow actors up here, were here at the very beginning, before we went into Iraq, because you *knew* and they *knew* what was in store. Thank you so much for the courage to stand up against this mean-spirited, vengeful administration. (*cheers*)
>
> Your actions are proof that the most precious part of this country, its soul, is alive and well, so thank you. Your ongoing commitment to ending this war allows people in other parts of the world to remain hopeful that America has the stuff to become again a country they can love and respect. Thank you. (*cheers*)
>
> I especially want to thank and acknowledge the servicemen and -women and the military families and Gold Star Mothers that are here. (*cheers*)
>
> A lot of press people have been asking me today what's the difference between now and during the Vietnam War. And I'll tell you, one *huge, crucial* difference: it took *six years* for Vietnam veterans, active-duty servicemen, Gold Star Mothers, and military families to come out against the war. It has happened now within three years of the war.* Their presence here is critical, and we should acknowledge their courage. (*cheers*)
>
> I haven't spoken at an antiwar rally in thirty-four years, because I've been afraid that because of the lies that have been and continue to be spread about me and that war, that they would be used to hurt this new antiwar movement.† But silence is no longer an option. (*cheers*)
>
> My daughter, who is here with me today—come here. (*Fonda waves Vanessa Vadim forward.*) She was a little girl when she would come with me to the anti–Vietnam War protests. She's

* Fonda had made the same observation earlier, in a 2005 speech at the National Press Club as the war's two-year anniversary marked a substantial demonstration: "People are realizing today that we can oppose the war and support the troops."

† The range and depth of anti-Fonda rhetoric has been chronicled in books by Carol Burke, Mary Hershberger, and Jerry Lembcke.

> here today with her two little children, my grandchildren. I'm very proud that they're here, but I'm so sad that we still have to do this, that we did not learn the lessons from the Vietnam War . . . that we've made the same mistakes—blindness to the realities on the ground, hubris and arrogance in dealing with the people and culture far older than we are—and that we understand so little; carelessness in our approach to rebuilding a country we've destroyed, allowing billions of dollars to be stolen, squandered at the hands of private contractors, just as this administration has done in our own gulf, in the post–[Hurricane] Katrina era. (*cheers*)
>
> So thank you, thank you for being here, and we'll continue to be here for as long as necessary. God bless.

The ghosts of Vietnam are raised. In the coverage to come, the *New York Times* will mention her with the other Hollywood celebrities, but the hard right will want her in the brig. Fox News will scroll "Hanoi Jane" footage and segue to her titillating 1968 sci-fi cult hit *Barbarella.* Celebrity guest Danny Bonaduce will declare, "I believe Jane Fonda believes in what she was saying, and she has a right to say it. Just if I were in charge, she'd be saying it from a prison cell from 1972 on."

Nasty woman. *Lock her up!*

Back at the rally, Susan Sarandon follows Fonda with data on the psychological toll: two hundred suicides and a 70 percent divorce rate among Iraq War vets. Robbins does an impish routine about impeaching Bush. Craggy-faced Sean Penn, in General MacArthur–esque aviator sunglasses, vows that if Congress can't heed the results of the recent midterm election and stop the war, "We won't support those politicians."

The stars know this "scenario," as performance studies scholar Diana Taylor labeled "meaning-making paradigms that structure social environments, behaviors and social outcomes" in *The Archive and the Repertoire.* The public, too, understands this part of the repertoire (another Taylor term), the oft-repeated, rowdy-but-orderly art of an afternoon's public protest, with mildly agitating speeches and maybe an arrest-free march.

Fonda's 2019–20 Fire Drill Fridays, though, are next level: thirteen weeks, sustained on one topic. Fonda led rallies every Friday morning at the Capitol, *plus* the Thursday-night teach-ins livestreamed on Facebook.

On October 11, 2019, clad in what immediately becomes her trademark red "Here I am!" overcoat, a wrap as bold as John Hancock's signature—"So bright it looked as if it might be warming the planet," Fredrick Kunkle will write in the *Washington Post*—Fonda is trailed by cameras, an eighty-one-year-old striding at workout speed past the Supreme Court to the Capitol. She arrives at a tiny stage, speaks forcefully, then hands the platform to scientists and activists supplying cold facts about the urgent threat of climate change.

This will be the DC pattern into January 2020, and elsewhere afterward. Jane coaxes out cameras and crowds. Experts take the stage.

Greenpeace and Code Pink are co-organizers, but it couldn't happen without Celebrity Jane. The media is on alert: Fonda plans to get arrested! The *Washington Post* has produced a stylish two-minute video of Fonda explaining the climate emergency and why she plans to protest it; she looks

Fonda addresses a Fire Drill Friday rally at Los Angeles City Hall, February 2020. *SOPA Images Limited / Alamy*

tremendously chic, tapping into her 1960s Paris years—beret, scarf, all black. Hanoi Jane footage is spliced in, and that persona seizes the frame: Activist Jane. (Who probably won't be remembered for her movies.)*

At the Capitol, Fonda's civil disobedience is no joke, even if it's not exactly Chicago 1968, where her soon-to-be husband Tom Hayden became part of the Chicago Seven, charged by the feds with inciting riots during the Democratic National Convention. After an hour of speeches, the Capitol Police mass on the steps, braced as if Fonda and her allies aim to storm the place.

The protesters are warned to move back or disband. Fonda and several dozen people are arrested. The handcuffing is orderly, and very slow. It will grow more efficient.

After the next week's rally (subject: the Green New Deal), police block access to the Capitol steps. The crowd is herded away. Police vehicles cut off return access to the Capitol grounds. The protestors, including an elderly man in a wheelchair, are corralled onto First Street SE, in front of the Library of Congress. Demonstrators teem in the street, where Fonda is arrested again with dozens more supporters.

"The house is on fire!" someone yells as Fonda gets zip-tied.

"Put the fire out!" the crowd responds.

Chants blare, bullhorn and choral response:

"*Show me what democracy looks like?!*"

"*This is what democracy looks like!!* "

"*Hey-hey. Ho-ho. Fossil fuels have got to go, Hey-hey. Ho-ho . . .* "

The next week the focus is oceans. Activist and longtime TV star Ted Danson (*Cheers*, *The Good Place*) genially invites more people to join the movement.

Fonda is not genial. "The fossil fuel industry wants us to think it's our fault," she says in her closing remarks. She pauses, then explodes: "*Bullshit!*"

* Fittingly, the same day as the first rally, the front page of the *Post*'s Style section featured an interview with director Steven Soderbergh promoting *The Laundromat*, a satire based on the 2016 Panama Papers scandal that serves as a scathing exposé of shell companies. Soderbergh continued his years-long lament that serious movies for adults—the kind Fonda once made—are all but dead.

The next day Jane goes viral. The Los Angeles wing of BAFTA (the British Academy of Film and Television Arts) gets more than two million views for a tweet of Fonda being arrested and shouting her acceptance speech over the din.

"BAFTA, thank you! For the Stanley Kubrick Britannia Award for Excellence in Film! Thank you! I'm sorry I'm not there!" She holds her handcuffed wrists near her chin as an officer shuffles her toward a paddy wagon. "I'm very honored!"

Jane Fonda Just Accepted a BAFTA Award While Being Arrested, and the Internet Is Impressed, a headline gushes.

MTV Australia's take: The Indisputably Badass Jane Fonda Accepted an Award While Being Arrested. The story's lede: "Jane Fonda is possibly the coolest octogenarian we have ever seen."

Weeks later she's sentenced to a night in jail. The *New York Times* is now on the story. The *Washington Post* reports that a guard advised her against using a prison mattress, likely bug-infested. Instead, she sleeps on her famous red coat.

She gets a court date. She smacks down conservative pundit Abby Huntsman on *The View*. She draws guff from Trump, on the stump in Louisiana, where he is campaigning for the Republican gubernatorial candidate the night before his loss to the incumbent Democrat. She's on CNN for the concluding ten-minute block with Don Lemon. It's a lovefest.

"Jane Fonda," Lemon says, beaming, signing off on the segment.

"Don Lemon," she replies, beaming right back.

PBS gives her the final ten-minute slot on a Thursday—programming that, in Washington, at least, conflicts directly with her livestreamed 7:00 PM virtual teach-in on war and the military. (The PBS segment is pretaped.)

"We've known each other a long time," Fonda says as anchor Judy Woodruff introduces her.

"Jane Fonda," Woodruff says at the end.

Again, Fonda returns the salute: "Judy Woodruff!"

Sally Field is the arrestee of the week December 13, when the topic is transitioning the economy to new climate-friendly jobs—a suitable theme for the Oscar-winning star of the 1979 labor movie *Norma Rae*. The day is wet and cold, yet a diehard spirit takes over. The rally soldiers on even as the House Judiciary Committee forwards Trump impeachment articles to the full House.

Field speaks off the cuff, and with conviction. "If those people don't listen," she says, waving at the Capitol behind her, "because they're all fighting other battles against each other—they're *not* listening. If we can't get them to listen and move, then do it yourself! . . . I'm soaking wet, I'm freezing cold, and I'm proud as hell to be here!"

"Indigenous people had the original Green New Deal," declares Winona LaDuke, economic and environmental activist and presidential candidate Ralph Nader's running mate in 1996 and 2000. LaDuke is part of the cadre of what Fonda calls "front-line communities" testifying about what's happening and what can be done:

> We've spent seventy years fighting a pipeline that has not happened and is not gonna happen. We remember when you could drink the water from every river, fifty million buffalo, passenger pigeons that blackened the sky; that's when America was great. . . . You may not notice that in DC because you're so self-absorbed; let's just say that one. But the rest of us know what's going down, and we're doing it.

The December 20 rally takes place one day before Fonda's birthday, when she'll turn eighty-two. The crowd is the biggest yet, easily thousands. Gloria Steinem shows up and gets arrested, along with over a hundred more willing to go beyond the rally and on to jail. Annie Leibovitz snaps photos for *Vogue*. The *New Yorker* tags along and writes about the "star power" of the Fire Drill Friday events. Fonda speaks first and last and makes most of the introductions.

Lower key but as critical to Fonda are the livestreamed Teach-In Thursdays. Shades of *Wayne's World*, the homemade videocast spoof from *Saturday Night Live*: in a small room, Fonda chats with experts arrayed on a couch. Everyone speaks toward an iPhone on a tripod, which wobbles as it pans. Volunteers try to maintain decent sound and light levels. Almost every week a boom mic dips into the shot.

"Talk loud," Fonda stage whispers to Hana Heineken of Rainforest Action Network on December 27. Guiding the dialogue, Fonda's homework shows. "Name names," she prods Heineken. The theme is forests, and Heineken says certain companies are notably bad when it comes to deforestation. Fonda wants them on WANTED posters.

"Unilever, Nestlé," Heineken begins.

"Those companies are bad on plastics too," Fonda interjects. The crisis of plastics is an ongoing motif, especially during Oceans Week.

Rolf Skar of Greenpeace mentions the "epidemic" of Indigenous land defenders being murdered. Fonda nods, and immediately adds data: "A hundred in the last ten years have been killed in Brazil."

As questions come in from around the world during the January 2 teach-in on corporate accountability, Fonda asks, "Anyone want to talk about the critical infrastructure law?"

Ellen Dorsey of Wallace Global Fund, Tamara Toles O'Laughlin of 350.org, and Katie Redford of EarthRights International all vigorously agree. States are passing laws making it a felony to protest at fossil fuel infrastructure sites.

Fonda, disgusted, says it's a Catch-22: "So right at the time when the scientists are telling us we have to stop fossil fuel expansion, it's been made criminal to protest the expansion of fossil fuels."

Toxify the polluters, Redford suggests. These sessions are very much about strategies and tactics, answering the viewers' inevitable *What can we do?* One answer: use the playbook that ultimately made a pariah of Big Tobacco and lately crippled opioid makers.

"It is a beast that has been gored but not killed," Redford says, going on about what "we" must do.

O'Laughlin pauses the conversation to make sure "we" means *everybody.*

"It's a beautiful opportunity, isn't it?" Fonda says, leaning in, ablaze with purpose. "It's a great challenge. We're so lucky to be involved right now, and healthy enough to fight. Right?" She pauses hopefully, both fists clenched in front of her.

Cut to 2024, moments after the presidential debate between Trump and Kamala Harris; Fonda is the first guest on *Jimmy Kimmel Live!*, and they are reacting positively to Harris's slam-dunk win. (This is the debate when Trump lashed out about immigrants eating dogs.) More than once she pivots to the audience, lifts those fists and urges immediate action on climate.

During the first teach-in, a viewer asks why Fonda, sitting next to *Grace and Frankie* costar Sam Waterston, doesn't make a climate emergency movie to instruct the public and mobilize support.

"Movies take time," Fonda responds. "And we don't have time."

In a bonus clip added to HBO's 2018 documentary *Jane Fonda in Five Acts*, Fonda recalls the moment, just before filming *Klute* (1971), when she realized "what kind of activist" she wanted to be: one who doesn't simply hose money and words but spends time on the front lines.

"You want to know how people organize? You go to Detroit and you go to meetings with union organizers. You want to find out what it's like to live near a toxic dump? You go there . . . A voice said to me, *You don't want to be someone who lives at the top of the hill, helping people down at the bottom of the hill. You want to be down at the bottom of the hill with the people. Otherwise how do you know what to do?*"

"I wanted to learn," Fonda explains as she hosts yet another teach-in. At the January 10 finale, Greenpeace USA executive director Annie Leonard, a pivotal organizer of Fire Drill Fridays, announces that Greenpeace and Fonda will continue the Fire Drill Fridays in California, and that grassroots chapters are springing up all over.

"Fueled by the power of Fonda's celebrity and a growing sense of urgency about the warming planet, the campaign has exploded in size and scope," the *Washington Post* will judge later that day.

"We're building an army, folks!" Fonda claims from the stage, avid and fashionable as ever in a sporty red fedora and her signature red overcoat. Joaquin Phoenix, Amber Valletta, June Diane Raphael, Susan Sarandon, and Martin Sheen supply celebrity wattage. The two-speaker sound system is still disappointingly meager, which shortchanges the authoritative contributions from speakers including activist and author Naomi Klein, community banker Kat Taylor (married to then-current Democratic presidential candidate Tom Steyer, with climate his top campaign issue), Lakota grassroots activist Ta'Sina Sapa Win Smith, and 350.org cofounder Bill McKibben. McKibben is occupying the JPMorgan Chase bank branch a few blocks away to launch his 350.org's #stopthemoneypipeline campaign. The statement he transmits remotely is barely audible.

With Fonda, though, you hear every word. "We've got to make it big!" she exhorts.

"She is well fortified now against charges that she doesn't know what she's talking about," Molly Haskell wrote of Fonda in 1974.

At that point, *Klute* Oscar in hand, Fonda had been largely absent from the Hollywood screen. She was stumping for causes and returning to Vietnam, even after the Hanoi stumble, to make the little-seen documentary *Introduction to the Enemy*.

When Haskell asked about the mainstream movies Fonda might again make, the actress philosophized, then got practical. "They are important in framing our minds," Fonda said. "I don't want to make heavy movies, though. I've read about everything that's come along, but they are written so irresponsibly. I notice that a lot of actors are producing their own films, so why shouldn't I?"

4

KISS KISS BANG BANG: LESSONS FROM THE '60S, PART I

Hurry Sundown • The Chase

> *Movie making is like fighting a war. Soldiers are good when they believe in what they're fighting for. The same is true for an artist: You must really want to express some dream or vision. Without that, eventually all the juices begin to dry up.*
>
> —Jane Fonda

Hurry Sundown OPENS WITH AN aerial shot from inside an airplane as bombs are dropped almost lyrically, blowing up dikes on the ground. Even without Fonda in mind, the first impression now is hardly of the American South, specifically Georgia, immediately after World War II. The mind's eye sees Vietnam, churned up and burned by the American bombing campaign.

Fonda was neither a full-throttle activist nor an actress with any substantial clout when she appeared in the star-studded *Hurry Sundown* in 1967, and the similarly social-minded all-star drama *The Chase* the previous year. Arrestingly, both movies—real political pictures, received as flops, yet deeply fascinating artifacts of mid-twentieth-century

America—are set in the South. Both feature landscapes blatantly resembling the war-torn images emerging from Vietnam. Both eventually combust, channeling the violent unrest beginning to define the decade.

Hurry Sundown (1967)

Hurry Sundown is an overheated civil rights movie directed by Otto Preminger, the prolific, esteemed, often abusive auteur on a career downslope after such topically themed hits as *Carmen Jones* (1954), *The Man with the Golden Arm* (1955), *Exodus* (1960), and *Advise & Consent* (1962). The cast is A-list—Michael Caine, Faye Dunaway, Diahann Carroll, Beah Richards, Robert Hooks, Burgess Meredith—and Fonda's name is high in the mix. She plays Julie Ann Warren, the ultimate high-society figure in a 1946 Jim Crow town, an object of privilege and elegance, clad in a series of stylish sleeveless dresses and wide-brimmed hats. The accent isn't as broad as in *Period of Adjustment*, but Julie Ann's drawl is massively musical.

"You know I was ten years old before I knew *damn* and *Yankee* were two separate words?" she coos to a northern industrialist, her voice sweet as a peach. Julie is serving up the sugar to promote her husband's business chances.

Julie is positioned early to be a heroine. At a social gathering after the pompous redneck judge played by Burgess Meredith storms out of his sharply segregated church (Black worshipers are relegated to the back of the sanctuary), the racist judge irrationally seethes that a Black woman who'd taken Communion just before he was offered the cup was "drunken, syphilitic." Fonda's Julie has a smooth reply. "Do you know this woman?" she says with a smile, her voice up high and innocent. "Then how come you're so sure she's drunken and syphilitic and all? Unless, of course, you're especially qualified in those fields." Fonda delivers the dart lightly. The poison is withheld until the last phrase, the chin lifted slightly.

Hurry Sundown will complicate Julie, but while the role has its moments, the long picture is not really about her; Fonda exits with twenty-three minutes to go. But, as in *Walk on the Wild Side*, it's her character's moral recognition that drives the turgid movie's climax.

The movie is drawn from the bestselling, thousand-plus-page 1964 novel by K. B. Gilden, the pen name of wife-and-husband writers Katya and Bert Gilden; the screen adaptation was by Thomas C. Ryan, whose only other notable credit is for adapting Carson McCullers's *The Heart Is a Lonely Hunter*. Cowriting with Ryan was playwright Horton Foote, who had already earned an Academy Award for adapting Harper Lee's *To Kill a Mockingbird* in 1962, and who would go on to a major stage and screen career—another Oscar for *Tender Mercies* in 1984 and the 1995 drama Pulitzer for his play *The Young Man from Atlanta*. Despite the writing pedigree, *Hurry Sundown*'s White villains are bulgingly caricatured southern zealots—though how gross the caricatures really are can be debated, when in real life America was somewhere on the road between Bull Connor's harsh tactics defending segregation in Birmingham in the early 1960s and the 1968 presidential run of George Wallace, who as Alabama governor had proclaimed, "Segregation now! Segregation tomorrow! Segregation forever!"

Distractingly, Michael Caine is massively miscast as Fonda's good ol' boy husband. Caine was hot off his Oscar-nominated performance as the Cockney womanizer of *Alfie* and was in the thick of three British spy pictures based on popular Len Deighton novels when he took on the part of an amoral land developer in *Hurry Sundown*. In his memoir *The Elephant to Hollywood*, Caine recounts the advice he got from fellow Brit and *Gone with the Wind* star Vivien Leigh: to handle American Deep South speech, Leigh counseled, say "Four door Ford" as "foah doah Ford," and go from there. But the diphthongs don't glide convincingly off Caine's ineffably English tongue.

Worse, he's playing a rough, off-putting egotist. Henry Warren is a greedy racist spewing slurs, buttering up Meredith's cracker of a judge, sleeping with the judge's daughter, negligently hospitalizing his small son, inadvertently killing his adolescent nephew, and raping his wife. The wife is Fonda, enduring what *New Yorker* film critic Richard Brody in 2011 labeled "one of the longest, and most repellant, screen kisses ever filmed." Preminger, not one to shy away from sensationalizing, tactlessly presses his camera as close as he can.

The melodrama hinges on White developers trying to wrest the last parcels of land they need from two holdouts: a poor White farmer named Rad (John Phillip Law, soon Fonda's opposite in *Barbarella*), and an elderly Black woman named Rose (the formidable Beah Richards, an Oscar nominee that season for the far more digestible *Guess Who's Coming to Dinner?*). Neither Rad nor Rose wants to sell, but Julie may actually control Rose's land—especially in the eyes of the crooked southern court.

Caine expects his wife to take this advantage. Julie won't do it. She adores Rose, who practically raised her. Caine, unafraid of playing unlikable characters, gently presses Julie, leaning in from slightly above, a predatory position at odds with the reassuring smoothness of his voice. In this long take, a medium close-up on the plush couch of their estate, Julie grows defensive. Fonda stammers: "She . . . she loved me. There was a time when she was the only one in this whole world I knew really loved me."

Looking straight ahead, visualizing a mean past, Fonda gives us an early glimpse of her ferocious loneliness in 1969's *They Shoot Horses, Don't They?*, playing another woman trapped in an America rife with deadly injustice. "And I can't go against her," Julie concludes.

But she does. Julie, finally channeling her husband's underhanded ways, claims that the property was never really sold to Rose's family. Fonda shows that Julie is uncomfortable playing the snake, but play it Julie does, growing slightly haughty.

Rose rises in fury to refute the lie, and Preminger's melodrama is so pulpy that Rose all but dies on the spot. Even so, Richards is rather awesome in the scene—tears and shock and heartbreak, fast and furious. Richards is tasked with embodying the vast American racist betrayal, and she squeezes it into a tremendous gush.

Like Rad, Rose's son Reeve (Robert Hooks) is a returning World War II vet, and he knows how to use dynamite to blow irrigation ditches into the earth. If Reeve and Rad work together—Reeve's radical idea—they could farm profitably. But in 1946 Georgia, as 1967 audiences would well understand, Jim Crow and KKK forces would conspire to put that dynamite to more reactionary use.

Diahann Carroll, renowned for her tremendous poise, ultimately becomes the movie's moral center as Vivian, the local teacher and Reeve's love interest. When Vivian follows Julie into the courthouse's

Fonda with Diahann Carroll, the moral center of *Hurry Sundown*. *SIGMA / RGR Collection / Alamy*

Whites-only ladies' room to tell Julie her husband has lied, Julie slaps her.* Fonda plays the instant shame convincingly, tearing up and begging forgiveness. It's Julie's wake-up call, the sort of social epiphany Fonda's characters will experience again and again.

An indignant White woman comes into the ladies' room and asks what Carroll is doing there. "Cleaning up," Carroll quips, nailing the satisfying one-liner with coiled composure.

* This precedes by six months *In the Heat of the Night* and the year's most famous interracial slapping scene, when Sidney Poitier's Philadelphia detective, stuck working on a case down south, is smacked by a White plantation owner. Poitier immediately slaps him back, right in front of the chesty sheriff played by Rod Steiger, whose perplexity is at the core of the movie, and the year. See Mark Harris's terrific movie history of 1967, *Pictures at a Revolution: Five Movies and the Birth of the New Hollywood* (New York: Penguin, 2008).

There is a mischievous bit of business as Carroll's Vivian shows up at the county building to examine historical records. Burgess Meredith, the wildly bigoted judge, is outraged that a Black woman simply walked in. But Carroll coolly flatters him while he fulminates in his office, and as he calms down he grabs a small inner tube—his hemorrhoid pillow—and blows into the valve. The sight gag: the tube briefly encircles his face, making a crude ass of the judge.

The parade of stars keeps you watching. Faye Dunaway, making her movie debut and on the cusp of an Oscar nomination and superstardom with *Bonnie and Clyde*, released just six months after *Sundown*, fascinates in her brief appearances as Rad's spirited, earthy wife, dressed in the drab fabrics and tones of the dirt poor; even her khaki hair lacks color, contrasting with rich Julie's henna-red mane. (Dunaway makes up for the dusty patina with fierce, upright loyalty to Rad and a vibrant grip on the camera.) Robert Hooks, riding high as a Tony nominee for Broadway's *Hallelujah, Baby!* and a lead actor with enough magnetism to play the super-competent title figure in the 1972 Blaxploitation movie *Trouble Man*, is a grave, dignified match for Carroll as the noble war vet with progressive plans. And Richards, after her great swoon, gets a brief, intense deathbed speech that she delivers with quiet force and belated anger, recognizing that she should have opposed White supremacy more vigorously. She urges Hooks to stand tall.

This is fast company, and Fonda keeps up. She conveys easy polish and a lively mind, even in a gothic characterization that paints Julie as both angel and devil. Julie is an abused wife, a manipulative one-percenter, and eventually the righteous story's courtroom savior. Fonda mostly is offhand and reflective, giving Julie's shifting facets a cool grounding.

But she's stuck in a potboiler, and Preminger, despite his social high-mindedness,* has a lurid streak. Early in the story the bored Julie drunkenly tries seducing her husband. She drinks suggestively from a

* Stories abound of Preminger's cruelty to actors, but it's worth remembering his peak value. Director/historian Peter Bogdanovich, in his 1999 book *Movie of the Week*, rated Preminger as "one of the finest and most influential filmmakers of the Forties into the Seventies who almost single-handedly broke down the walls of movie censorship and blacklisting."

liquor bottle, then grabs her husband's saxophone. (Somehow this lout is a lapsed musician; late in the picture he laments the soulful jazzman he might have been. Remember: the novel was a thousand pages long.) Fonda is directed to recline Caine. Slowly, with maximum innuendo, she blows his horn.

Possibly this was a reason the *New York Times* branded the film "an offense to intelligence."

Again, it's not really her picture: the movie finishes with the marriage that works (Dunaway and Law) and the promising union that's just starting (Carroll and Hooks). But *Hurry Sundown* shows a Fonda whom audiences would come to know—one who learns about the wicked world and consciously strips herself of privilege to work for justice. The justice she pursues in the movie's subplot involves standing up for her disabled son, who is ruinously treated by Caine. The justice she pursues in real life would soon involve bombed dikes flooding farmland—only not in Georgia, as in *Sundown*'s climax, but in Vietnam.

Julie's courtroom recognition is not that she can "save" Reeve and his land, but that she can at least stop lying to herself and abandon her role in perpetuating systemic harm. She nearly gets a *Frankly, my dear, I don't give a damn* exit line, as Fonda tells Caine, the embodiment of reckless White power, that she's done with him. Desperate, he asks, "Where am I supposed to go?"

"Back to the shrimp boats," Fonda's Julie says, practically disinterested, cutting him down to size. "Or anywhere you like."

The Chase (1966)

As *The Chase* was being put together in 1965, the Watts neighborhood in Los Angeles erupted into a four-day riot, with nearly three dozen people killed. *The Chase* isn't about that—it's based on an early-1950s Texas-set play by Horton Foote—yet the movie feels concussed by current events. It's a more explosive, more clairvoyant, and substantially more nuanced American panorama than *Hurry Sundown.* "I had written what I thought was a good, small picture about twenty-four hours in the life of a Texas town," screenwriter Lillian Hellman said of her intentions after the film's release, when it was regarded as a massive mess.

If the declining Preminger was old Hollywood, Arthur Penn—a veteran of the Actors Studio and the director of playwright Hellman's 1960 Broadway drama *Toys in the Attic*—was about to become the face of New Hollywood. Penn had already earned acclaim for directing Paul Newman in *The Left-Handed Gun* (1958), and Anne Bancroft and Patty Duke in their Oscar-winning 1962 performances in *The Miracle Worker* (he also directed them onstage in the story's original Broadway run). Warren Beatty starred in Penn's 1965 film *Mickey One*, a visually striking, narratively jangled oddity in the manner of French Nouvelle Vague icons François Truffaut and Jean-Luc Godard.

Mickey One is an intriguing, stark black-and-white warmup for *The Chase*, with Penn and Beatty—emerging Actors Studio mavericks about to shock old Hollywood with the bullets and bluegrass of *Bonnie and Clyde*—taking sinister views of showbiz, America, and human existence. *Mickey One* is not an easy picture. But it is clearly descended from the hip, juddering tactics of Truffaut (*Shoot the Piano Player*, *Jules et Jim*) and Godard (*Breathless*, *Contempt*)—both of whom were approached before Penn to direct *Bonnie and Clyde*. It's not a movie that deserves to be as buried as it is.

The catchy credits feature a jazzy saxophone (Stan Getz is the soloist) underscoring an absurd image: beefy, toweled men with mobster faces laughing in a sauna at Beatty, puffing a cigar, fully clothed right down to snappy gloves and a Chaplinesque bowler hat. Beatty plays a stand-up comic in league with the mob, and in the opening montage life is good: elegant sports car, women galore, nightclub applause.

But the setup is Kafka: Suddenly he owes his bosses everything he has. For what? The messenger won't say.

Beatty runs for his life. He goes underground, where the blighted, malevolent American landscape is rife with trashy alleys and dim, grubby rooms. The design, pivotal in this absurdist exercise, is by George Jenkins, who would play a role in four key Fonda pictures and would design director Alan J. Pakula's 1970s "paranoia trilogy" of *Klute*, *The Parallax View*, and *All the President's Men*.

Beatty picks up an assaulted man's Social Security card and has the Polish name truncated by an employer to Mickey One. Inevitably, he tries to work his way back into the stand-up game, and Beatty performs his comedy with a nasty edge. Even telling jokes, he's a bit of a mobster himself. The rich imagery in the movie's first moments includes a shot of heavies beating a guy in a room while Beatty watches. Then a dame on his lap distracts him with a kiss, and he literally looks the other way.

Like his character in *Bonnie and Clyde*, Beatty's Mickey is a fugitive. But Mickey *believes* he's guilty. Of what? asks Jenny (Alexandra Stewart), the young woman he shacks up with for a time. "Of not being innocent," he says.

Questions pop up now and then about signs from God, suggesting, but not embracing, a religious through-line.

An auto junkyard looms large as a hellish American graveyard, and a street fire suggests civic decline. Bursting into wild flame is a machine called "Yes" that looks like a giant white Erector Set of motion, the artistic display of a Felliniesque mute who sporadically shadows Mickey. What is art? Is Mickey an artist? In a black-comic scene rippling with menace, Mickey auditions for a gangster sitting in the blackness of an empty theater. Alone onstage, Mickey feels sure he's about to be murdered. A long shot shows Beatty pinned onstage by a harsh spotlight, a tiny figure in a single white shaft. It looks like we're viewing him through the barrel of a gun.

"I mean, I heard of tough audiences, but I think this is illegal," Beatty says into the microphone, hunching slightly, staring nervously into the blinding light. The gallows-humor punch line: "I don't even know if I'm in season."

Mickey One flopped with audiences and confused Hollywood honchos, but it was an early missive from the European-influenced New Hollywood that would land with force in 1967, thanks in part to the irreverent style and violence of the Beatty-produced, Penn-directed *Bonnie and Clyde*.

But between *Mickey* and *Bonnie* came Penn's *The Chase*, a movie with authorship that, notoriously, is impossible to untangle. Hellman was adapting Horton Foote's 1952 play, which he made into a novel four years later. Penn biographer Nat Segaloff notes that producer Sam Spiegel hired blacklisted writer Michael Wilson to work big themes into "his unsigned first draft dated March 11, 1959"; he dates Hellman's "final script" to March 30, 1965, when Spiegel hired Ivan Moffat "for a polish."

In a twist worthy of a David Mamet or Coen brothers Hollywood satire, Foote confirmed to Segaloff that at the end, the playwright himself was brought back as a screenwriter, to rework his now-unrecognizable original story.

The movie took shape as part of producer Spiegel's Hollywood comeback, and his reputation for such "important" films as *The African Queen*, *On the Waterfront*, *Bridge on the River Kwai*, and *Lawrence of Arabia* helped draw top actors. (The reputations of the sturdy Hellman and in-demand Penn were a plus too.) The lore of *The Chase* is that Penn, still fairly new to filmmaking, made a fatal Hollywood mistake: he departed after shooting wrapped to stage the Broadway-bound musical *Golden Boy* starring Sammy Davis Jr. Spiegel then had the picture edited in a way Penn hated.

"It was not a happy experience," Hellman summed up, even as she allowed that "certainly most of my script was there."

So a timely picture (in color, like *Hurry Sundown*) about a nation out of control was shake-'n'-baked by a Hollywood process that nobody controlled.

Still, as a document of everything mixed up about the '60s, *The Chase* exerts a deep allure. Writing an excited book about Penn in 1969, British critic Robin Wood declared it "Penn's first indisputable (one would have thought) masterpiece." The plot hinges on another fugitive: an escaped convict named Bubber played by Robert Redford and vaguely positioned as a martyr. Bubber and a fellow escapee scamper through the Texas night as the opening credits roll, with a crackling main title design by the James Bond franchise's Maurice Binder and moody, suspenseful music by Bond's John Barry. Together the convicts carjack a passing motorist, but the sidekick kills the motorist with a rock and takes off with the car.

"Hey! What'd you do it for? You bastard!" Bubber yells as the other man vanishes. Bubber's a good guy, we will learn. He was jailed for drunkenly flying a helicopter belonging to Val Rogers (E. G. Marshall), the rich man who runs the town, but Bubber also took the rap for things he didn't do. Though he is about to vanish until the climax of the film, we are primed to like him because, sensibly, he is appalled by the careless killing.

In Foote's play, the Bubber character is heading back to his hometown for vengeance on the sheriff who sent him away. In the movie, Marlon Brando plays the sheriff as the lone reasonable figure in a very wild small town, where the throng of strivers and haters emerge as a rococo portrait of American decadence.

"Some of those people out there are just *nuts*," Brando murmurs with authentic feeling as threats rise through the story's lone action-packed night. "They're just nuts," he repeats, as his wife (Angie Dickinson, who makes her character a cool, stable partner for Brando's rational lawman) listens with concern. Pauline Kael wrote that the 1966 audience laughed at that line, but it's hard to imagine audiences laughing fifty years later as *The Chase* displays a combustible public that is either overzealous—novelist Philip Roth's "indigenous American berserk"—or apathetic, with no functional, sensible middle.

The movie's hard kernel of *people are nuts* derives from 1952 Foote, whose even-handed Sheriff Calder—called Hawes in the play—tries to hold the line against a lynch mob. "The chase" is the race to see whether institutional justice can outrun the crazed public.

Foote's depressing answer: *No.* The movie shows that a public aflame with fear will, with righteous fury, trample law and order.

Anna, Bubber's wife, is played by Fonda with a flat Texas accent, common sense, and tensile emotional strength. She tries to protect her fugitive husband from the horde. But it's a challenge for this loosely drawn, wrong-side-of-the-tracks woman to trust Brando—the law.

The sexual revolution is in full swing in town, and it's tangled up with free-ranging violence. Emily Stewart (Janice Rule, in a money-green dress the same shade as one that the rich Val Rogers bought for Dickinson's character) sashays through the bank where her nebbishy husband (Robert Duvall) works, and she makes an unapologetic beeline for her lover, Damon Fuller (Richard Bradford). A birthday gala for Rogers is afoot, and since the social climber Emily Stewart and her cipher of a spouse aren't invited, they throw a party of their own. It's a racy blowout, mirrored by yet another party populated by teenagers next door.

The Stewarts' party spins up so drunkenly that the guests shoot at each other with pretend handguns and automatic weapons, foreshadowing

Fonda and Marlon Brando in *The Chase*. *ZUMA Press Inc. / Alamy*

the ungovernable cataclysm of *The Chase*'s big finish. Someone lobs a high-heeled shoe as a "grenade" that "blows up" a bucket of ice. Someone else fires a real gun, and Brando's Sheriff Calder arrives to settle folks down. As he leaves, Emily invites him to stay, grinning some innuendo about his "pistol."

Then Calder's in town narrowly keeping Damon and two sidekicks from lynching Lester (Joel Fluellen), the Black man who runs the vast car junkyard where Bubber is hiding. The open terrorism of the Jim Crow South is brutally displayed as the White men tell Lester to "put your knife away," when, as the hapless man tries to point out, he doesn't *have* a knife. Minor frightened Black characters populate the edges of the picture until Lester—who once was done a favor by Bubber and now is cornered into paying it back—becomes pivotal.

Calder is disgusted by the tenor of the town, and Brando meanly murmurs insults. "Why don't you go on home and open another bottle, and get back in bed with your friend's wife," he tells Damon after breaking up the lynching party. Another time, he mutters about whether any of his citizens can read.

Calder locks up Lester for his own protection, but it doesn't work. Val Rogers, the moneyed E. G. Marshall character, shows up at the jail demanding to know where Bubber is. Damon and his gang follow. They beat Calder into submission, pulverizing Brando until he looks like his punch-drunk, truth-telling Terry Malloy at the end of *On the Waterfront*. Then the rich man's gang beats the information about Bubber's whereabouts out of Lester.

Fonda's work comes during the back third of the film. Anna is a plot device: Bubber, on the run, will make his way to her. Wide-eyed, guarded, and as attentive as a fox, Fonda's Anna also becomes the ears for men explaining how society works.

Calder gives a speech that Brando imbues with realpolitik about how he's bending the rules so he can protect Bubber. Bubber gives a speech that the earnest Redford fills with conviction about how he's too *free* now, *inside*, to suffer any longer the indignities of unjust imprisonment. "Bubber makes the movie's point," Redford told biographer Michael Feeney Callan. "The role was also the renegade, done-down kid, and that was easy for me, since I'd considered myself an outsider to convention for a lot of my teens."

Fonda's job is to listen, mixed up to the max. Anna is conflicted about justice: "But you didn't do it! You can't be convicted!" she blurts to Bubber, as Redford scowls at her naïveté. Anna is also conflicted about her lovers: she's married to Bubber, but she's been seeing upper-class Jake Rogers (James Fox), son of Val; Jake was her first beau, and now he's married and cheating. During their usual Saturday-night hotel-room tryst, Anna rebuffs Jake's talk of any sort of dreamy future for them together.

Jake asks why she never asks for anything. "Because I wouldn't get it," Anna says. (The bleak utterance anticipates Barbara Loden's 1970 film *Wanda*, an enigma in its day but entered into the National Film Registry in 2017.) Fonda, shot in close-up, the light low, lying on the carpeted hotel room floor, delivers the line with just the slightest whisper of resignation. She's too tough to waste time feeling sorry for herself; her Anna maintains a psychologically protective edge. This will be sharpened and hardened in *They Shoot Horses, Don't They?* and *Klute*.

As in *Casablanca*, morally, a) there's no genuinely wrong choice for Anna between Bubber and Jake, and b) their romantic problems don't amount to a hill of beans. In this formulation, of course, Fonda's Anna, our dusty Texan Ingrid Bergman, tilts slightly toward the noble rebel on the run. (The Texas accent here, by the way, is less lavish than the pronunciations in *Period of Adjustment* or even *Hurry Sundown*. After drawling her way through much of the '60s—a decade in which, as the next chapter will explore, she also often acted in French—in the '70s Fonda would play no southerners.)

For emerging stars Redford and Fonda, about to hit it big as the *Barefoot in the Park* newlyweds, the chance to work with the mighty Brando was too good to pass up. As a rational sheriff in a hedonistic town bent on mob rule, Brando, acting half as fast (or twice as slow) as everyone else, deliberately sucks the flamboyance out of the sheriff's sardonic one-liners. As a character trait it eventually makes sense, even if at first it seems like scratch-and-mumble run amok. In his 1986 memoir, French director Roger Vadim comically describes Fonda at home during their marriage doing a two-minute impersonation of Brando, in character as Calder, pondering a question and fidgeting: "Seated at a desk, she sighed, scratched her nose, failed to find an answer worthy of a California [*sic*] sheriff, tilted the chair back, belched without making noise. . . . She thought about the question, closed her eyes, opened them, threw back her head as if about to laugh, but didn't laugh."

Indeed, there's a pensive moment in the film during which Brando picks up a pipe, rubs both sides of his nose with it, tells his wife to give back that green party dress Marshall's character bought for her, then, ending the scene, looks again meaningfully at the pipe.

Yet Brando's turn is not a throwaway. *New York Times* critic A. O. Scott later rated *The Chase* with other 1960s Brando "flops" *Reflections in a Golden Eye* and *Burn!* as "three of Mr. Brando's subtlest and most unnerving performances . . . each one an exploration of the frustrations, corruptions and compromises of power." Brando's weary way of entering a scene as if he's already had a long day works to the character's advantage.

"The state of Texas says anybody can own a gun and most of you've got two but deputies you ain't," Brando's Calder says flatly, without commas, as angry citizens demand to join the hunt for Bubber. Brando, with a ten-gallon hat to tilt around and with a big belt buckle to clasp, keeps these lines laconic but law-based as Calder tries to douse the burning fuse.

As audiences knew at that moment, Brando was *the* great Hollywood figurehead of mid-1960s acting and activism. (By this point Harry Belafonte was fully on the barricades with Martin Luther King and had retreated from the screen.) Still, even with the civil rights movement and early Vietnam discontent percolating under the action, the high-minded intentions of everyone from producer to writers to celebrity activist-actors couldn't bring solid political coherence to *The Chase*, especially given a heavy-handed ending in which a minor character slides in practically from nowhere to assassinate Bubber on the jailhouse steps as Calder whisks him toward the safety of the jail.

Disturbingly and unmistakably, the image evokes Jack Ruby shooting Lee Harvey Oswald. "Bubber, for me," Penn told Redford biographer Callan, "was a representational figure who symbolized the purity that was lost after Kennedy's assassination. He became a golden martyr." Yet there is no satisfying way for that political history to scan with the story on the screen. The JFK evocation muddies the transmission of an already hard-to-read picture.

That violent climax comes on the heels of sheer anarchy as the whole town flocks to Bubber's hideout in the vast auto junkyard that, as in *Mickey One*, plainly stands for American decay in a decade already torn by Vietnam. Torches are lit, Molotov cocktails are tossed, and soon the blazing, bizarre extravaganza calls to mind *Apocalypse Now*, with roughly the same level of adrenalized mayhem. "*The horror*," Brando as the depraved Kurtz famously purrs in Francis Ford Coppola's 1979 film, and the actor's hypnotized vocal timbre as he utters that line isn't far from the way he breathes "Some of those people out there are just nuts. They're just nuts" in *The Chase*. As the great American junkyard burns, a thrilled teenage girl tosses an earring into the flames and then practically shrieks to a nearby boy, "I'd love you forever if you got my earring for me through fire, through *war!*"

The Chase radically scaled up the social injustice in Fonda's oeuvre, and her Anna watches in alarm, unable to leverage any kind of change.

The movie's final shot is of Fonda's sooty-faced Anna waiting outside Val Rogers's house; Jake was wounded in the melee. When Rogers comes out and says dully, "My son died at five o'clock," Fonda simply gets up and walks away, toward the camera and then out of the frame as the credits roll and the mournful soundtrack plays chords of *Amen*.

The Chase rates only a paragraph in Fonda's first memoir. "What a package, right?" she gushes as she lists the cast. She also calls the picture "Lillian Hellman's *The Chase*." Mainly she laments how big her own hair is.

Still: *The Chase* had its finger on the country's racing pulse. But if Penn lost control as Spiegel edited it, what might a Penn cut have been? Penn would go on to direct the wonderfully garrulous 1970 western satire *Little Big Man*, but he would muddle Arlo Guthrie's winsome, cheeky protest song "Alice's Restaurant" into the bloated, cynical 1969 movie of the same name, showing no kinship with hippies.* The ur-'60s experience of *The Chase* surely helped brand impressions upon Fonda about how to make, and lose, meaning in movies. Say what you want—and later, Penn would say disparaging things about Fonda's explicitly political pictures—but when Fonda got around to making movies, they would say what she wanted.

* A disappointed Arlo Guthrie walked out on the *Alice's Restaurant* premiere, and for a bitter take on the '60s, see Penn's glum, damage-filled *Four Friends* (1981).

5

VIVE LA DIFFÉRENCE: LESSONS FROM THE '60S, PART II

Any Wednesday • Les Félins (Joy House) • La Ronde (Circle of Love) • La Curée (The Game Is Over) • Spirits of the Dead • Barbarella

> *"There was a time," her father, a more intuitive and less flexible actor, groans, "when Jane would have bored the hell out of anybody, talking about the Method." The days of theorizing are long over. "With Vadim I learned to relax," she says, "and not let the cerebral machinations show."*
>
> —*New York Times,* 1974

IN HOLLYWOOD, THE SECOND HALF of the 1960s were cataclysmic. Studios were devoured by conglomerates; public taste lurched from the box office dominance of the shiny *The Sound of Music* in 1965 to a Best Picture win for the X-rated *Midnight Cowboy* in 1970. Reflected in this arc was the country's convulsion under the weight of riots, assassinations, and the quagmire of the Vietnam War.

The counterculture was in full purple flower. "Cinema" was blowing up. Hippies were making pictures. A leader of the pack: Jane's little brother, Peter—"Captain America" in the out-of-nowhere indie hit *Easy Rider* (1969).

Jane sensed the "meaning" gap between their projects as early as 1966. Peter was making a rebel biker flick called *The Wild Angels*, yanking its conflicts right off the streets. She was making yet another vanilla pudding romantic comedy: *Any Wednesday*.

Any Wednesday (1966)

Casablanca cowriter Julius Epstein, back with Fonda after *Tall Story* and lugging along some of the same bad habits, adapted *Any Wednesday* from Muriel Resnik's 1964 four-character bedroom farce, a Broadway hit at 983 total performances. In the film version, director Robert Ellis Miller slides split-screen panels around to push couples together or split them apart—a tired cliché by 1966 (though juiced in a caper context for 1968's *The Thomas Crown Affair*). The title song is pure sap, with these not-quite-rhyming lyrics from Alan and Marilyn Bergman: "When we surrender / The whole day's agenda / To love." That's the tone.

Fonda plays Ellen Gordon, suckered into covering up businessman Jason Robards's serial philandering. She bats her eyes in huffy indignation, but soon enough they're involved. The plot is pinched from the 1961 Best Picture winner, *The Apartment*: Robards gets his business to purchase a flat for "entertaining," only the company doesn't really need it. Robards uses it, with Fonda. She is "kept." He visits every Wednesday.

In the first of three movies he would make with Fonda, Robards is irascible and charismatic, easy to watch, delightful to root against. But this is a melodrama, and he's in a one-note role: the villain, a titan of industry who's equally domineering in his romantic acquisitions. The splendid Rosemary Murphy, reprising her Tony-nominated turn from the Broadway production as Robards's winning, worldly wife, Dorothy, eventually leaves this cad, saying with a complicated smile that he's exciting, but not "husband material."

Dean Jones, as a plain-speaking Ohio inventor battling Robards's takeover of his small company, is annoyingly folksy, adopting the kind of James Stewart routine that made Jim Hutton a pest in *Period of Adjustment*. (The overanimated Jones's costars just then were often animals: surrounding this were *That Darn Cat!*, *The Ugly Dachshund*, and *Monkeys, Go Home!*, and then came his adventures with a sentient Volkswagen Beetle in *The Love Bug*.) To keep the suddenly omnipresent Dorothy from discovering Robards's tomcatting, Jones pretends to be Fonda's husband. Gene Hackman played the role on Broadway, and his offhand style likely felt more adult.

That ace Broadway cast included Sandy Dennis, who won a Tony playing Ellen. But in the movie, Ellen is not much of a role. Fonda is stuck as another spacey ingenue, an anxious ditz.

At first, at least, Fonda looks more like herself, with her long hair down and wearing appealing, unfussy earth-tone clothes; it almost begins to feel like the actual 1960s, not the leftover 1950s. Fonda's Ellen works in an art gallery, giving the flick a touch of Manhattan style, but this career is dropped as soon as she becomes "kept." Two years into her tenure as a "kept" woman, she has a shorter, more conservative upswept housewife hairdo.

Comedy is hard, and it breaks a heavy sweat here. Fonda fights the wacky long sleeves of a fancy nightgown Robards has bought for her. She faints when Dorothy first surprises her in the apartment. She pouts, she whines, she guzzles champagne from the bottle. Director Miller weirdly has her acting as if to a balcony while she blows out her thirtieth birthday candle alone, gushing a string of sad lines and kitten-mewl cries.

Yet flapping ingenue roles were common in the mid-1960s. The cooler, freer "kooks" embodied by the likes of Julie Christie in *Petulia* (1968) and Goldie Hawn in *Cactus Flower* (1969) hadn't quite come in.

"Do you want to know what your hang-up is?" Jones's character blurts at Ellen. "You're a thirty-year-old child."

Fonda plays that—emotional, flighty—because the heart of this thirty-year-old woman-child is won with bouquets of bright balloons. Fonda throws herself into it. But what was the use? "One night I'd come home from some idiotic scene I was doing and Peter comes rolling in on his motorcycle," Fonda told *Newsweek* in 1977. "He was at the beginning of his counter-culture trip. He'd just finished a scene where there was this huge fight in a church and he had this guitar with him and was writing songs."

His film, *The Wild Angels*, was from producer-director Roger Corman, with Peter starring as Blues, leader of a group of Hells Angels bikers. The movie features plenty of real Hells Angels, and Peter's character and his pal Loser (Bruce Dern) flaunt iron crosses and swastikas among their denim and leather outfits. Picking a fight then fleeing from the cops, Dern's character gets shot; he dies when his buddies break him out of the hospital. The church scene that Jane mentions is Loser's funeral, with Peter railing against the priest and declaring the bikers as being pro-"freedom." The finish is unhinged: drink, drugs, and rape, society cracking at its foundations. As the late 1960s reeled, the pictures grew feral.

"And," Jane continued to *Newsweek*, "I realized that at least he was relating to *something* that had to do with the American culture, while I was making this ridiculous movie about a young mistress of a married executive."

If Fonda was reaching a Hollywood dead end, she also was just about done with her lessons abroad as a semi-expat half based in France. ("I lived all over Paris," she told the Parisian magazine *Numéro* in 2020, recalling her eight years with Roger Vadim.) The international body of work she compiled through the '60s offered a piquant array of Continental flavors, but thanks to her husband and main collaborator, Vadim—the noted French playboy director of *And God Created Woman* (1956) and *Dangerous Liaisons* (1959), author of the 1986 memoir *Bardot, Deneuve, Fonda: My Life with the Three Most Beautiful Women in the World*—this oeuvre, too, was drenched in sex.

Her five European pictures, ending with the indelibly cult-y, quintessentially Vadim-y *Barbarella* . . .

Les Félins (a.k.a. *Joy House* in the US, *The Love Cage* in the UK, 1964)

Emerging French star Alain Delon—handsome and edgy, bedroom eyes and hardwired sneer—had played the shifty lead in director René Clément's 1960 film *Purple Noon*, an effective thriller in color, notable as the first screen version of Patricia Highsmith's endlessly adaptable thriller *The Talented Mr. Ripley*. Teamed with Delon and Clément in a new black-and-white mystery, Fonda was slated for a workout in style.

In *Les Félins*, Delon is Marc, a jaunty playboy who fools around with a rich thug's wife and gets chased by the thug's goons from New York to Nice. In Nice he hides among the down-and-outers in a church's soup kitchen.

Enter Fonda and Lola Albright: twin angels of death, in stunning silhouette, matching black dresses and scarves, generously bringing home-cooked food to the drifters. Albright—sophisticated, calculating—is Barbara, Fonda's rich cousin. Barbara hires Delon to be the live-in driver on her weirdly isolated mansion. Fonda's character, a poor relation named Melinda, is basically a scullery maid racked with envy and ambition.

"If I were Barbara, I'd be able to get what I want," Fonda's Melinda confides to Delon.

Lola Albright, Fonda, and Alain Delon in *Les Félins*.
Photo 12 / Alamy

Fonda is instantly smitten by the roguish, hunted Delon. She flirts, joking about the ticklishness of the mansion's front gate lock. Fonda pops the lock open with a comically large key.

The Big (and weird) Secret: Barbara is concealing her lover, Vincent, *inside* the mansion's walls, because together Barbara and Vincent murdered Barbara's husband several years earlier. Delon is their patsy. They will kill him to steal his identity, pawning off the fugitive Vincent as the nobody Delon. The drifter, they reason, will never be missed.

The rub: a) Delon quickly catches on, and b) Fonda's Melinda has eyes for Delon. She doesn't want him killed. With ambitions that would please Highsmith's Tom Ripley, Melinda tries to outfox Barbara.

As Melinda asserts herself, Fonda acts out like a teen against her mother. She dons one of Barbara's glamorous white dresses and models herself for Delon, revealingly backlit by the light of an open refrigerator. She naughtily strips down to lingerie while Barbara's away, preening as the wall-trapped Vincent watches from behind two-way mirrors throughout the house. She goads him, wiggling seductively, dancing "the surf" to composer Lalo Schifrin's jazz music.

"It's beautiful outside. You should see the sun," Fonda says with a mischievous smile. She shimmies her hips. "Do you like this dance?"

Clement's camerawork is maximally suggestive here, with Fonda's hand drifting down the frame of a closet mirror to pelvic level, and Melinda's transformation is complete: ingenue to femme fatale. The sexuality is a power grab, her stab at becoming like Barbara . . . even beginning to think of taking Barbara's place.

Barbara has promised the villa to Melinda when her scheme with Vincent is complete, and Melinda badly wants it. But she also wants Delon. The plot arranges for her to have both, while giving Fonda an exercise in playing an innocent who evolves into a deceptive, dangerous Delilah. Fonda gets a lot of silent business to do, eavesdropping and skulking, holding the screen without talking; the film is not nearly as dialogue-driven as her comedies and dramas thus far. (The movie was filmed in English, though a dubbed French version is also available; the English track is better, adding—especially in the European performers' acting—an extra level of role-playing to a picture rich with slippery identities.)

Fonda's inquisitive, wary face holds its close-ups. The body language finds new expressions. Fonda's first French work is a very healthy stretch.

La Ronde (a.k.a. *Circle of Love*, 1964)

Like *The Chapman Report*, this is an ensemble study of sexuality, again with Fonda entering in a strikingly large hat—in this case, not a massive white bloom to be deflowered but a layer of veils to be peeled away.

Director Roger Vadim had emerged with the scandalous *And God Created Woman*, a big, primary-colored (abundant blues and reds), boundary-pushing melodrama with Brigitte Bardot as a barefoot orphan woman (not yet twenty-one, but marriageable) of such unbridled passion that she drives three lovers to extremes. The early, widely celebrated image of Bardot sunbathing nude on the seaside bluffs of Saint-Tropez, stretched out on her belly across the full CinemaScope frame, declared Vadim's bold determination as a voluptuary, and for most of that picture's ninety minutes the camera slavishly follows the magnetically pouty Bardot and her terpsichorean swivels. The movie shows off her dance training with Bardot gyrating to jazz as her near-insane lovers beg her to be still.

Vadim's black-and-white 1959 version of *Dangerous Liaisons* again used jazz (Thelonious Monk, Art Blakey, and the Jazz Messengers) as a hip, menacing underscore for romantic intrigue. Jeanne Moreau is the mature Juliette de Merteuil to the younger Marianne Tourvel of Annette Stroyberg, identified in the credits as Annette Vadim. Stroyberg was Vadim's second wife, after Bardot. Fonda would be number three.

In 1950 Max Ophüls had made his own version of Arthur Schnitzler's 1897 play *La Ronde*, a risqué exploration of sexual encounters linked, partner by partner, across social strata. Ophüls's deliberately stagy movie is guided by a suave narrator who cranks a literal merry-go-round; it's set in 1900 Vienna as a knowing, elegant, *ooh-la-la* affair with long, patient tracking shots and music by operetta composer Oscar Straus. Simone Signoret plays the young prostitute who opens the story, and Danielle Darrieux has the role Fonda will embody in Vadim's remake: a young wife embarking on an affair.

Vadim's color update borrows bits of Ophüls's style. The opening credits whirl like a carousel to waltz music and prewar Parisian scenes (it's 1914), and a garden tryst amplifies a dainty Ophüls gag by cutting to nude statuary figures that look like they're watching, or blushing.

Fonda's sequence is the last twenty minutes of the first hour; she plays Sophie, the wife who meets a single young man in a rented apartment. She is curious. She clearly craves a sensual encounter. "I have to go," she says as she arrives, but she sends a wholly different message by reclining into a chair. Her hat has jumbo wings and dense veils. Vadim moves the camera close and penetrates the layers, revealing Fonda with relish.

Acting in French, Fonda makes Sophie delicate and almost painfully hopeful throughout the light comic scene. Her eager but fairly naive lover (Jean Paredes) nervously fumbles around the plushly appointed apartment until he picks her up and carries her into the bedroom; she purrs his name ("Alfred . . . "). A bout of performance anxiety is resolved after a heady little discussion of French novelist Stendhal and a touch of affection, with Fonda caressing her illicit lover's thighs through the covers as her wedding ring glints.

Fonda gets to be more playful and knowing in the ensuing scene with her husband (Maurice Ronet), who believes a wife must be a Madonna while other women may be whores, as he needs. They are in bed, and it's spotlighted, as if in a theater, with darkness all around; nothing exists in this milieu but Man and Woman. Vadim's soft-focus camera stays close on Fonda's face as Sophie conceals secret smiles. She coaxes her husband to share his experiences, perhaps with earthier women. Slyly, she guides him toward a more fulsome understanding of female desire.

The dialogue is by classically grounded French playwright Jean Anouilh (the 1964 film *Becket* is from his stage drama, winning Edward Anhalt an Oscar for adapted screenplay, the lone win of the prestige hit's twelve nominations), and the pillow talk and its sexual politics have bounce. Fonda gingerly steers the discussion with lively eyes and kinetic friskiness, eventually leaping like a kitten to curl into her husband's lap. Her repertoire of Hollywood wives and ingenues steps up in class.

In French, Fonda successfully plies a little savoir faire. "I love dessert," she murmurs in her closing line. The confidence is to us, not to him. She settles contentedly into her pillow.

Vadim goes in for period opulence and soft-focus effects; the light is conspicuously caught by the sparkle of an eye or a champagne flute's rim. Inevitably, too—though it's done with other characters more than with Fonda's cat-with-the-cream character—Vadim goes in for a helping of nudity.

Exploitative nakedness is largely what Fonda recalls in her memoir, as an eight-story Times Square billboard displayed a nude sketch of her figure to promote *Circle of Love*, as *La Ronde* was titled in the United States. DRAWING OF JANE FONDA IS DRAPED WITH CANVAS, read a 1965 *New York Times* headline as Fonda sued the advertisers for $3 million.

La Curée (a.k.a. *The Game Is Over*, 1966)

Then they were married, Fonda and Vadim, and in this treacherous romantic morsel, the husband's first shot of his wife finds her reclined on the floor pedaling an exercise machine. Her outfit: leg warmers and a white T-shirt over a leotard (an unwitting preview of the world-famous 1980s *Jane Fonda's Workout* couture). Looming over her: her sneering son-in-law, soon to be her lover.

The story is adapted from Émile Zola's 1872 political novel of the obscenely rich. Vadim's film—he directed and cowrote—narrows the story to a sharp romantic triangle. Fonda, as Renée, has been cheating on Saccard, her older husband. She confides her infidelity to Maxime (Peter McEnery), Saccard's university student son by a previous wife. That's natural enough: Maxime is closer to her own age.

The husband's chateau, guarded by German shepherds, is a riot of tension, bristling with museum-quality objets d'art but also adorned with pop artifacts. The production design is by Jean André, who similarly decorated Clément's *Les Félins*, and the cinematographer is Claude Renoir, grandson of painter Pierre-Auguste Renoir, nephew of filmmaker Jean Renoir. Their sumptuous greens murmur jealousy, their purples purr passion and '60s youth. The look is warm and clear, lean yet plush—a stylish step up from Fonda's Manhattan apartment comedies. (The movie is in French, though this was also shot in an English version, released as *The Game Is Over*.)

The dangerous games include Fonda demanding the young man's attention by firing a rifle into his bedroom, and Fonda handles the gun as confidently as she would fifteen years later hunting Dabney Coleman in *9 to 5*. Maxime plays at ravishing Fonda, donning a Genghis Khan costume and makeup. Her face is theatrically covered too, shiny white with beauty cream. When they kiss, it's a smooch of two masks.

Vadim has Fonda skitter through these encounters in bikini panties and little else. Pushing the boundaries of screen nudity, Vadim films Fonda seducing McEnery's handsome Maxime with a topless veiled dance behind an opaque shower wall. Further, he shoots a nude love scene as reflected in a funhouse mirror, getting an effect like those in the paintings of cinematographer Renoir's *grand-père*. Eventually Vadim shows the duo lolling naked in a greenhouse grotto, evoking Eden by way of Hugh Hefner's Playboy Mansion, the lovers barely covered by their embraces.

No! declared Italy, banning the film.

Fonda's Renée, like Jean Racine's tragic Phèdre, is hopelessly in love with her son-in-law, and the pool in their greenhouse foretells her metaphorical drowning. When Saccard figures out what's going on, he leverages his financial power. He compels his son to marry a potential business ally's daughter—the old story.

"Well done. Nice goal, Dad," Maxime tells his father, giving in, game over. "Right between the posts."

Positioned between McEnerny's excitable young Maxime and the politic reserve of her husband (performed with edgy poise by Michel Piccoli, France's knowing Everyman answer to Gene Hackman), Fonda deftly switches between sexiness and doom. In one shot we see both gears: Maxime initiates a role-play with her as whore, so Fonda drops a shoulder, takes on a sultry air, and makes up a burlesque name for herself. But then she panics, running into his arms to be sure that that's not *really* how he thinks of her, that this is *love!* Fonda's quicksilver intensity is worthy of Greek myth—this would be a tidy "Classical Passions" double feature with *In the Cool of the Day*—and again she is willing to go all out. Watching Maxime announce his engagement from behind a window, Fonda's Renée presses herself to the glass with an agony like Ben's wailing *"Elaine!!!"* in *The Graduate*—still a year away.

Also released the next year: Jean-Luc Godard's *La Chinoise*, the ideology-saturated study of young 1960s Parisian Maoists. In *La Curée* Maxime studies Chinese and jokes that the future is China's. But Vadim the sensualist is hardly the hardcore theorist Godard. Vadim obsesses on Parisian upper-class opulence and decadence without much comment, despite the rich husband's quiet ruthlessness and the trained, snarling German shepherds meant to be windows to his predatory soul. The ideological Godard packs his pictures with politics, not least his lone project with Fonda (an implosion still several years hence). Lucky stiff Vadim stuffs his flicks with sex.

Spirits of the Dead (a.k.a. *Tre Passi nel Delirio*, 1968)

Thirteen Edgar Allan Poe–based movies were released in the 1960s, more by far than in any other decade (ladies and gentlemen, Vincent Price!). This ends that string: it's a high-gothic, low-budget triptych of shorts from Vadim, Louis Malle, and Federico Fellini. Vadim adapts the story "Metzengerstein" for his wife by transforming Poe's Caligula-like nobleman Frederick into a woman, Frederique.

"I love this place," murmurs Fonda's Frederique (this, again, is in French), gazing at one of her castles by the shore. In the background, blithely ignored by Frederique, is a hanged man.

She's a degenerate aristocrat who coddles a leopard cub, lures a young maiden into a threesome, and presides over orgies of food and lovemaking. She wears leg- and midriff-revealing costumes that would not be out of place in a lingerie shoot, or in *Barbarella*. This "petty Caligula" (Poe's phrase) is rejected by a tall, haughty, rail-thin lad who has captured her fancy, and this rake is played by Peter Fonda (who appears in this awkward project to be speaking English, though the voice is dubbed). He scorns Frederique. She has his barn burned. But then she's distressed that he's dead, and she's haunted. Read into this medieval erotica what you will: his big, wild horse survives and comes to her. Her gorgeous horse tapestry mysteriously burns. Driven mad, the contessa mounts the horse, galloping into fire.

Fonda, whose humongous blonde mane rates its own end credit ("JANE FONDA's hair styling by CARITA"), radiates attitudes—lust, disdain, despair—while saying very little in this terse scenario. Many scenes are simply Vadim's tableaux of debauch, or of Fonda's Frederique galloping across the countryside, or along a beach.

This is Fonda's narrowing track with Vadim. More to see. Less to act.

The triptych is better to its other stars. In Malle's "William Wilson," thief-faced Alain Delon is haunted after murdering his rival, while cagy Brigitte Bardot appears as a courtesan dueling Delon at cards. And Fellini's "Toby Dammit," the lone contemporary entry among two period pieces, looks like a riff on *8½*; adapting Poe's "Never Bet the Devil Your Head" with cowriter Bernardino Zapponi, Fellini has Terence Stamp playing Dammit, a fading English star (the lean, stylish, restless, offhand Stamp is perfect) looking for a career rebound in Rome. Dammit is haunted by the image of a leering lass: "To me the devil is cheerful, agile," he says morbidly during a flippant TV interview. "He looks like a little girl."

The hollow-eyed, mustachioed Stamp ultimately tears away in a Ferrari toward the apparition of the grinning girl, driving like a maniac off a crumbled bridge, looking like Poe, cackling at his own madness. The Ferrari apparently was Stamp's fee for the project, which, under Fellini's guidance, allowed him to rip through a nutso story with zeal.

Fonda, atop a steed and under Vadim, did not get nearly as much from the gig.

Barbarella (1968)

In a project devised by Vadim and produced by Italian impresario Dino De Laurentiis, Fonda plays a character who defeats evil with her infinite capacity for love, or something like it. Fonda's plucky, foxy heroine navigates through space in a capsule lined with Wookiee fur, on a mission to track down the mysterious appearance somewhere in the peaceful cosmos of a *weapon!* Her superpower is sex; perforce, Barbarella's adventures involve popping in and out of *beaucoup de* go-go outfits.

Barbarella is hardly the beginning of Fonda's gig as a sex symbol, but this film rocketed that persona beyond the moon. The famous title sequence (by the Bond franchise's Maurice Binder, though the screen credit says "Arcady") finds her floating in her tin can and strip-teasing out of her space suit. She starts classy, à la Gypsy Rose Lee, with just the fingertips of her astro-gloves. When the credits are done, she's in the buff.

"Just a minute, I'll slip something on," Barbarella says as she tunes into a communications screen held by a half-nude classical statue. (Go figure: her upscale capsule also includes Georges Seurat's painting *A Sunday Afternoon on the Island of La Grande Jatte*. Vadim!)

"Don't trouble yourself," replies serious Claude Dauphin, President of Earth. The dry punch line: "This is an affair of state."

Barbarella sprang from the 1962 French adult comic strip by Jean-Claude Forest, a jamboree of racy situations and revealing drawings; Forest's title character has the courage of an action hero and the carnal energy of a Playboy Bunny. By 1968, the satiric possibilities of a *Barbarella* movie seemed fizzy: James Bond, Vietnam, and the sexual revolution all might swing through the crosshairs. Vadim and Fonda landed a true '60s zeitgeist writer in high-riding Terry Southern, adapter of the subversive hits *Dr. Strangelove* and *The Loved One*; Southern had been around at the California parties thrown at Fonda and Vadim's, and a black-and-white photo of Jane and Terry in an enigmatic embrace graced the book jacket of his 1967 collection *Red Dirt Marijuana and Other Tastes*. Southern's satiric novel *The Magic Christian* would become a Peter Sellers–Ringo Starr comedy in 1969, and his and Mason Hoffenberg's "dirty book" parody *Candy*—the Voltaire-y trek of an innocent, gorgeous, wide-eyed young woman bumbling through the corrupt and cockeyed world—would hit screens just two months after *Barbarella*. With teenage Swede Ewa Aulin careening through antic incidents and phases of undress, *Candy* is *Barbarella* kin with a killer cast (Richard Burton as a rock-star Romantic poet, Marlon Brando appearing to float in the back of a semitruck as a guru, James Coburn as a wildly hip brain surgeon, and Walter Matthau as a gung-ho, sex-starved air commander).

But Southern works no magic with *Barbarella*, which credits another half-dozen writers after Southern and Vadim. (*Candy* the movie wasn't top Southern, either; Buck Henry wrote that jokey screenplay.) There is no target, and barely a subject. The "peace and love" vibe isn't even punched up much. Vadim devises his movie strictly as eye candy, wedging his wife into Wonder Woman wear.

Roger Vadim directs wife Jane Fonda in *Barbarella*.
Courtesy Everett Collection

"Barbarella has no sense of guilt about her body," Vadim explained to the *New York Times* in a joint interview with Fonda, discussing their sci-fi plan in 1966, as *The Game Is Over* was released stateside. "I want to make something beautiful out of eroticism."

The *Times* pressed on with a question for Jane:

> How does an actress trained in the technique of the Method and Lee Strasberg project herself into a futuristic heroine? "I'll leave the working out of that to Vadim," she said, putting an affectionate arm around his shoulders.

Well.

When Barbarella reaches the Tau Ceti system seeking the rogue Durand-Durand and his dangerous new positronic ray, she's tossed around by the crash landing. She also tumbles to the ground as—let us count the ways—two creepy young twin girls hit her in the head with a rock; she trips over her tail while wearing a tiny fur getup; she exits the spaceship after a second crash; she is assaulted by the Black Guards of Tau Ceti's Grand Tyrant; she unexpectedly slides down a hidden chute; she's pecked by birds; she unexpectedly slides through a second chute; and she plops into the decadent court of SoGo (think Sodom and Gomorrah, and behold the dude inside the giant bong while women laze around and smoke "essence of man"). The part is largely costumes and pratfalls.

The creepy twins cage Barbarella and sic their mechanical dolls on her, steel teeth chomping away (a bit, like a fair amount of the movie, pulled straight from the original comic). She's freed by the local "catchman" (Ugo Tognazzi), and she's willing to reward him with lovemaking. Diverging from the comic, Barbarella has to be coaxed into doing it the old-fashioned way—in the flesh, not with the "advanced" nonphysical technique she's accustomed to. Obviously, she explains, that old kind of sex was "pointless to continue . . . when other substitutes for ego support and self-esteem were made available." Fonda handles the Freudian jargon as she handles dialogue about peace and militarism in the opening scene: lightly, with familiar aplomb.

But hey, the catchman saved her. She gives in. When it's done, Barbarella sings.

Continuing her hunt for Durand-Durand, she's discovered by the blind angel Pygar (John Phillip Law) and Professor Ping (world-class mime Marcel Marceau, cast for a joke in a speaking part), who explains the *Inferno*-style stone labyrinth where good people are exiled by the Great Tyrant. Professor Ping also explains that Pygar is too depressed to fly. With a gleam in her eye, Barbarella makes the angel airborne again.

While Ping fixes her spaceship, Pygar flies her into SoGo, where she's cooed at by the piratical Black Queen (Rolling Stones muse Anita Pallenberg, coolly leering at Fonda and calling her "Pretty-pretty").* This Black Queen turns out to be the Great Tyrant, and her servant turns out to be Durand-Durand (Milo O'Shea, seething with stock megalomania).

* Pallenberg was in *Candy*, too, thanks to the Southern connection and her knowing, of-the-moment vibe; Pallenberg's brief movie flurry also included Nicolas Roeg's riveting 1970 *Performance* with Mick Jagger.

One of Barbarella's many random rescues comes courtesy of Dildano, leader of the Revolutionary Forces. He has Earth's sex pill and is dying to try it. Barbarella is agreeable as ever. Soon they are aquiver, palm to palm. Her hair curls. His does too.

Dildano is played hilariously by David Hemmings, the sullen, swinging photographer of Michelangelo Antonioni's pivotal 1966 film *Blow-Up*; Hemmings even looks funny, sporting gladiatorial leather straps and chains and a leather bikini bottom. His intensity is undermined by the fact that none of the movie around him works; it's the lone witty bit, and with Hemmings gracefully sputtering and covering up, barking into his transmitter and pleading for the pill-sex experience, it's the only chance for an actor to actually *perform*.

Fonda should have so much to do. Instead, her big scene involves surviving Durand-Durand's sadistic Exsexsive Machine, which looks like a sweatbox with a keyboard the mad scientist pounds, driving it to a crescendo that will kill her with pleasure—but her limitless capacity for *love* fries the thing.

Fonda's ecstatic face-making—what else can you call it; what else could she do?—is not entirely to be sneezed at. In the frank, serious 2008 study *Screening Sex*, film scholar Linda Williams inevitably comes to Fonda.* Williams claims Fonda was "the very first to play characters whose orgasms mattered," and she credits *Barbarella* with "the first (American) face of female orgasm on the American screen."

So stipulated. Still: for Fonda the actress, Vadim's direction was turning into a dead end.

In the *Times*, critic Renata Adler had concerns:

> For a while, the audience catching all the pointless, witless modernist allusions feels in on something chic, and laughs. Then it is clear that there is nothing whatever to be in on—except another uninspired omnispoof. Women have been treated very strangely

* Williams's introduction of Fonda echoes Patricia Bosworth's "won't be remembered for her movies": "Best known today for two roles played out not in film but in highly mediated public life: first as 'Hanoi Jane,' the antiwar activist whose opposition to the Vietnam war was demonstrated in a highly publicized visit to Hanoi in July 1972; second, as the guru of the home video workout."

> in movies lately—from the ancient biddy rapists with sticky, sandy eyes in "The Producers," through Doris Day mocked, all the actresses oddly cast and photographed from unattractive angles, to Barbarella, bruised and chewed about. Maybe it is an anti-Mummy reflex, no good, decent women on the screen. It is as though the medium, particularly in mechanistic science fiction and pseudo boffo bachelor comedy, has grown to hate them.

Even so, *Barbarella* landed big and left a mark, from posters on dorm walls to the 1974 launch by German students of an experimental hybrid rocket using solid and liquid fuel, a project they dubbed *Barbarella*. The allure endures: a long-contemplated remake got a bump in 2024 with the notion of Sydney Sweeney, popular star of *White Lotus* and *Anyone but You*, potentially stepping into Fonda's boots.

"I mean, that's a big swing," Josh Horowitz said as he interviewed Sweeney for his March 22, 2024, *Happy Sad Confused* video podcast from New York City's 92nd Street Y; the live audience buzzed happily at the new *Barbarella* prospect. "It's wild. You're obviously going to have to give that a different spin. The gender politics are going to have to be way different, obviously, with where we're at today."

"Barbarella is such a fun character to explore," replied Sweeney, whose big credits at the time included the *Spider-Man* spinoff *Madame Web*, since superhero comics are twenty-first-century Hollywood's lingua franca. "She really embraces her femininity and sexuality, and I love that. She uses sex as a weapon, which I think is such an interesting way into a sci-fi world. We'll see what happens."*

Acting in France cut no ice for Fonda in Hollywood. *Barbarella* was fine midnight popcorn but no way forward for a committed actor and evolving activist. It would be more than a year before her scorching breakthrough in *They Shoot Horses, Don't They?* She needed that big, mainstream, sneakily topical, daringly serious, profoundly American drama.

* The other Fonda movie unendingly rumored as ripe for a remake is the progressive workplace comedy *9 to 5*, with Fonda as a secretary sheathed in conservative dresses right up to her chin. Jada Pinkett Smith had long been attached to that, and in spring 2024 Jennifer Aniston emerged as a potential driver, with *Juno* writer Diablo Cody said to be involved. Surely betting pools exist about which pic hits screens first.

6

WILD IN THE STREETS: LESSONS FROM THE '60S, PART III

They Shoot Horses, Don't They? • *Klute*

> *I still believe that there was a narrow window (from about 1967 to 1975) in which the prospect of a grown-up cinema . . . came into being.*
>
> —David Thomson, *The Whole Equation*

As Fonda was making *They Shoot Horses, Don't They?*, movies were breaking wide open politically. A fractional sampler of 1968–70 pictures slugging it out over hippies, student protests, the youth movement, the women's movement, civil rights, gay rights, Native American rights, prisoners' rights, and Vietnam would include *The Boys in the Band, Burn!, Cotton Comes to Harlem, Diary of a Mad Housewife, Getting Straight, The Great White Hope, Greetings* (and its follow-up *Hi, Mom!*), *Halls of Anger, In the Year of the Pig, Joe, The Landlord, The Learning Tree, The Liberation of L. B. Jones, Little Big Man, Popi, Psych-Out, Putney Swope, The Revolutionary, Riot, The Scalphunters, Soldier Blue, The Strawberry Statement, Tell Them Willie Boy Is Here, Uptight, Watermelon Man, Wild in the Streets, WUSA, Z,* and *Zabriskie Point.*

They Shoot Horses, Don't They? was certainly political, but its subject was broad and its setting was historical, a 1930s drama with 1960s implications. Developing her own stories just a few years later, Fonda would not embrace such indirectness. She would work fairly intently in the present, following the blazing examples of two moviemakers quite close to her, both of whom pulled together legendary topical pictures just months before *Horses*. Hardcore lefty and Oscar-winning cinematographer Haskell Wexler fought through the teargas of the 1968 Chicago riots and came out with *Medium Cool*, while Jane's brother Peter zoomed out of low-budget biker flicks and into history with *Easy Rider*.

Easy Rider was initially Peter Fonda's vision, following a string of B pictures involving sex, drugs, and motorcycles; he was looking to make a big, true movie about the mixed-up American moment. "The film is really a lecture-demonstration on the conclusions Peter Fonda has come to regarding the United States of America in 1969," Elizabeth Campbell wrote in a *Rolling Stone* interview.

Indeed, the "lecture" was stitched together from earnest but sketchy impulses. It was shot without much of a script, depending on which report you believe; in *A Grand Guy*, Terry Southern biographer Lee Hill contends that a lot of it actually was penned by Southern, who, true to his easygoing nature, allowed his contribution to be shrouded in the subsequent myth.

The movie, with writing credit shared by Fonda, Southern, and Dennis Hopper, follows Fonda's Wyatt (a.k.a. "Captain America," because his helmet and gas tank are painted with the stars and stripes) and Hopper's Billy, a pair of hippie motorcyclists, smuggling cocaine from Mexico with the American Dream goal of one big payday. It's an inverted western trekking east past Monument Valley—John Ford country—not on horses but straddling horsepower as the soundtrack revs into Steppenwolf's "Born to Be Wild," maybe as iconic a movie image as exists in the late 1960s zeitgeist. The shaggy story racks up side trips as the bikers get arrested, get high with a New Mexico lawyer (Jack Nicholson), and acid-trip through New Orleans crypts during Mardi Gras before randomly being gunned down by southern rednecks. Sometimes, goes the lore, scenes were riffed under the influence as Nicholson, Fonda, and Hopper—the picture's inarguably erratic director—toked under great western skies. Sometimes it was like an Actors Studio psycho-exorcism: during the crypts sequence, Hopper goaded Peter into dredging up his deepest pain and weeping over his real mother's suicide.

Easy Rider was a rebel effort, financed by Bob Rafelson and Bert Schneider's new Raybert Productions, soon to become the maverick outfit BBS. In short order BBS generated Rafelson's *Five Easy Pieces* and Peter Bogdanovich's *The Last Picture Show*, swift emblems of New Hollywood's refreshingly artful style, but *Easy Rider* was first off the mark, ratifying the mandate to break with studio strictures and make indie/outsider work. Peter Fonda told Campbell at *Rolling Stone* that he considered the movie "cinema verité in allegory terms"—a very blurry thing to say. The Hollywood studios, Fonda told Campbell, "still hold me in contempt on the one hand and in awe on the other. In contempt, because I've shown them a mirror of their own greed, and in awe, because I was able to do something they can't do, which was simply to make a motion picture honestly."

Honest was wielded to reflect the preferences of forward-thinking audiences, as opposed to the frequently invoked studio "squares." When *Village Voice* rock critic Robert Christgau praised *Easy Rider*'s groundbreaking soundtrack of rock hits, he invoked the morally loaded word: "[Hopper] knew he could not make his movie honestly without real music."

Fake music might be, say, the drippy "Raindrops Keep Fallin' on My Head" montage of 1969's big hit, the comfortingly comedic, easygoing *Butch Cassidy and the Sundance Kid*—on screens two months after *Easy Rider*, and like *Easy Rider* (yet so unlike it), a buddy picture about American antiheroes with no way out in the end. And *dishonesty* might be *Butch Cassidy* director George Roy Hill offering the puffed-up claim that William Goldman's slick outlaw script was "about Vietnam. Not literally, of course, but it symbolized a whole contingent of society that was bailing out." Sure.

Easy Rider had the right rock for its antihero jam. But did it have the right idea? Google *Easy Rider* and the search engine reveals a popular query: *What was the point?*

"A man went looking for America and couldn't find it anywhere," the *Easy Rider* advertising explained, again in a kind of blur. The picture is too neatly summed up by an exchange driven by George Hanson, Jack

Nicholson's lawyer character. "This used to be a hell of a good country," he tells Hopper, lamenting that mainstream society has become a menace. "Don't ever tell anybody that they're not free, 'cause then they're going to get real busy killing and maiming to prove to you that they are," Hanson says. "Oh yeah, they gonna talk to you and talk to you and talk to you about individual freedom. But they see a free individual, it's gonna scare 'em."

"It don't make 'em running scared," Hopper's character replies.

"No," Hanson agrees. "It makes 'em dangerous."

Not much else of note is spoken aside from Captain America's disenchanted "We blew it" near the end, just before he and Billy hit the road one last fatal time. Obviously, Fonda, Hopper, Nicholson (emerging as a star screen presence after getting his hands dirty with Roger Corman as a B-movie producer and writing *The Trip* and *Head*) and Southern grasped exactly the American tensions they were living through, and they concluded with a catastrophe that still shocks because that violent schism is extraordinarily in play today. But they captured a lot of it in image, song, and tone and not in crafted words and well-planned, storyboarded glory. In the 1960s, *writing* wasn't as trustworthy a gateway to truth as improv and devising, and nobody knew better than actors that "acting" could be treacherously false. Ergo, Method men Fonda and Hopper vibed their way into a phenomenon.

"One must talk about a film like this in terms of what audiences enjoy it for or one is talking gibberish," Pauline Kael wrote in her 1968 essay "Trash, Art and the Movies." The target of that sentiment was *The Graduate*, but the thrust of the passage was movie criticism, and the needlessness, even in the face of an increasingly serious film culture, of analyzing technique. "Taking it apart is far less important than trying to see it whole," Kael declared.

In fact, in *Easy Rider*'s ripped-apart social moment, powered by amped and distorted rock, shot the year of the MLK and RFK assassinations, the Tet Offensive in Vietnam, and President Johnson bowing out of a reelection bid, the whole is the only way to see why the movie clicked. "Hoppe always quoted Jean Cocteau," Peter Fonda wrote of Hopper in his memoir, recalling their zigzag process; "98 per cent of true art was accident, 1 per cent was logic, and 1 per cent was intellect." It's a convenient thing for a surrealist like Cocteau to believe, and a tactic that would be disastrous for an activist, but Fonda trots out the many lucky outcomes of the shambolically manufactured *Easy Rider*. Hollywood historian Peter Biskind wrote that Buck Henry, invoking Dadaist technique, called the movie "the automatic handwriting of the counterculture."*

As for specific politics—well, it was all baked in, right?

Christgau's 1969 critique praised *Easy Rider* as "the only film I know that not only uses rock well—though that is rare enough—but also does justice to its spirit." (The movie's bleakness is set by the opener, Steppenwolf's "The Pusher," barking its "goddamn" as a promise that this contested Americana will be no blissed-out strawberry field.) Christgau's kicker is a beauty as he describes the "love-hate thing" about America shared by rock and the hip new picture, "glorifying the outcasts and detesting and fearing the straights. You could even say that its dark side was anticipated spiritually by all those teen death songs that don't seem quite so funny after all. Think about it: Isn't Tom Hayden the leader of the pack?"

Very soon, Jane would ratify that.

At least Peter was making his own meaning. Sister Jane wasn't, yet, at least not in features. (Documentaries would be another story—the first fertile terrain for activist-artist Jane, and soon.)

One of her key fellow travelers in the 1970s, particularly as she grappled with Vietnam, would be Haskell Wexler, a devotee of cinema verité, a cranky truth-teller, and a whiz with lenses and light. When George Lucas needed help on location and on deadline in Petaluma, California, filming cars cruising around at night for *American Graffiti*, Wexler would figure it out; Wexler had a Best Cinematography Oscar for the black-and-white *Who's Afraid of Virginia Woolf?* (1966), was director of photography on the kinetic, sultry *The Thomas Crown Affair* (1968), and won the cinematography Oscar again for *Bound for*

* Screenwriter Tom Mankiewicz's shading: "A cinematic accident committed by extremely talented potheads."

Glory (1976). Wexler was supposed to be on the *Easy Rider* team and had been in the thick of preproduction. With *Medium Cool*, released a month after *Easy Rider* in the late summer of '69, Wexler—working not only as cinematographer but also as writer and director—one-upped his actor pals Peter Fonda and Dennis Hopper in terms of leaving his script open to events and capturing the madness of the streets.

Just as *Easy Rider* timed its shooting schedule to Mardi Gras for maximum reality, Wexler planned to film *Medium Cool* in the thick of the bound-to-be-wild 1968 Democratic National Convention in Chicago. Oddly, he had been given the directorial job to adapt Jack Couffer's 1967 novel *The Concrete Wilderness*, about a country boy and his dog braving cruelty in New York City. (Couffer was a WWII vet turned filmmaker, soon to be Oscar nominated as the cinematographer of 1973's *Jonathan Livingston Seagull*.) That story is largely abandoned in *Medium Cool* as Wexler vamps through roughed-in scenarios that boil down to how a cynical news cameraman gets involved with a single mother whose young son goes missing in the DNC riot, a framework for Wexler to hang questions about media ethics. Wexler tracks his apprehensive-looking star, Verna Bloom, through the police beatings and tear gas chaos, as she searches for her boy.

All credit to Wexler for knowing that America was cracking, and for doing his cinematic work from the hot, hot inside out. But his story is terribly elastic. You have to pull the picture apart, because this much-debated landmark doesn't always hang together.

It is a media critique that is brutally sarcastic about the quality of news, opening with John (Robert Forster), the cameraman, filming a car crash *before* calling an ambulance. At a cocktail party, journalists grouse: "I've made films on all kinds of social problems," a newsman says. "And the big bombs are the ones where we went in in detail and showed why something happened. Nobody wants to take the time. They'd rather see thirty seconds of somebody getting their skull cracked."

"The point I resent very much," goes another journalist's improvised line, "is the fact that wherever I go, I'm beat up."* Nineteen seventy

* Compare/contrast half a century later with the mainstreamed rhetoric of "*Fake news!*" and "*Enemies of the people!*"

would be the year Nixon's vice president, Spiro Agnew, would target the press as "nattering nabobs of negativism," an aromatic phrase from speechwriter William Safire. Nixon's "enemies list," first formulated in 1971, would be less waggish, as it included swaths of journalists and, of course, Jane Fonda.

Keeping it real, Wexler uses actual journalists in a lot of the roles; scoops young Harold Blankenship, playing the son of Bloom's character, out of an Appalachian-populated slum in Chicago's Uptown; films actual police "war games" at Minnesota's Fort Ripley; shoots a date sequence at a real roller derby; and follows John to Washington and the mud-drenched "Resurrection City" of Martin Luther King's Poor People's Campaign.* Historian Studs Terkel is credited as "Our Man in Chicago" for providing connections to actual Chicagoans.

Wexler's documentary bona fides were already well established by this point, chiefly by *The Bus*, an hour-long chronicle of Black Americans traveling to the 1963 March on Washington. (He would also shoot the 1979 No Nukes concerts at Madison Square Garden.) By 1968, his obsession with reality and media also owed something to independent actor-director-writer John Cassavetes, and to French Nouvelle Vague leftist Jean-Luc Godard. The former's influence is so overt that Wexler named *Medium Cool*'s cameraman John Cassellis. (He named another cameraman Pennybaker, for his comrade-in-documentary-arms D. A. Pennebaker, of the earlier *Jane*.) As for the latter, *Medium Cool* ends with a car crash alluding directly to Godard's hyper-meta *Weekend* (1967), famed for a seven-minute tracking shot of a traffic jam that ends with protagonists speeding by the bloody bodies once the road opens up—*Medium Cool*'s exact frame.

Godard's presence looms again in a giant poster of *Breathless* star Jean-Paul Belmondo on John's apartment wall. Also on that wall: Eddie Adams's iconic, horrific February 1, 1968, news photo of a South Vietnamese general executing a man at point-blank range.

Wexler, like Godard, wants the fiction, then wants to crack it open with reality. (The influence is Brecht; more on that in the next chapter,

* Among the most galvanizing speakers during Jane Fonda's 2019–20 Fire Drill Fridays: Rev. William Barber II, reviving King's Poor People's Campaign.

when Jane collides with the didactic Godard.) When Chicago's cops started clobbering people, Wexler used it to jolt his "story." "The Democratic Party fell into place by ignoring the American public," he said later, "and giving me a scene to build a film on."

He had known Chicago would be wild and scripted the riot scene back in January. Everyone knew what was coming: During Godard's 1968 US speaking tour, critic Richard Brody writes, "students invited him to film their activities that summer at the Democratic National Convention in Chicago, where, they said, they intended to bring about nothing less than 'the destruction of the United States as we know it.' Godard demurred, recommending newsreel cameramen instead."

Medium Cool splits the difference.

Not surprisingly, though—and corresponding with that first newsman's complaint at the top of the movie—the violent footage overwhelms the comparatively trivial story of Bloom as the mother, in a yellow summer dress and low heels, gingerly jogging through the streets, looking for her lost child. How could it not? The actual unrest has what Wexler's slender fiction doesn't: dynamic immediacy and unimpeachable *honesty.*

"We felt we were there for a higher purpose, you know," Marianna Hill, who played the cameraman's girlfriend, says in the movie's DVD commentary. "To tell the truth about something that was happening that we weren't even clear about, but we knew Haskell had kind of an insight into."

That sounds like a tricky place to be. The slipperiness, both willful and unintentional, is confirmed by critic/filmmaker Olivier Gruner's view of Wexler's "dense assemblage of social commentary, intertextuality and visual puns." In Gruner's analysis of the movie's political weaknesses and strengths, "It was conceived as both a filmic document of the times and proponent of the idea that there *can be no filmic document of the times*, for the camera creates its own reality" (emphasis in the original).

In 1968, Wexler later claimed in the DVD commentary, the electricity of the country's friction "was not being reflected through anybody's cameras." He admired *Easy Rider*, but whatever that revolution was "got co-opted very quickly and very easily. [*Medium Cool*] hit them where they live."

If so, it was because the movie co-opted a real riot for visceral effect. While it captured the scandal of police brutality and a federal-local political negligence akin to the laissez-faire malfeasance that permitted the January 6, 2021, US Capitol insurrection—also wildly predictable—the dominant subject of *Medium Cool* is the media (taking its title from Marshall McLuhan's influential 1964 theories on the topic), and the corrosive ways news seeks heat. In a sense, *Medium Cool* suffered from *The Chase*'s problem all over again, with a society blowing up, ideas firehosing in several directions, and the camera capturing striking images that the script can't quite knit together.

Medium Cool and *Easy Rider* drove countercultural attitudes to the limit and stretched narrative boundaries with valiant creative and social instincts. It denigrates neither picture, both of them American essentials, to note that while they are soaked in politics, neither was built to advance a particular political point.* And the moviemaking lesson is this: in resisting *writing*, their generic resistant politics turns to purple haze.

That's not a liability unless you're trying to send a message. Sending messages would become what Jane was all about. Watching her brother and Wexler, Fonda—who was about to establish herself as an extraordinary actor—could begin to figure out which cinematic tools would work.

They Shoot Horses, Don't They? (1969)

"*Yowza, yowza, yowza! Welcome to the dance of destiny, ladies and gentlemen! . . . On and on and on. . . . When will it end? . . . One couple and only one will waltz out of here, over broken bodies and broken dreams. . . . Those who give up, those who give out, those who give in—out! Tough rules, but these are tough times!*"

That's the carnival-barker patter of the Depression-era dance marathon's emcee, played by Gig Young with showbiz flair and a gangster's edge. His excited hard sell is the American Dream as twisted torture—dancing for dough, if you don't die first.

* As a matter of habit, critics and audiences often view this absence of an agenda as an artistic plus; see my 2014 study *American Playwriting and the Anti-political Prejudice* (New York: Palgrave Macmillan, 2014).

Fonda gets top billing and earns her first Best Actress Oscar nomination with *They Shoot Horses, Don't They?*, arguably director Sydney Pollack's first prestige picture—prestige being the throughline as Pollack mastered everything from weepies (*The Way We Were*, 1973) to thrillers (*Three Days of the Condor*, 1975) and farce (*Tootsie*, 1982). Pollack, fresh off the sly, race-aware western *The Scalphunters* (1968) and the intellectually pretentious war-as-chess *Castle Keep* (1969), whips up a pressure cooker and tasks Fonda with carrying the ensemble project through to its excruciating finish. It was her biggest lift yet, and she shouldered it with style. Fonda's bleak, unrelenting rage inspired Pauline Kael's famous prediction about Fonda "personifying American tensions" and "dominating our movies in the seventies."

The story of *They Shoot Horses* is based on the 1935 novel by Horace McCoy, who once worked as a bouncer at the Santa Monica Pier; the Pier's old Aragon Ballroom was the model for the movie's sunless seaside dance hall overcrowded with hungry down-and-outers, a bum's Grand Hotel. With the characters locked indoors, racking up hours in its grueling endurance contest, the saga is savage and the metaphor is heavy. The leading voice is Gloria's—Fonda's, that is. When we first see her in line to register for the contest (eyebrows penciled, short hair marcelled in 1930s waves, a forelock swirling insolently down over one eye), she's poor and starving, barely able to hold her head upright. She's perceptive and wary, a cornered animal. And she's suicidal, with clues to her despair slipped in from the start.

Her gallows humor is mirthless, and relentless. An upbeat old navy man (Red Buttons) compares the sign-up line to a cattle roundup, and Gloria grunts that cattle have it better: "There's always somebody feeding them." Her boyish young partner (Michael Sarrazin) asks Gloria why she came to California. "You don't freeze while you're starving," she says bitterly.

Gloria always has a quip in defense. Warned that her attitude could get her thrown out of the marathon, she's unimpressed: "I've been disqualified by experts," she reports, and Fonda's tired smile hangs with grim history. Could the pivot from the indomitable Barbarella be more complete?

During one of the marathoners' cruelly brief breaks, this is the patter, with Gloria swatting replies:

"You should be sleepin'."

"I'd just wake up."

"You want anything? Something for your feet?"

"How 'bout a saw?"

The contestants—desperate souls with almost no backstories—dance for days, weeks, more than a month. Someone complains at Gloria, "What the hell *do* you want? Anyone ever tell you—"

"Yeah, they told me," she snaps; Gloria always grabs the last rough word. But she knows she's helpless, and the picture accrues utterance after utterance that life on current terms ain't worth it. She routinely targets the young pregnant woman played by Bonnie Bedelia, insisting that it will be better if the kid isn't born. And speaking of a woman in her sixties, Gloria says with feeling, "God, I hope I never live to be that old."

With the exhausted Gloria half-asleep against his chest as they dutifully shuffle to yet another tune, the boyish, sad-eyed Sarrazin asks what

Fonda as desperate, despairing Gloria in *They Shoot Horses, Don't They?* *Album / Alamy*

she would do with the money if they won. "Maybe I'd buy some good rat poison," she murmurs. It's a reasonable reaction to her circumstances, given how Pollack ratchets up the despair, sucking possibilities and even air out of his milieu.

The miracle of the performance is how Fonda plays fatigue with such ferocious emotional energy. During a glum sexual encounter with Young's emcee, she's as intimidating as a Doberman, snarling, "Don't touch me!" Fonda spins lines with flinty 1930s flair, and reacts to hardships and scams with layers of unspoken hurt and outrage. Pollack, coming into his own as one of Hollywood's best directors of stars, is the right guide for this.* It's a big performance, yet it's never overplayed.

Illustrating what an actor's director Pollack was becoming, it's worth noting how many characters register early and deeply in this marathon. The movie's nine Oscar nominations included three for acting: Fonda's; Susannah York's, for her silvery, fragile turn as an upscale platinum blonde; and Gig Young's supporting actor win for his flamboyant, corrupt marathon host (a veritable type at that moment, given the Broadway success and, soon, the movie triumph of *Cabaret* with Joel Grey's leering Master of Ceremonies).

Befitting the dancing and delirium, Pollack orchestrates a lot of blurry color, hallucinatory sound, and fancy camerawork. The camera glides through the ballroom, spinning dizzily, angling high and low, sprinting with the inhuman race scenes, practically passing out over collapsed bodies. The second race actually climaxes with Fonda dragging a dead character called the Ancient Mariner—the navy fellow played with endearing, melancholy panache by Red Buttons—over the finish line so she can make the cut and dance on. The competitors are abused with sadistic flair as Young purrs all-American platitudes into the microphone about can-do moxie and plucky determination. You watch in horror as

* Pollack, of course, was a sometime actor himself, especially later in his career, and best remembered as Dustin Hoffman's agent in *Tootsie*. You can see the kind of grounded, simple, convincing performance he favored in his supporting turn as a sergeant in the small, smart 1962 film *War Hunt*, set during the Korean War, directed by Denis Sanders, and with Robert Redford in his first leading role.

the contestants gradually melt down, and as Gloria finally begs Sarrazin to put a bullet in her head.

"They got it all rigged before you even show up," Gloria observes lifelessly.

Near the end Pollack catches Fonda in a spotlight after more than a thousand hours of competing, suddenly stranded without a partner, standing solo, still moving, if barely, looking pitifully weak and hopeless. Fonda's anxious, flayed despond recalls the haggard Migrant Mother of Dorothea Lange's famous 1936 Dust Bowl photograph.

"If you think of 'They Shoot Horses, Don't They?,' you'll remember Jane Fonda, so desperate and defiant and sad as she pushes herself through a Depression-era dance marathon," critic A. O. Scott wrote in his 2008 appreciation of Pollack. Scott was praising the late director's generally unobtrusive style, but that Fonda-first analysis undersells the overwhelming tone Pollack created in this instance. The hall is so light deprived that Sarrazin's boyish character occasionally strays through a side door to glimpse the Pacific Ocean and sniff the wind, and at one point, trapped inside, he strains on tiptoes to keep a tiny shaft of sun on his face for just an extra second. The close camerawork hugs actors' bodies, emphasizing the nowhere-to-go claustrophobia of the contestants' poverty. The juxtaposition of contestants' tormented faces as they strain around a track to the whiplike rhythm of the "cancan song"—Offenbach's "Infernal Galop" from *Orpheus in the Underworld*—is typical of the movie's devilishly controlled audiovisual messaging. The picture feels like a lethal merry-go-round even before Gloria calls it that near the end.

It is true, though, that Fonda slices through with an especially steely edge.

For the climax, Pollack lets the camera stare as Gloria makes her morbid final plea to Sarrazin. Her eyes sear and moisten; her voice quavers with fatigue and longing, finally soft. Gloria is incurably unhappy. She begs for relief. Strangely and sadly, since Peter Fonda had just shared his own familial grief in *Easy Rider*, it's hard not to see some measure of the final, futile anguish of Fonda's mother in dog-tired Gloria's misery and yearning for rest.

In this final reckoning outdoors on the brownish nighttime pier, three showbiz lights glow just beyond Sarrazin's shoulder: one red, one white, one blue. That's the only color, and it's not an accident. It's been true of the Depression-set story all along: it hates the country's rat race. And, inarguably, the movie's fury—Gloria's fury, made palpable by Fonda's growing power—taps into the 1969 berserk of war, assassinations, and accelerating protests.

Kael's lengthy *New Yorker* review, the one that singles out Fonda as the actress best poised to dominate the 1970s, says a lot about the novel and nothing of Vietnam. Vincent Canby's piece in the *Times* didn't invoke the war, either. But in *Jane Fonda's War*, Mary Hershberger points out what a powerful metaphor *They Shoot Horses* is, with the dancers exhorted and abused, "regimented as soldiers," strewn like battlefield corpses. Hershberger writes, "Fonda's strong performance in the film, in which her character rejected a system of suffering and exploitation, was the political image of Fonda that her audiences brought with them when they came to hear her speak about the war in Vietnam. The film established Fonda as a person to whom politics mattered before she first spoke out publicly on the war."

Tom Hayden would later write, "About the Depression, it could as well have been about the spiritual exhaustion induced by Vietnam."

Consider it Jane's analogue to her dad's parched *Grapes of Wrath*. Tom Joad soldiers on. Facing different disillusions about America, Gloria gives up.

Klute (1971)

The Halloween weekend of 2019 treated the world to a fresh Jane Fonda media blitz. This was her viral BAFTA-award, *Thanks!*-in-handcuffs moment, and London's *Guardian* newspaper leaped on with a new listicle ranking Fonda's best films. On top, as usual: *Klute*.*

Klute endures as an artful suspense picture, even though its sudden climactic action sequence, with Donald Sutherland's detective Klute

* While *Klute* conventionally tops these exercises, this particular list has a frivolous streak, or maybe a malevolent bent. In the British press's bloody style, Godard's poison pen documentary *Letter to Jane*—a 1972 sour grapes exercise in which Jane Fonda does not "act" and did not willingly participate, explored in the next chapter—unreasonably barrels into fourth place.

jabbing in to quickly finish the job, is an abrupt blur. As Pollack was hitting his stride with *They Shoot Horses*, so was Alan J. Pakula maturing with this, his second feature and the first installment of what would be known as his "paranoia trilogy," with *The Parallax View* (1974) and *All the President's Men* (1976). *Klute* bristles with fear, with furtive watching . . . and with arrestingly frank talk about sex.

"There's nothing wrong," Fonda's throaty voice says as hooker Bree Daniels, heard over the opening credits as we watch a miniature tape recorder's revolving reels. "Nothing is wrong. I think the only way that any of us can ever be happy is to let it all hang out, and do it all . . . and fuck it."

The tone is edgy; this is sex at the top of the '70s, and Fonda's Bree is a proud swinging pro—hip, cool, and free. Fonda's got her famous shag haircut at last; *at last* she's in a contemporary drama playing a character so real she had to do research. Even more than Pollack, Pakula relies on her, trusting Fonda to anchor the drama with presence and style. A wordless scene in the middle of the movie tracks Bree through a noisy club, where she enters, angles up to a guy and begins her smooth, party-ready *Let's groove* come-on. She abruptly drops the flirtation with an unhappy frown, then pastes the smile back on and jives through the crowd. (She might be high—she's just fled a rattling encounter with an old associate, now a strung-out junkie.) Pakula, maybe as star-smitten as any major director in the '70s, watches Fonda for long stretches without cutting, and in this bit alone her fluidity, spontaneity, and swift masking—since Bree, of course, is a very fancy sort of *actor*, rejected several times for "straight" jobs as a model or a performer—illustrates how she earned this first Oscar.

But if the picture feels progressive in the control it gives Fonda's prickly, seemingly liberated Bree, it also feels backward as it thrusts her intro a romance with the most morally straitlaced cop possible: John Klute of Tuscarora, Pennsylvania, played like a forbidding priest by the glaring Donald Sutherland. Equally retrograde, the moviemakers threaten Bree with Jack the Ripper retribution for her freedom, as a maniac exploits the new permissiveness and blames Bree (prostitutes, swingers) for hang-ups he swears he never knew he had. The screenplay by Andy and David Lewis is a genre thriller, rippling with horror tropes—tinkling chimes and a breathy voice singing creepily to send chills up our spines.

In the early '70s, detective flicks were evolving. The old-fashioned brand included Paul Newman as the gum-chewing title dick in 1966's *Harper* as rich Lauren Bacall gives him the runaround; Frank Sinatra's hard-boiled PI in *Tony Rome* (1967) and its sequel *Lady in Cement* (1968); and James Garner's oddly bland title character in the 1969 Raymond Chandler reboot *Marlowe*. New blood was around the corner with Richard Roundtree in Gordon Parks's suave Blaxploitation fountainhead *Shaft* (1971); Robert Altman's jazzy, irreverent *The Long Goodbye* (1973), with a dry Elliott Gould as Chandler's Marlowe navigating a modern, morally foggy L.A.; and Roman Polanski's juicy, punishing noir revival *Chinatown* (1974), reeking of the Holocaust and the Manson murders (atrocities that both scorched Polanski personally).* *Klute* belongs with the hip new movement not for its story twists but as a delectable exercise in composition and style. Fonda's character is rewardingly complex, but on top of that, she's framed with extraordinary cleverness. Pakula's movie is the best-looking, most visually savvy picture Fonda ever was in.

Shooting in New York, *Klute*'s designers created a Manhattan that's both recognizably realistic and styled with a slightly fantastical edge that repeatedly puts its characters in subtly cramped, threatening spaces. The dialogue is extremely terse. The acting is understated. The color palette is restricted.

Cinematographer Gordon Willis made some of the most appealingly composed dark-toned movies of the 1970s, including the *Godfather* pictures and Woody Allen's newly serious films from *Annie Hall* through the Ingmar Bergman homage *Interiors* and the majestic black-and-white *Manhattan*. *Klute* shows Willis's particular gift for blacks and tans, negative spaces, and opaque backgrounds; it's a masterwork of shadows and silhouettes against occasional rich colors—yellow taxis blooming through Manhattan's concrete, or bright stacked produce animating a street market.

* See Sam Wasson's history *The Big Goodbye: Chinatown and the Last Years of Hollywood* (New York: Flatiron, 2020) for a dissection of that picture's production and influences.

Production designer George Jenkins, an art director going back to *The Best Years of Our Lives* and *The Bishop's Wife* in the 1940s, would do four more Fonda movies and lots with Pakula, including *All the President's Men* and *Sophie's Choice* (he won an Oscar for the former). *Klute*'s quiet opening scene—eerily formal, visually destabilizing—takes place in an upscale suburban dining room. The dinner party's peaceful order is threatened by the startling riot of green jungle growth behind a giant window. A body could get lost in that thicket.

Sure enough, the host becomes a missing person. An investigation begins.

On a protective stakeout, Sutherland's cadaver-faced Klute inhabits a basement apartment beneath Bree's place, and it registers like a cave. It's next to a funeral home with a cool-blue neon sign that Bree walks underneath as she returns to her flat upstairs. The foreshadowing is milder than it sounds, and so is the tracking shot of Bree leaving her building and heading toward the climactic scene, filmed from across the street from the funeral home, with flowers and a hearse briefly obscuring our view of her. Adding menace, the camera's point of view is the killer's, stalking her.

The cave where Klute, the prude from Tuscarora, sleeps on a cot looks primitive compared to the sleek hangout of Klute's foil, Frankie, a stylish pimp and drug addict played by Roy Scheider. The ancient city/country binary looks so plain to Bree that she needles Klute about it: "Tell me, Klute, did we get you a little? Huh? Just a little bit? Us city folk? The sin, the glitter, the wickedness? Huh?"

"All that's so pathetic," Sutherland's Klute replies, above it.

"Fuck off," she says, hurt.

But Bree's not wrong about the scheme. The movie is so intensely about *place* that the final image is of Bree leaving her apartment, and New York, as Klute grabs her luggage and they begin a life together. Bree's typically vacillating final lines, in a voice-over that's clearly one of the character's sessions with her therapist (more on them later), are "I have no idea what's going to happen. I just can't stay in the city, you know? Maybe I'll come back. You'll probably see me next week."

Scheider's Frankie, the quintessential evil city figure, lives in a glossy apartment that looks like 4 AM the night disco was dreamed up. Showing this room is initially more important to Pakula and the designers than showing Scheider's face. Frankie is silhouetted as we absorb his hedonistic milieu—a large wall grid of five-by-three black squares divided by thin white light, plus abstract paintings, sculptures slightly aglow, white leather furniture that's immaculate in the shadows. It's a synthetic sensation.

When Pakula cuts to the actors in the scene, a small, round lamp with slowly changing colored lights gives Scheider's shots a druggy buzz. A sculpture of long, thin metal reeds quivers next to Sutherland, as if this detective has antennae.

You could examine *Klute*'s compositions all day, from the headless dressmaker dummies in the garment shop where Bree flees in the climactic *don't get killed* scene to the repeated stark solo shots of Sutherland, pensive and judgmental, pressed near walls, watching with an aura

Fonda as hooker Bree Daniels alongside Roy Scheider's pimp Frankie in *Klute*. *RGR Collection / Alamy*

of severity, shadowed like a Rembrandt.* The slightly exaggerated reality allows for one of the most elegant, morally complicated sequences in the film, when Bree, on the job, visits the seventy-year-old Goldfarb (Morris Strassberg), who runs the garment shop. It's after hours, and the camera tracks Fonda as she enters in the movie's most famous dress—long, high-necked, silver like jewelry, and tight and scaly like reptile skin, suggesting Bree as cold blooded. (The great, prolific costume designer Ann Roth gives Bree sophisticated looks throughout the picture: she's in long, soft fabrics with a wide belt during an upscale fashion audition, and as she backslides toward Frankie's hookers-and-addicts underworld she's in miniskirts and go-go boots.) Bree's "performance" for the old man is a monologue, an extremely old-fashioned, even genteel seduction. Her flattering, stagy saga paints young men as callow, and Fonda speaks low, generating formal intimacy, slowly unzipping her dress. It's one of the rare scenes in which Fonda's acting is underscored: Bree unspools her erotic tale to a delicate European waltz.

The camera recedes, leaving us to imagine. It's believable when Bree later says that Goldfarb never touches her.

Then Pakula cuts to Klute, watching from outside, disgusted. But Bree convincingly finds kindness in her act. Fonda, outraged at Klute's puritanism, blurts, "Goddamn you!"—blushing as much for Goldfarb as for herself.

Fonda understandably fretted that playing a prostitute would be retrograde in 1971.† But the role of Bree seemed alluringly complicated, and

* This is Sutherland as Tragedy; earlier in 1971 he was Comedy, a sunny hippie reverend whack job in Jules Feiffer's *Little Murders*, starring Sutherland's *M*A*S*H* pal Elliott Gould (who produced it, and at one point thought of Jean-Luc Godard to direct it). *Little Murders*, too, was shot in New York by Gordon Willis.

† A note on movie prostitutes: PLAY A HOOKER AND WIN AN OSCAR, read a 1996 *New York Times* headline surveying that long history as Elisabeth Shue, Sharon Stone, and Mira Sorvino simultaneously earned Academy Award nominations for such roles. In 2025 Mikey Madison, playing a young sex worker in Sean Baker's *Anora*, was a surprise Best Actress winner over the prognosticated favorite and Screen Actors Guild / Golden Globe winner, sixty-two-year-old Demi Moore as an aging actress ravaged by a younger iteration of herself in Coralie Fargeat's body horror movie *The Substance*; that Oscar upset was widely seen as life imitating Fargeat's brutal plot. In 1971, Warren Beatty's costars *both* played hookers: Julie Christie in Robert Altman's *McCabe & Mrs. Miller*

Fonda committed to late-night research with hookers set up by the production team. The zeitgeist was rumbling: Fonda's gripping Bree presaged the "porno chic" era inaugurated by the X-rated *Deep Throat*, explicit porn and the fifth most popular movie of 1972. Her brash, hip character is an entertaining contrast—in perfect sync with 1971's brawling sexual politics—with Sutherland's restrained turn as the throwback detective.*

"Operating on alternating currents, Bree is a dynamic study in contradictions," critic Melissa Anderson wrote in 2018, "an imperfect yet indelible symbol of second-wave feminism, the cresting of which nearly coincides with *Klute*'s release." *Klute* followed twin towers of early 1970s feminist writing, Kate Millet's *Sexual Politics* and Germaine Greer's *The Female Eunuch*, by less than a year; by the end of 1971, Gloria Steinem would launch *Ms*.

The activist content of *Klute* is undeniable in the bravura static close-up of Fonda, two minutes and ten seconds long, as Bree listens to the tape of bad guy Peter Cable (Charles Cioffi) killing one of her friends. Fonda quietly, thoroughly breaks down, weeping through her eyes and nose. Remarkably, Fonda expands beyond Bree's immediate fear—which is palpable, with the murderer standing over her, forcing her to listen to his cruelty, surely winding himself up for more violence. The

---

and Goldie Hawn in the Richard Brooks heist picture *Dollars*. As Molly Haskell pointed out three years later in *From Reverence to Rape*, by 1971 skin was in, but Hollywood didn't know what to do with the new freedom. "From a woman's point of view," Haskell wrote, "the ten years from, say, 1962 or 1963 to 1973 have been the most disheartening in screen history. . . . Whores, quasi-whores, jilted mistresses, emotional cripples, drunks. Daffy ingenues, Lolitas, kooks, sex-starved spinsters, psychotics. Icebergs, zombies, and ballbreakers. That's what little girls of the sixties and seventies are made of." Unhappily furthering this representation, Fonda—whose early credits, let's recall, included the role of Kitty, a runaway confined to Barbara Stanwyck's brothel in *Walk on the Wild Side*—would follow *Klute* by playing yet another prostitute in actor-producer Sutherland's drab good-time outlaws project *Steelyard Blues* (1973).

* For a spectacular time capsule of the era's battle of the sexes, see the Chris Hegedus–D. A. Pennebaker documentary *Town Bloody Hall*, which chronicles the 1971 summit pitting novelist Norman Mailer defending his "The Prisoner of Sex" *Harper's* essay—a masculine manifesto, swinging hard at the women's liberation movement, published later in the year as a book—against critiques from Germaine Greer and a glittering, seething roster of public intellectuals.

victim screams; Bree sheds reverent tears. This is deep cultural mourning, women rendered helpless before men. It's carried by the sadistic recording, and by Fonda's trapped, empathetic face.

Pakula gives Fonda a wide berth to establish exactly how Bree struggles, and largely succeeds, to exert control in her world. The brusqueness of business is deftly depicted at a pay phone; Bree calls in and says, "I could use a quick fifty; you got a commuter for me?" At the subsequent hotel meetup we see how Bree coolly gets the upper hand with the john, running the show. Fonda half reclines and stretches her right arm across a couch, displaying herself, claiming territory. Then, with the camera not cutting, observing behavior in real time, and with no musical underscoring, we watch Bree penetrate his personal space. He's not exactly ready. Further surprising him and us, Fonda/Bree playfully bites his shirt at the biceps. He's too bashful to state what he wants; she cajoles, and suddenly her ear is at his mouth. (Such a small, beautiful piece of business—you never know if that comes from actor, director, or maybe someone else. But it's on the actor to pull it off.) Best to get money out of the way up front, she purrs. As she stands, the camera backs up and discreetly observes from behind as Bree takes off her top, further unnerving the man when he turns and sees her. He is perpetually challenged, and coaxed, to keep up.

The next scene is a celebrated gag, the john huffing on top while she gasps and checks her watch. But you sense that even this was as realistic, as *honest*, as the director and actor could make it.

"It made me feel, uh . . . that I had some control over myself, that I had some control over my life. That I could determine things for myself," Bree explains of her profession in one of the therapy sessions threading through the narrative. Fonda convinced Pakula that the therapist should be female, and Vivian Nathan is sublimely quizzical in the role, listening from the shelter of a plush wingback chair that's oddly perpendicular to her client; like so much else in *Klute*, the formal, static composition is noticeably painterly. In another Fonda suggestion—she begins to have auteurist fingerprints on the film—the therapy scenes were improvised at the *end* of the shoot. Pakula told biographer Jared Brown that he shot scads of footage as Fonda and Nathan dialogued, angling for the apt revelations.

The therapy sessions are a borderline cliché, but they give Bree a critical vent for frank expression and reflection that otherwise would not exist in this narrative about a mixed-up loner. The picture shows Bree's paradoxes—her ambition, her intellect, her verbal skills and stumbles (reading for a play, she dons an Irish accent), her self-destructive choices. It also shows how New York does *not* see her, especially on those theater and fashion auditions. (A visually spectacular early scene dehumanizes women both with staffers who barely glance at the model job applicants and with three colossal blowups of female faces obscured by makeup and jewels, before the fashion editors swiftly reject Bree as having "funny hands.") Bree seems free spirited and commanding at first, striding through town, jockeying men. But she wears a lot of protective turtlenecks. Her shag haircut is a helmet pushed low toward her eyes.

"Don't hide your face," an agent tells her, not really caring. If Bree swaggers like she's independent, she also hardens her shell.

An image of hypersexuality has trailed Fonda all her long life, and far from flinching, she embraces it, mostly owning it at least from *Klute* (she even claims *Barbarella*) through the exercise videos, the 2011 self-help book *Prime Time*, and the ultralight yet purposeful 2018 Hollywood comedy *Book Club* and its 2023 sequel, playing an older version of the sex-positive Samantha figure from *Sex and the City*—free, unattached, unapologetic. (Candice Bergen, Diane Keaton, and Mary Steenburgen are Fonda's *Book Club* costars, inspired to rev up their love lives after diving into the popular erotic thriller *Fifty Shades of Grey*.)

Still, despite *Klute*'s reputation for frankness, the sex in the film is demure. The lovemaking scenes (with the john, with John Klute) are brief and shadowed, discreetly cloaked. (The 2025 Oscar winner *Anora*, by contrast, is an immersive sex-club parade.) Skirting exploitation, Fonda and Pakula dramatize prurience without becoming prurient. It's Bree's attitude that matters, the emotional masking or openness, not the physical display.

Fonda and Sutherland fit snugly into the terse, efficient milieu. Neither star projects sentimentality, even when, in character, they shop together at a street market, shot in shallow focus with city traffic lights blurring romantically behind them. Falling for Klute, Fonda's Bree lightly tugs the back of Sutherland's windbreaker. That's it for affectionate displays. Understatement drives the *Klute* allure.

Fonda has called *Klute* pivotal to her sense of activism via performance. "It was the first time as an actress that I had made a movie that was about broader social issues," she said, not entirely accurately. "God, it felt so good, it felt so good that I said I don't want to do anything else. This is what art is supposed to be, this is what I'm supposed to be doing. I had these new thoughts and new ideas. I had to learn more and deepen them, and then express this through my work."

As the 1960s became the 1970s, movies evolved into "our national theater," Pauline Kael persuasively claimed in the introduction to her 1973 review collection *Deeper into Movies*. Kael, still jazzed by Fonda in the full-throttle dramatic key of *They Shoot Horses*, accurately diagnosed her "special kind of smartness," writing in her review of *Klute*: "She has somehow got to a plane of acting at which even the closest close-up never reveals a false thought and, seen on the movie streets a block away, she's Bree, not Jane Fonda, walking toward us." Wishing there could be two Janes—one bubbling with light comedy, one rippling with adult complexity—Kael gushed anew:

"There isn't another young dramatic actress in American films who can touch her."

Major actors were increasingly forming their own companies and developing material, and with *The Candidate* in 1972, Robert Redford scratched his political itch. The Oscar-winning screenplay was by Eugene McCarthy speechwriter Jeremy Larner, with direction by Redford's *Downhill Racer* (1969) collaborator Michael Ritchie. But the idea was Redford's; he was the uncredited executive producer. Playing straight-talking young California activist/lawyer Bill McKay as he runs for the

US Senate against a three-term incumbent, Redford grouses cynically at the cynicism of the system, deploying the classic Redford cadence. He furrows his brow, takes a beat—the pause is an unstated, usually unmistakable *WTF?*—and generally looks smarter and more serious than everyone else. Redford, almost always more comfortable alone outdoors than inside with people, also generally looks like he can barely abide American culture.

Redford's McKay is humorless, even though he learns to start his speeches with safe jokes, and though he giggles uncontrollably when laughter is inappropriate—that is, while he is blowing an opportunity for free airtime with a local broadcaster. "Maybe people aren't ready to listen," McKay says gravely at another point. Although he is the son of a longtime California politician (played by the wily Melvyn Douglas, real-life spouse of Helen Gahagan Douglas, who coined the moniker "Tricky Dick" as she lost a California Senate race in 1950 to Richard Nixon), somehow McKay is surprised and annoyed by everything, from fundraiser small talk with Natalie Wood to getting outmaneuvered by grandstanding incumbent Republican Crocker Jarman (Don Porter) at a devastating California wildfire. (As Jarman, Porter is pitch perfect with campaign boilerplate that still sounds playable, and with evergreen dog whistles that align mightily with MAGA.)

McKay's campaign experience: Philip Roth's indigenous American berserk.

Campaigns are depicted as being molded way ahead of time by opinion polls and donated cash—which, as Redford's campaign manager Peter Boyle would explain, is *just the way it works until the public votes.* The durability of this character is uncanny: the campaign manager as played by Boyle, bearded and soft-spoken until he explodes, is a dead ringer for Toby Ziegler, the White House communications director on Aaron Sorkin's TV hit *The West Wing* as played by Richard Schiff, bearded and soft-spoken until he explodes.

Still, in *The Candidate*, Redford's McKay is the sincere youngish dude, looking almost exactly like a Kennedy in one striking shot at a podium, in dark suit and tie, seen from slightly above, the angle accentuating the square jaw and shock of hair. We are drawn to McKay because of his candor and *hope* when he impetuously goes off script, riffing from the heart in his TV debate closing statement:

> We've completely ignored the fact that this is a society divided by fear, hatred, and violence. And until we talk about just what this society really is, then I don't know how we're going to change it. . . . We haven't discussed race in this country. We haven't discussed poverty. In short, we haven't discussed any of the sicknesses that may yet send this country up in flames. And we'd better do it. We better get it out in the open and confront it, before it's too late.

Plus ça change . . .

Somehow, McKay is stunned when he wins. The movie's vague ending, aping *The Graduate*, echoing "We blew it" in *Easy Rider*, is a cop-out as McKay wonders, "What do we do now?"

If you win, you go to work. You leverage power, drive change.

In the misapplied lyrics of pop rapper Mickey Avalon's 2006 song, you "do the Jane Fonda."

At the 1972 Oscars, winning Best Actress for *Klute*, Fonda delivered an unexpectedly diplomatic twelve-second acceptance speech. "Thank all of you who applauded," the Hollywood daughter said to the Academy after bowing twice, suggesting that portions of the audience were sitting in disapproving silence. After a breath, she concluded simply, with assurance and composure, if without audible punctuation: "There's a great deal to say and I'm not going to say it tonight I would just like to really thank you very much."

At that moment, Fonda had become an actress with Hollywood power, though that was not necessarily saying an awful lot. Yet she let go of the studio rope; the slackening, she often says, was mutual, if her suspicions of graylisting were accurate. Mentally and emotionally she was already working in the activist field. With a stronger sense of direction than brother Peter's easy rider Captain America—and in one brief, indelible moment, wearing a helmet that failed to protect her—she hit the road.

When you win, what you do next, if you are Jane Fonda: literally, you go to war.

After *Klute*, she wouldn't be in another top-flight Hollywood movie for six years.

7

FIGHTING FOR IT

Steelyard Blues • F.T.A. • Tout Va Bien • Letter to Jane • Introduction to the Enemy

Soldier, we love you. Yeah, soldier, we love you.

—Lyric by singer-composer and *FTA Show* costar Rita Martinson

On the road in 1971, the rude gesture called the *bras d'honneur*—an *up yours* uppercut, also known as the Italian salute—was swung with verve by Jane Fonda.

"Foxtrot, tango, alpha," Fonda bellows with comrades in her documentary *F.T.A.* The movie chronicles a political vaudeville led by Fonda and Donald Sutherland, a counterculture alternative to Bob Hope's increasingly out of touch sexy-jokey USO shows. Fonda punches up "foxtrot" with the defiant *bras d'honneur*, arm bent and fist lifted. The FTA ensemble hisses the final "F" like a fuse before detonating the kicker: "*FUCK* the Army!"

Sung before a rowdy crowd of GIs living America's Vietnam disenchantment, the *up yours* was cathartic.

As the war soldiered on, Vietnam was a rare Hollywood subject; it was practically off-limits until the seal was broken late in the '70s, with Fonda in the first wave. Yet *up yours* became a common attitude toward America's increasingly questionable war machinery as World War II receded and the Cold War and Vietnam became the new realities.

"Tell MAA to go fuck himself," Jack Nicholson blurts in his first full sentence as Buddusky, aka "Badass," in *The Last Detail*. The 1973 movie depicted a pointlessly sadistic military culture sending teenage Randy Quaid to the brig for stealing forty dollars from a charity fund, miffing an officer's wife; Nicholson and Otis Young play the navy lifers assigned to "chase" Quaid from Norfolk, Virginia, to Portsmouth, Maine. Paradoxically, the duo (Nicholson especially; Young's Black American character is more reluctant to risk what he's gained in life) bend the rules and teach the kid to be a free spirit just as the military is locking him up—a metaphor for the era if ever there was one. Innocence (Quaid) gets hammered in the picture.*

The Last Detail was directed by Hal Ashby, the man who would direct Fonda's 1978 Oscar-winning Vietnam breakthrough *Coming Home*, and who in 1973 was emerging as one of the extraordinary decade's best moviemakers. An Oscar-winning editor for *In the Heat*

* This story looked strikingly ironic as Fonda protested in Trump's DC, with Trump taking a stab at being a Nicholson "Badass," only as a reactionary. Trump's aim? Protecting soldiers' abilities to be "killing machines," as he tweeted in October 2019. Apparently, he missed Fonda's *Winter Soldier*.

He squelched rules in the case of Navy SEAL Edward Gallagher, who was acquitted by a military court of all charges, including murder, except one: posing illegally for photographs with an enemy body. Trump, poseur extraordinaire, of course is pro-pose.

Secretary of the Navy Richard Spencer got fired for quietly asking the grandstanding Trump to let the military justice system do its job. "A shocking and unprecedented intervention in a low-level review," Spencer wrote in a *Washington Post* op-ed, explaining his ouster and characterizing Trump's actions. "It was also a reminder that the president has very little understanding of what it means to be in the military, to fight ethically or to be governed by a uniform set of rules and practices." It's *The Last Detail*, only through the looking glass.

This contextual contrast invokes cinema's Kuleshov effect, in which a neutral image gains meaning depending on what image is edited next to it. Intercut with 1973 Jack Nicholson, military justice looks petty and vindictive. Intercut with 2019 Donald Trump, military justice looks Solomonic.

Back to *Winter Soldier*, and an inversion of the Gallagher incident: a slide show in the 1972 documentary illustrates torture techniques, and a vet displays a photo of himself grinning with a buddy over a slain Vietnamese victim. "I'm showing it in hopes that none of you people that have never been involved ever let this happen to you," the vet says. "Don't ever let your government do this to you. It's me. I'm holding a dead body, smiling."

of the Night (1967), Ashby made his directorial debut with *The Landlord* (1970, with cinematographer Gordon Willis yet again capturing greater New York) starring a free-spirited Beau Bridges on the verge of gentrifying a predominantly Black apartment building in Brooklyn's Park Slope, then directed the blissful, suicide-themed black comedy *Harold and Maude* (1971), with Warren Beatty's *Shampoo* (1975) and the Woody Guthrie biopic *Bound for Glory* (1976) ahead. In *The Last Detail* Ashby channels melancholy and antics as the doomed journey winds north by train and bus. The story, by navy vet Darryl Ponicsan (from his novel) and Robert Towne, is Bertolt Brecht's great war tragedy *Mother Courage*: everyone is too far into the system to brawl or wisecrack any kind of way out.

That doesn't make *The Last Detail* the bull goose looney of the *up yours* pack. It's too detached from the actual war, unlike the unshakably rattling, absurdly grand black comedy *Catch-22*. Joseph Heller's novel is set during World War II and was published in 1961, yet with America becoming inseparable from the word *quagmire*—soggy land that bogs you down forever—1970 was an ideal year for a picture grimly satirizing atavistic boondoggle. The war as rendered by Heller (a WWII bombardier in Italy), and then by screenwriter Buck Henry, reuniting with director Mike Nichols after *The Graduate*, was one the country didn't need, didn't want, and couldn't stop.

Catch-22 is a dry, adult, sophisticated, hilarious, impeccably composed series of *moving pictures*—long takes with space for actors to perform, for jokes to develop, for punch lines to land.* The deep, vivid cast, led by Alan Arkin as the seriously baffled Yossarian, includes Anthony Perkins, Martin Sheen, Charles Grodin, Orson Welles, Austin Pendleton, Bob Balaban, Jack Gilford, Bob Newhart, Richard Benjamin, Peter Bonerz, and Norman Fell, all relishing gallows humor. One gloriously nonsensical scene involves Newhart, as the anxious Major Major, instructing Fell's Sergeant Towser to tell visitors he can only be seen

* Do not expect as much from the sad, tan-toned, six-part 2019 streaming series *Catch-22*, with George Clooney among the executive producers and stars. "Can't overcome the dullness of the screenplay, with its very un-Hellerian tendency to moralize," wrote Mike Hale of the *New York Times*.

when he's not in. The camera follows Newhart left and right, with the subject of the framed portrait on the wall behind him changing each time the camera pans: it's Roosevelt, then Churchill, then Stalin.

Nichols's cinematographer was David Watkin, fresh off the satire *How I Won the War* and the history *The Charge of the Light Brigade*, and later an Oscar winner for *Out of Africa*. Perhaps Watkin's most daring, uproarious, and complicated *Catch-22* shot—it's hard to say which one's best; the team tops itself all the time—follows Martin Balsam as Colonel Cathcart and Jon Voight as the commercially minded Milo Minderbinder, whose business success turns him into a fascist tyrant. They stride down the tarmac of a seaside Italian airstrip (the location was actually Mexican, built for the movie), and the camera follows Cathcart and Minderbinder, panning left as they walk. An aircraft lands, whizzing in from the right, then left out of the frame. Out of sight, we hear it blow up. The shot continues panning left until we are behind Cathcart and Minderbinder, casually climbing into their jeep. The crashed plane comes into view, ablaze. SNAFU! No biggie!

This is black comedy in a stunning nutshell from a comic whiz at his confident peak, even if the depressive Nichols felt he'd been beaten to the punch by *M*A*S*H*.

In yet another indelible image, an airplane propeller scissors a character named Hungry Joe as he stands on an offshore raft. His legs and waist remain standing as his top plops into the sea, with—grisly to say—perfect comic timing.

In a pinnacle of the era's blow-up climaxes, *Catch-22* detonates the Mexican compound that the studio built. Heller's plot has Americans destroying their own base as part of a sales contract Minderbinder engineers with the Germans—his *rivals*, sure, but also new business partners, and profit is profit. Nichols's effects crew rigged concussive explosions, igniting towering fireballs that provided all of the scene's mouth-of-hell light.

Ingeniously, the base is consistently devoid of extras, which creates a peculiar hollowed-out, through-the-looking-glass aura. But the bombers were real enough that actors shouted their lines over engine roar, and real enough that Nichols apparently said things on set like "Don't fuck with me. I have the fifth largest air force in the world."

Voight's golden-haired First Lieutenant Minderbinder, initially a bright-eyed kid, not only masters the art of the deal but also leads Italy into fascist-controlled shambles. Standing on top of a chauffeured jeep, he surveys the chaotic streets and indulges a brief, crushingly cynical side conversation (penned by Henry, an exchange Heller admired, according to Nichols on the DVD commentary) with Yossarian, distressed about his dead comrade Nately (Art Garfunkel):

"But he died a rich man. He had over sixty shares in the syndicate."

"What good is that? He's dead."

"Then his family will get it."

"He didn't have time to have a family."

"Then his parents will get it."

"They don't need it, they're rich."

"Then they'll understand."

Yossarian can get the discharge he craves if he acquiesces to a quid pro quo, saying nice things about the military when he gets home. "*Like* us," Balsam's Cathcart says simply, with Buck Henry, as Colonel Korn, grinning next to him.

Steven Soderbergh interviewed Nichols on the 2001 DVD as they watched the film, and at one point he began to ask to what extent Vietnam was in mind during the shoot. Nichols did not pick up the cue, but he later told the story of snubbing John Wayne because "he was so reactionary." Wayne, flying to Mexico, asked permission to use the production's landing strip, "And we were such prigs, such righteous schmucks, that when he landed, we didn't go out to say hello," Nichols said. He and Buck Henry later apologized, and the anecdote answers Soderbergh. When Yossarian lifts up a strip of parachute silk to reveal the ripped abdomen of his fellow bombardier, the slow ooze of guts—which apparently took days for the crew to perfect—is lingering and graphic. It's calculated to disturb, and to bring the laughter to a stop.

The movie version of *M*A*S*H*, coming out a few months before *Catch-22*, was as meticulous in its alarming handling of wartime viscera. Recognizing the world of escalating casualties in which its American audience lived, Robert Altman's comedy framed the recessed ribs and squirting arteries as powerfully as the subversive slapstick.

"Goddamn army," goes a muttered refrain, and the story—like *Catch-22*, initially penned by a veteran, based on a 1968 novel written by former mobile army surgical hospital (MASH) doctor Richard Hooker—shows blundering, hypocrisy, and self-importance that begs to be lampooned.

The setting is Korea, where the makeshift operating theater is dim and bloody and only partially brightened by the dry banter. Donald Sutherland's offhand style as Hawkeye Pierce, dashingly complemented when the mischievous clown Trapper John McIntyre (Elliott Gould) swaggers in, defines the piece as they disdain their "regular" army rivals. It's the irregulars who hold all the charm.

That charm is partially tainted when watching the film today: her shrill hypocrisy notwithstanding, who still wants to see Sally Kellerman's Hot Lips Houlihan humiliated via the big shower reveal? In virtually all exchanges with women, the lusty men of *M*A*S*H* are mashers. *Catch-22* has its own scene of drooling military men without women, and in *The Last Detail*, Carol Kane has the most prominent, if brief, female role, identified as Young Whore.

Slightly ripened for television, though, where the sitcom adaptation of *M*A*S*H* first aired in September 1972, it's clear how the Marx Brothers anarchy, especially as led by the sensitive Alan Alda in the Hawkeye Pierce role, became a resistant (and inevitably more carefully righteous) *up yours* mainstream vehicle. The edges of *Catch-22* were too jagged to be squished into TV.

Steelyard Blues (1973)

There was almost zero room in these movies for women, a pattern that held in Fonda's oddly chosen, nonmilitary *bras d'honneur*, the comedy *Steelyard Blues*.

Sutherland, who had an executive producing credit, is a freedom-loving demolition derby nut fresh out of prison for petty crime. His brother (Howard Hesseman) is the district attorney, mean-spirited and law-and-order, the villain. The mustachioed Sutherland becomes the ringleader of a band of misfits (including an antic Peter Boyle as a circus veteran and mental ward escapee) trying to refurbish an abandoned plane so they can fly to "where there ain't no jails." Sutherland serves up a devilish grin and a slow, almost taunting twirl as he saunters out of the joint in the first scene. As in *M*A*S*H* and *The Last Detail*, the conflict will hinge on conformist society trying to confine free spirits. "Bein' different ain't never been a crime," goes a lyric to one of the movie's bluesy roots-rock tunes.

But the shaggy antiestablishment target is mushy. The movie fights a generalized fight. For Sutherland—and more acutely for Fonda—it's a dismal follow-up to *Klute*. "A whore with a heart of gold, how new," producer Julia Phillips, making her first movie, later wrote of Fonda's character, Iris.

Fonda's acting lifts the character. Her Iris is quick-witted, wry, and unfailingly likable. Of all the misfits, it's Iris who gets the proverbial joke. She's the most natural figure in a movie that shouts its quirkiness, with Boyle so madcap that at one point he's on all fours, barking like a dog at the "straight" authorities. Strained comedy is uniquely uncomfortable to watch, and with the cast laboring to be off-the-wall (or up the wall, as Boyle's Human Fly scales an air force storage facility during a break-in), it's consistently a relief to be back in Fonda's sensible presence—though even Fonda gets stuck with lame clichés, as when, torpedoing Hesseman's anticipated sexual pleasure, she pours an icy drink down his pants.

Iris is warm-hearted and willing to pitch in with rebels even though, as Sutherland's Jesse Veldini cruelly jests, Iris's clients *are* City Hall. Iris has spine enough to quietly resent it when Veldini assigns her the task of decorating the plane; Fonda looks away, nonplussed, refusing to ratify her conscription into a stereotypical "women's work" role. There's little more she can do, though, until a climactic dialogue that firmly places Veldini in the tradition of Redford's Bubber in *The Chase*.

"I'm not a criminal, Iris," Veldini says. "I'm an outlaw."

"What's the difference?"

"I don't know." What comes next is pure Bubber: "When I got out of the joint this time, Iris, I made a decision to go straight. You can't do it."

Veldini's brother rigs the system against him every time. We've seen it, as Hesseman's henchmen, like E. G. Marshall's thugs in *The Chase*, hold Sutherland down for a solid beating. "He didn't like my attitude,"

Veldini tells Iris, with Sutherland applying the lightest possible dusting of sarcasm.

Iris relates. Maybe this rang true for Fonda as well, after her trumped-up 1970 drug arrest in Cleveland, which led to her famous fist-raised mug shot. In the scene's remaining lines, Iris tries to figure out how to stake her claim.

"I don't belong to anybody," she says.

"Terrific!" Veldini replies. "That makes five of us."

"You're a loser."

"You are a whore, Iris."

Pause. "Don't push me."

"Push back."

"You're a bum."

"Right. You're fantastic, Iris." She smiles, clinching the inevitable comic romantic resolution and the political *up yours* alliance, vague as that is.

A few viewers were seduced by the picture's innocence. "I like its earnestness, its brow furrowed with mission," Vincent Canby wrote. "It reminds me of the little boy who covered himself with vanishing cream and then walked through a dinner party in the fond belief he was invisible."

"Clearly no one involved intended *Steelyard Blues* to be taken even half-seriously except as a gesture in behalf of joy and fellow-feeling," Richard Jameson wrote in *Movietone News*, going to bat for the widely maligned picture.

But the general naïveté and sloppy craftsmanship put most critics off. First-time movie director Alan Myerson had roots in sketch comedy and improv via Chicago's Second City and San Francisco's the Committee (which he cofounded, with Howard Hesseman and Peter Bonerz as mainstay performers, and which worked itself into the city's activist/protest scene). Myerson was headed for a long career in TV; subsequent film credits would be scarce, ending with *Police Academy 5*. He worked from a script by young writer David S. Ward, who would do far better in 1973 with *The Sting*.

The film's fledgling producers deemed Myerson's original cut "static and unfunny. It is unreleasable," Phillips recalled. So the producers recut the picture, to little avail. Gags are belabored: see Veldini inadvertently breaking everything he touches in his brother's office. Set pieces are rushed: there is no payoff after the outrage of zookeepers needlessly shooting a lion in its cage, where Veldini, in his parole-assigned job at the zoo, was goofing off with the animal. The editing itself is shockingly inept: Fonda greets Hesseman at her door in two clumsily mismatched shots. The ending feels puny as the outlaws run away on horseback. Behind them, inevitably, their hippie airplane blows up.

"It may be because Miss Fonda's and Sutherland's soberly humanitarian left-wing political views are so well known that they lend a heaviness to 'Steelyard Blues' that it would not have if we were not so aware," Canby judged. "I doubt it, however. They are two performers I admire very much, but this film, which may be up to their politics, is not up to their talents."

Boyle got good notices for his cockeyed sidekick routine, which included an impersonation of Brando, but the badly stereotypical supporting role and the politically blurry mission of *Steelyard Blues* should have been beneath the Oscar-winning Fonda in a year when Glenda Jackson was starring in *A Touch of Class*, Marsha Mason was in *Cinderella Liberty* (albeit as yet another prostitute, in a story by *The Last Detail*'s Darryl Ponicsan), and Barbra Streisand—playing an indomitable political activist—debated with Redford in Sydney Pollack's *The Way We Were*.

Still, Molly Haskell found Fonda's performance "remarkable—light, offhand, witty, and touching in some impossibly cute situations—all qualities I was afraid she had lost when she turned herself into a political propaganda machine."

Indeed, if Fonda was making a perversely tiny impact on-screen, there were two good reasons. As Haskell made clear in *From Reverence to Rape*, Hollywood wasn't offering women much. And as presumptive ally Haskell noted in her sour description of Fonda not as an activist but as a propagandist, the *stupid fucking actress* was fully engaged in the real-world trenches.

F.T.A. (1972)

In one of the live performances captured for the documentary *F.T.A.*, Jane Fonda plays Pat Nixon opposite actor Michael Alaimo as Pat's husband:

"Mister President, there's a terrible demonstration going on outside."

"Oh, there's always a demonstration going on outside, Pat."

"Yeah, but, Richard, this one is completely out of control."

"What are they asking for this time?"

"Free Angela Davis and all political prisoners," Fonda says, flashing the crowd of eager GIs a knowing, mischievous grin. "Out of Vietnam now, and draft all government officials."

"Well, we have people to take care of that, they'll do their job, you do your job, and I'll do my job."

"Richard, you don't understand, they're storming the White House!"

"Oh, in that case I better call out the Third Marines."

"You can't, Richard."

"Why not?"

"It *is* the Third Marines!"

The soldiers roar, and that's the tone of *The FTA Show*, the alt-USO road show cooked up by Fonda and colleagues, aligning themselves with the GI movement increasingly voicing resistance to the war.

Before larking into its comic skits and satirical tunes, though, the *F.T.A.* film, shot during a December 1971 tour, conscientiously frames itself as pure *Winter Soldier* (that documentary appearing in New York the next month, January 1972, with Fonda's Oscar win for *Klute* a few months away). The opening shot is a close-up of a real marine in uniform saying, "I mean, how can you write your mother and tell her that her handsome young darling marine, her hero, is anti-military, you know? But I sat down and wrote her a letter and told her exactly how I felt. And my mother wrote back and she said that she fully understood and she was happy that I felt that way, that I was anti-military."

Such testimonies are spliced in with *FTA Show* performances headlined by Fonda through much of 1971, culminating in the December tour to Hawaii, Okinawa, the Philippines, and mainland Japan. Performance-wise, there isn't a lot for Fonda to do onstage, and director Francine Parker's no-frills movie captures the ramshackle tour without really converting the footage to art. (As with *Steelyard*, Fonda found herself working with a director whose chief asset seemed to be less a sterling résumé than a shared attitude; this was Parker's only feature film.) The documentary, with cameras typically looking up from the front row or getting a view from the wings, preserves this history of Fonda being plucky and defiant in skits that play like *Beetle Bailey* bits with edge. She holds her own in a high-spirited four-woman kick line protesting sexism, singing at the top of her voice with the chorus of "*I'm tired of fuckers fuckin' over me.*" Fonda and singer Holly Near sport top hats and canes for the knockoff "Nothing Could Be Finer than to Be in Indochina."

"*Bomb another city today!*" they harmonize in the big finish before scampering off a makeshift stage.

Though she is the headliner, billed above Sutherland and everyone else, the "show" on-screen is anchored chiefly by singer-guitarist Len Chandler, leading original protest songs like the crooned, defiant "My Ass Is Mine" and the urgent, catchy "We Will Not Bow Down to Genocide"; on-screen, Chandler's at the microphone more than anyone. Rita Martinson, her voice light, tuneful, and heartfelt, quietly sings the memorable ballad "Soldier, We Love You"—a song that feels like the heart of the show, separating disdain for the war from support for the

Left to right: Rita Martinson, Pamela Donegan, Holly Near, and Jane Fonda perform their antiwar revue in *F.T.A.*
Courtesy Everett Collection

troops. Pamela Donegan performs a long poem that melds Vietnam resistance with Black Panther action. Sutherland recites from Dalton Trumbo's *Johnny Got His Gun.*

At one point a few GIs in the audience resist FTA and heckle the performers. One soldier, a drink in his hand, prowls the edge of the stage and yells at Sutherland, "You want to fight 'em over in Vietnam or you want to fight 'em in your own backyard?" Backstage, the ensemble huddles. Fonda asks what they should do. Sutherland takes the stage and tells the disruptive contingent they'll have to go. The audience agrees. "Out! Out! Out!" they chant, clapping along. Eventually a familiar protest anthem breaks out: "*Move on over or we'll move on over you . . .* "

Fonda plays a bigger role offstage as the activist, sometimes moderating impromptu conversations and structured rap sessions, frequently making public statements as the troupe alights at the next destination. In Okinawa she promotes "the understanding that the American GI is not the same as the American government. The American GIs don't know why they're here, don't want to be here, don't want to be in Vietnam *or* Japan *or* the Philippines *or* Hawaii, anywhere in the Pacific Rim or anywhere in the world where they don't belong."

When they land in the Philippines, the camera watches the Jane Gang deplane while we hear her a voice-over from another public statement about the tour. "It is not raising any new issues," Fonda says of *The FTA Show.* "It is just simply saying to people in the service, 'We recognize that the majority of you are against the war, don't like the kind of oppression you're experiencing, and we support your struggles.' How they struggle and in what direction is not up to us to say, to direct, to teach or anything like that. That's their job. But we support them."

The picture's rhetorical climax doesn't come from *The FTA Show.* It features Fonda at the Foreign Correspondents' Club in Tokyo, talking fast and sounding harsh, claiming chemicals, defoliants, and automation are continuing to make conditions worse, even if US casualties are down.* "They know it," Fonda tells the press, speaking of the GIs. "And

* "There was something shrill and perhaps memorized in her brief, impassioned call to 'stop the government unless it stops the war,'" Tom Hayden would later recall of his first encounter with Fonda, sharing the stage at a 1971 rally.

they're beginning to say no. We will not load bombs anymore, we will not kill Vietnamese people anymore, and we're beginning to ask why and in whose interests are we here?"

Parker's picture cuts to the December 18, 1971, scene at the US base in Iwakuni, Japan, with servicemen declaring, "We can no longer remain silent about the atrocities and injustice," and urging attendees to sign a petition.

Like *Winter Soldier*, *F.T.A.* is chiefly durable as a journalistic document—"The only film made at that time that really gives a vivid portrayal of this antiwar upsurge in the military," said director David Zeiger in his 2005 documentary *Sir! No Sir!*, which featured *The FTA Show*. But by 1972, other sorts of anti-Vietnam documentaries had been around for years, typically searing the audience with grounded critiques and damning images.

In 1968, Emile de Antonio's *In the Year of the Pig* opened with dissonant, mechanical sounds and graphic imagery that includes difficult-to-watch footage of burning bodies. What was apparently novel then, in that Academy Award–nominated documentary, looks conventional now: talking heads (journalist David Halberstam among them) and footage of state leaders. President Lyndon Johnson leans into a microphone during a speech to complain about American carping by saying, "I'm not saying you never had it so good. But that *is* the fact, isn't it?" and, rather plaintively, "I didn't get you into Vietnam. You've been in Vietnam ten years." Such statements are intercut with footage from the field, with sound sometimes at odds with image; note the claims of Vietnamese prisoners being treated in accord with the Geneva Conventions while we see them being brutalized. The shock-value testimonies of the Winter Soldier Investigation are anticipated by *In the Year of the Pig*, with soldiers describing the dehumanization of the enemy and ultraviolence quickly adopted as SOP.

Even more aggressively, the 1967 French compilation *Far from Vietnam* was straight-up agitprop. The French, having only recently retreated from both Algeria and Vietnam, cut to the chase, casting America as arrogant, rich, industrialist, imperialist. Right off the bat you get close-up looks at an aircraft carrier in the Seventh Fleet being supplied with heavy-looking missiles and bombs. The poor of the world cannot hope to match the rich in terms of materials and techniques—and you also must acknowledge, intones the French narrator, "on the American side, the same ignorance of the enemy." *Far from Vietnam* is gripping in reporting terms—lingering, for instance, on a 1967 Wall Street protest with antiwar demonstrators heckled by a large pro-war crowd looking like they're at a frat party, proudly holding up draft cards and chanting "Bomb Hanoi!"

But this being the French New Wave, and with directors including Agnès Varda, Claude Lelouch, Alain Resnais, and Jean-Luc Godard, its style and attitude elbow forward as well. Giant intertitles announce irony: JOHNSON PLEURE ("Johnson Cries"), reads one. That leads to a fascinating scene of Vietnamese street theater lampooning "our poor Johnson."

Theory is welcome, bog the action though it may. In Resnais's sequence, titled CLAUDE RIDDER, a fictional man prowls around in his own den and overarticulates his complex analysis of the war (framed as "bad faith" by the introductory voice-over narration) to a silent woman gazing at him impassively/skeptically.

What can art do?

Godard, who had established himself as the bad boy of the French New Wave with the jazzy, proto-punk genre bender *Breathless* in 1960 and had made more than a dozen influential features in the seven short years since, poses this question in the sequence CAMERA EYE. In a breathless voice-over, rapid as thought, Godard narrates with his face glued behind a camera. He is theorizing, talking it out, explaining that he had wanted to go to Vietnam, but Vietnam denied him: "Hanoi refused me permission to go to their country and they were right. I could've given them more problems than help."

This will be rehashed by Godard, only with Fonda in the camera eye, in *Letter to Jane.*

The camera is the subject of much of Godard's intellectual riffing as he ponders content and form. "We may say that our hearts bleed, but how? Our blood has nothing to do with the blood of anybody injured. So there was some kind of shame. They were shameful ideas, like when you sign peace petitions."

Therefore, he claims, *make films.*

"I make films. That's the best I can do for Vietnam. Instead of invading Vietnam with a kind of generosity that makes things unnatural, we let Vietnam invade us. And we are made to understand the place it takes in our lives wherever we are." He struggles against the "economic and aesthetic imperialism" of the dominant American film industry. He observes the irony that the working class, which he champions, does not see his pictures. Communication is strained between the artist/intellectual and a segmented audience. They exist in separate prisons—creative and economic.

This is the man who would make Fonda's first scripted movie post-*Klute*.

Tout Va Bien (1972)

On the vast map of Jane Fonda's life, Jean-Luc Godard, titan of international cinema, is but a blip. But in the 1972 French picture *Tout Va Bien* ("All Is Well," or "Everything's Fine"), Fonda is Godard's headliner, with a dual purpose in the movie's radical leftist machinery. As in Fonda's later *9 to 5*, the "story" involves workers taking over a workplace. Thoroughly unlike *9 to 5*, the frame, per Godard practice, is repeatedly broken and self-consciously analyzed.

Fonda plays a reporter*—*Steelyard Blues* would mark the end of her call girl roles, and the 1970s would find her playing a reporter or writer in four movies—but she also is used overtly as a star name making the project possible.

"I want to make a film," we hear in voice-over after the credits, coded in the red, white, and blue of the French flag.

"You need money for that," comes an answer. We see a close-up of a checkbook as a hand signs, one by one, twenty-one checks to various departments; the means of production are squarely foregrounded.

* Uncannily, the 1972 *Tout Va Bien* summarizes the twenty-first-century print journalism dilemma—papers collapsing in the Internet age—as soon as it introduces Fonda's character. Quoting a report from the Parisian magazine *Charlie Hebdo*, she says on a broadcast, "The written press is dying, a death it brought about itself. After years of building themselves a rat trap, they are caught, and they are screwed. How smart of the establishment press to maintain, thanks to advertising, such a low price that it doesn't even cover the cost of their raw materials."

"If you use stars then people will give you money," the dialogue continues.

"Then," the reply goes, "we will use stars."

Fonda is paired with Yves Montand, star of 1969's *Z*. We see them, shot straight on, as familiar stars, soon reannounced in all-caps titles as JANE FONDA and YVES MONTAND.

"You must pay them not to act," Godard said of movie stars in 1972, "then photograph them as if they are masterpieces." There is a certain amount of that sort of voguing through the picture. The voice-over dialogue continues, engaging in a brief, mocking love story. But *Tout Va Bien* will have none of that.

"We didn't want the vulgarity of narrative," Jean-Henri Roger told Godard biographer Richard Brody in 2001. "If there are characters, it's bourgeois." Roger was part of the Dziga Vertov Group created by Godard and chief collaborator Jean-Pierre Gorin in 1968, the year of France's

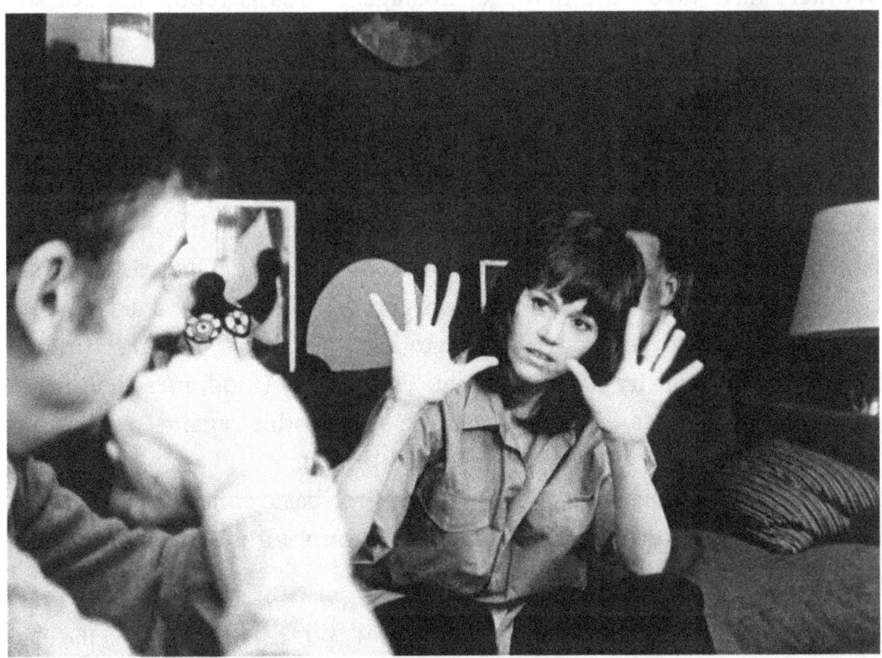

Fonda and Yves Montand, stars of Jean-Luc Godard's *Tout Va Bien*. *Courtesy Everett Collection*

May riots. Godard had fulfilled his *Breathless* promise by becoming a prolific, though seldom profitable, filmmaker through the 1960s, increasingly foregrounding politics.* *La Chinoise*, from 1967, follows a group of Maoist students studying doctrine and gearing up for action: In a corrupt culture, are violence and terrorism warranted to spur change? The question was amplified by the Paris protests.

Gorin became Godard's political-aesthetic sparring partner, and they produced a string of theory-driven works under the flag of the Dziga Vertov Group. (The name is drawn from 1920s–1930s Soviet filmmaker and theorist Dziga Vertov, whose concepts included "cine eye," consciously echoed in Godard's Camera Eye in *Far from Vietnam*.) That culminated with *Tout Va Bien*, which reckoned with the meaning of the 1968 French unrest and contemplated its lessons as of 1972.

Fonda plays a radio reporter romantically involved with a filmmaker played by Montand, who is disenchanted with movies and now making commercials. Montand goes with her to a meatpacking plant on strike. Workers have taken the manager hostage. Fonda is reporting, but she and Montand largely fade into the background.

Godard and Gorin make their meatpacking plant set deliberately theatrical. Twenty-first-century auteur Wes Anderson uses these kinds of stagy sets in his movies; in *Tout Va Bien* it's a brilliant cutaway of a two-story structure, giving us an organizational master view of the warren of various offices, hallways, and stairways. The floors are strewn with loose papers, illustrating the chaos of the workers' takeover. The workers wear bloody aprons. Sausages are seen on giant posters in the background. The camera slowly tracks from left to right and back again, letting us take in the complexity of the well-chosen industry (food, meat), allowing ample room for masses of bodies to be seen jostling against each other in a borderline slapstick vision of class conflict.

The movie listens, conspicuously, to three basic constituencies: management, the union, and the radical subgroup within the union. "*The*

* In an interview for the Criterion Collection's 2004 DVD release, Gorin said the filmmakers had no illusions about making money with *Tout Va Bien*, but added, "I think we had the hope that we could address more people than the three Christians in a cave we'd been addressing."

working class will kick your ass," the strikers sing, fists raised, as the camera dispassionately tracks back and forth, surveying the wide scene.* This briefly suggests a Brechtian musical. It's no accident.

Gradually, *Tout Va Bien* swings back around to the characters played by the stars, starting with Montand's filmmaker. In an unbroken six-and-a-half-minute take, Montand, seen in a medium shot, wearing a gray suit with his tie loosened, standing next to a film camera, answers unheard questions about his Godard-like life and career, explaining how he was a Nouvelle Vague scenarist but eventually felt trapped by the insipid tendencies of movies. He turned to commercials as a better choice: more honest, ridiculous though they are.

He plans a political film about France. But he's confused.

Writings by Bertolt Brecht begin to point the way. "Do you know his preface to *Mahagonny*?" he asks. "Isn't it brilliant?"

Ah, yes, the viewer thinks. *Brecht's preface to* Mahagonny.

In fact, that 1930 essay illustrates the problem of the artist-worker versus the means of production, an iron framework that Brecht termed an "apparatus." Godard's apparatus—his support, but also his nemesis—was the ministry-guided French film industry. Also, more dominantly, "apparatus" means commercial Hollywood. (Can't work with it, can't work without it.)

Brecht wrote of artists:

> By imagining that they have got hold of an apparatus which in fact has got hold of them they are supporting an apparatus which is out of their control, which is no longer as they believe a means of furthering output but has become an obstacle to output, and specifically to their own output as soon as it follows a new and original course which the apparatus finds awkward or opposed to its own aims. Their output then becomes a matter of delivering the goods.

* The French appetite for strike endures; as 2019 became 2020, demonstrators and tear gas collided on French streets, with President Emmanuel Macron's efforts to reform pension plans leading to the longest strike in the nation's history, with an encore of strikes and protests in 2023 as legislation raised the retirement age.

That last phrase, "delivering the goods," is the sort of sneering line Pauline Kael and many critics repeatedly wrote in the 1970s of formula movies made as if in a sausage factory and cynically marketed to a mindless mob trained and starved for "entertainment."

"They are not in fact free inventors," Brecht continued, roping artists and journalists into one category; "the apparatus goes on fulfilling its function with or without them; the theaters play every night; the papers come out so many times a day; and they absorb what they need; and all they need is a given amount of stuff."*

With Brecht duly invoked, Godard and Gorin shift away from Montand, though not before punctuating his malaise with a very funny ninety-second shot of the commercial he is making. The product isn't stated and doesn't matter, though razor blades were mentioned by the director in an earlier phone call to an unseen actress whose bare bum would be used, he explained as she took the job, for comparison with the smoothness of a man's fresh-shaved cheek. We see the commercial through the viewfinder and in the background, in "reality"; it's simply the legs of two women, one in red tights and a short dress, the other in yellow tights and a short dress, twisting and stomping arrhythmically to a bouncy *ba-bop-ba-bop-ba-baaa* tune (those are the choral lyrics) that sounds like late-1960s Herb Alpert, or the peppy *Barbarella* theme. *Tout Va Bien* is often amusing, if on-the-nose in its targets, as when the meat plant manager is made by the workers to time his bathroom break—but is kept out of an occupied bathroom by a worker loudly singing "The Internationale." *Désolé!*

Fonda gets her confessional turn in a three-minute close-up. Like Montand's film director, this American journalist, Susan DeWitt, is uncomfortable with what her workplace system—in her case, a news bureau—allows her to do. Both the news organization's house style and its "acceptable" subjects are suffocating. She is trapped by Brecht's apparatus.

"I had realized that for me to say what I want to say, their style doesn't work. Only I don't have an alternative," she says, speaking in

* Again, Trump's ongoing presence center stage for a second term is well understood in part as a continuing triumph of "delivering the goods," entertainment-wise. Trump stuffs the sausage.

English. Her editors refuse a piece about the factory strike, leading her to complain, "I am an American correspondent in France who doesn't correspond to anything anymore."*

Fonda's delivery has the introspective spontaneity of Bree's *Klute* therapy sessions. As she speaks fluent French, we also are reminded of Fonda's real-life experience as a semi-expat in France.

We then see Susan in a radio studio, a long shot with an engineer in the foreground. She fails to nail an English-language broadcast bit, struggling to articulate, in too theoretical terms, the historical moment.

"It's crap," she says of her copy, giving up.

At last comes the scene between the stars, their "love story." Like the other social arrangements we observe, it's failing. The French tricolor marks their small apartment—blue couch, red coffee pot, white walls, and a white robe for Fonda, although as they argue in French about the sexual tension in the relationship, she changes into a khaki shirt, the kind a journalist might don to meet Castro in the Cuban hills.

The problem, Fonda observes to Montand, is his limited headings for their relationship: Food, Movies, Sex. The camera cuts closer to Fonda as she pushes back, wanting her partner to understand what's outside those headings. As Fonda plays it, the invitation to communicate, to expand and deepen the relationship, is sincere; the eyes and voice plead lightly. But she also pulls no punches. The voice grows steely as she notes that he only has one interest.

The filmmakers cut to it: a large black-and-white photo of a penis, cradled by a woman's hand.

She revolts. She leaves.

The meatpacking strike, where Fonda and Montand were held hostage for two days, helps both characters realize their unsatisfying positions within the apparatus. So they change. Montand reengages with filmmaking, now with purpose. Fonda pursues a story in a supermarket,

* Fonda's character would be further frustrated by the journalistic apparatus of even the Internet era's most serious survivors, increasingly tabloid-y in their shock-and-controversy headlines, and often brazenly clickbait-y. On January 15, 2020, the top story under the *Washington Post*'s online "National" heading was like something Godard and Gorin would write: WATCH THIS CAT FIGHT OFF THREE COYOTES THAT WERE DEFINITELY PLANNING TO EAT HIM.

a capitalist-consumerist metaphor, figuring her news agency won't want this story either.

This is the movie's stunning, climactic, near-ten-minute tracking shot, moving from left to right, then back again, behind twenty-five cash registers, with customers unloading their absurdly piled grocery carts as we listen to the registers' whirs and clacks. (Brody writes that Gorin largely handled the film's direction, drawing from Godardian techniques, as Godard recovered from a devastating motorcycle accident.) Fonda observes but is largely subsumed into the action. In one of the grocery aisles, a communist author hawks his discounted books. A group of youthful rebels sprint into the store, challenging his thinking.

"Are you a militant?" he indignantly asks a young woman.

"Of course I am," she answers curtly, demanding answers when he tap dances about what his platitude-driven book actually means. The youths, as in 1968, bring rebellion, yelling that *everything is free*, leading customers to bypass the registers, meeting resistance from the police. It ends in a melee.

This Has Been an Account for Those Who Don't Keep Them, reads a title card.

As it exhorts citizens to recognize systemic structures and take more control of their own histories, *Tout Va Bien* also asks the question that Godard and the Dziga Vertov Group, "being interested in the grammar of cinema," as Gorin put it, had been wrestling with: How do you make a valid, or "honest," political movie? Godard and Gorin mistrusted "political films" in the conventionally understood sense, pictures that preached to the converted, denounced obvious evils, and celebrated easy moral victories; those movies suffered from predictability. The filmmakers' focus shifted to problems of form, subverting narrative and character, foregrounding *process*. On-screen, they attempted to overturn the fundamental assumptions and patterns they hoped to overturn in the world.

Fonda, like Montand a major star and a well-known activist, was ideal for this exercise. Her persona as Susan is on brand, and to the extent the movie needs a "performance" from her, she easily delivers. Proportionally, her role is about the same size as in *Steelyard Blues*, which, after delays, would arrive on screens the following year. And if *Tout Va Bien* is a heavy theoretical hammer compared to the useless cardboard spoon of *Steelyard Blues*, there is a nagging similarity in the roles' pivotal moments (Iris in *Steelyard* pouring ice down horny Howard Hesseman's trousers, Susan DeWitt in *Tout Va Bien* breaking with Montand as she sticks the photo of the penis over her face to complain that he thinks of nothing else). She stylishly snaps her face toward the camera like a model to break the fourth wall as needed. She's easy with the halting self-doubt about broadcasting; the reporting job neatly launches inquiries about social relations, and thus, as happens in reporters' tales from *Meet John Doe* to *Medium Cool*, to inquiries of her own complicity, and Fonda is terrific at simultaneously interrogating herself and frustrating systems. She is genuinely pained by the emotional distance of her romantic relationship. Fonda's characteristically quick-tempo acting, far more verbal than physical in Godard's largely static talking-head shots, is smart—alive to nuances of feeling, thought, theory. She is, for these Marxists, a magnificent foot soldier, never at odds with the experimental project's key.

Fluent as she is within the Godard-Gorin grammar, though, the Dziga Vertov Group tactics of Brechtian alienation and deconstruction would not become hers.* And the very next shot of the Godard-Gorin-Fonda relationship depicted an odd falling-out that endures, peculiarly, on film. Fonda was about to get fragged.

Letter to Jane (1972)

The shot was a photo of Fonda in North Vietnam—not *the* Hanoi Jane moment but a far less incendiary image.

The picture was taken by Joseph Kraft, published in *L'Express* and elsewhere globally, in August 1972. The problem of what role intellectuals

* Fonda plainly would have been a poor long-term fit with this band of outsiders, but she was apparently tempted by the prospect of submerging herself within an activist group. Hayden had blanched when Fonda, as he was getting to know her, considered renouncing her stardom and joining a film collective: "I remember cautioning her against giving up acting, knowing from experience how collectives could confuse professionalism with privilege," Hayden wrote, adding of his own time in an ideological collective known as the Red Family: "I could imagine the Red Family demanding that she work underground to shed her bourgeois leanings."

can play in revolution was postulated even more succinctly, Jean-Luc Godard and Jean-Pierre Gorin argued, in this *single photo* than in the entirety of *Tout Va Bien*, which poses the same question.

So together in *Letter to Jane*, Godard and Gorin clear their throats for the first twenty minutes of their chesty, windy fifty-two-minute essay. They ponder how to ask questions. They diagram positionalities. They use stills from *Tout Va Bien* and, very occasionally, from elsewhere, never resorting to moving images, often leaving the screen black as they talk.

As cinema, *Letter to Jane* is a chore, but it suggests what the Godard-Gorin lecture act may have been like. Together, they twice made tours of the United States, often on campuses, talking film and politics. A lengthy 1972 *New York Times* article by James Conaway chronicled how the philosophizing could slide into attitudinizing: "The effect can be numbing. I spent portions of several days with Godard/Gorin, in New York and at Rutgers University, the first leg of their money-making tour of American campuses; the discursive miasma was penetrated only fitfully by reality."

Godard appears particularly prone to put-ons and pranks. "In the end," Conaway wrote, "he asked me to make up this article."*

In the photo of Fonda that was driving them wild, she dominates the left side of the frame. She is seen from the torso up, her face an expression of concern verging on distress. On the right of the frame is the person she is listening to, seen from behind, face not visible. Another figure, a Vietnamese man, occupies the lower center portion of the image. He's in the background, therefore smaller in relation to Fonda, and slightly out of focus. He, too, looks vaguely concerned. His expression, and hers, are enough for Godard and Gorin to run with. They remain unseen, heard in voice-over, speaking in English. They eviscerate Fonda, reviling her desire for "peace." The concept, they spit, is meaningless. Nixon also says he wants "peace," and what is that worth?

* In 1968, Godard, working with documentarians D. A. Pennebaker and Richard Leacock, filmed Tom Hayden in Berkeley—as well as, at other times and in other places, such figures as Amiri Baraka and Jefferson Airplane—for a project called *One American Movie*, which never materialized.

The *L'Express* photo dissected in *Letter to Jane*.
Courtesy Everett Collection

Meanwhile, the expression on the Vietnamese man's face, they argue, is inescapably the expression of revolution, even if out of focus, born of day-to-day suffering.

Isolate the image of the "actress-militant"—though the film is addressed to Jane, Godard and Gorin disingenuously use the third person in their analysis, they say, to avoid seeming to attack Jane as they instead dissect this "function of Jane"—and the expression could indicate a pietà, "a hippie needing a fix," or other possibilities. Finally getting wound up, Godard and Gorin begin to sound like the Ricky Gervaises of the world who *just doesn't want to hear it* from actors:

> One must realize that stars are not allowed to think. They are only social functions. They are thought and they make you think. One just has to look at the acting of big thinkers like Marlon

> Brando [*a still of Brando appears*] or any other motherfuckers to understand why capital needs this sort of art to reinforce the strength of idealistic philosophy and its fight against the materialist philosophy of Marx, Engels, Lenin, and Mao, who represent their peoples.

The suddenly rapid finish is anticlimactic, stating that the proper approach for an American actress-militant in Vietnam is to "keep [your] mouth shut" and listen to what the Vietnamese mean when they talk about peace; "The rest is just masquerade."

Is it, though?

The ungallant, antibourgeois, indelibly personal teardown not only echoes Godard's "Instead of invading Vietnam with a kind of generosity that makes things unnatural" position of *Far from Vietnam*. It also articulates a similar anxiety as the one expressed by Godard in the 1972 interview, included in the 2004 DVD, fretting about whether making a film trying to be "in service of" workers risks being "to the detriment" of workers. Historically, movies have been controlled by power that oppresses labor. How dare movies risk presuming what long-silenced workers actually want to say?

Tout Va Bien dramatizes this with rigor and style. It highlights the creative process so we can see the filter. It questions class frictions and artists' and intellectuals' roles through its light, consciously stagy, flamboyant, composed images and fictions. It knowingly inserts a good deal of French reality circa 1968–72. *Tout Va Bien* is talky, yet it's also visually alive, spiky in its humor, and disciplined in its depictions. It is constructively provocative, not baldly, prescriptively didactic—the lone weapon in the *Letter to Jane* arsenal. The art of *Tout Va Bien* engages and dislodges.

In the end, though, the contrast to be drawn is not between *Tout Va Bien* and *Letter to Jane*. It's between *Letter to Jane* and Fonda's own activism, certainly in Vietnam but also at home.

What's remembered about Fonda in Vietnam are the photos of her within a North Vietnamese antiaircraft position, military helmet on—the capper, as it were, exposing her to the sticky charges of sedition. But that was not, as of 1972 and *Letter to Jane*, the dominant image it would later become. Eventually it was the unerasable mistake of her life: "Hanoi Jane," a stupid fucking photo. Her mission was to stop the threatened US bombing campaign targeting Vietnamese dikes, flooding rice paddies, creating widespread starvation. The stupid photo scrubbed that mission. It made Fonda appear to be something she was not: anti-soldier.

The distortions that followed have been vast, and they endure as simplistic fodder for cultural chat. In the 2018 documentary *Jane Fonda in Five Acts*, longtime TV host Dick Cavett is seen in the early '70s asking if, during World War II, Fonda would have gone to Berlin to protest American attacks—a blatantly absurd comparison. In the 1998 history *Traveling to Vietnam: American Peace Activists and the War*, Mary Hershberger notes that America rapidly lost its moral authority with the deeply irrational, astonishingly pulverizing assault on Vietnam: "No other country had ever exploded so many bombs on another—there was no military equivalence between the two countries."

Hershberger also explains in her introduction why Fonda only warrants two pages of her 231-page study, despite the fact that everyone presumed Fonda would be her primary subject. In fact, more than two hundred Americans traveled to Vietnam as part of a years-long antiwar effort.

"I was amazed, and still am, at the hatred and controversy her trip generated," Tom Hayden wrote in his 1988 memoir *Reunion*. In a 2004 article for the *Nation* as the Iraq War deepened and presidential candidate John Kerry faced a smear campaign over his Vietnam-era antiwar efforts, Hayden noted that Kerry historian Douglas Brinkley labeled Fonda's Hanoi visit "unconscionable." "Why should American atrocities be merely unsettling," Hayden asked, "but a trip to Hanoi unconscionable?" Fonda spent much of the rest of 1972 on a ninety-day speaking tour with Hayden and their newly organized Indochina Peace Campaign, doing what they could to keep Vietnam on voters' minds as the November presidential election approached.

In other words, the activist put her body on the line while her French confreres ran their mouths in a drive-by documentary, aggressively perpetuating the myth that "stars are not allowed to think." If she failed their purity test, she should not have cared.

Introduction to the Enemy (1974)

Fonda had already busied herself collapsing the gap between herself and the world, planting herself amid soldiers against the war with the Winter Soldier Investigation and with her *FTA Show* performances at home and abroad, and placing herself in Vietnam in 1972 and then again in 1974, making the documentary *Introduction to the Enemy* with Hayden.

Their cinematographer for *Introduction to the Enemy* was Haskell Wexler, the Hollywood radical every bit as committed as Fonda. Wexler had followed his ambitious *Medium Cool* with the twenty-two-minute 1971 documentary *Interview with My Lai Veterans*, and he would follow *Introduction to the Enemy* with cinematography for the Academy Award juggernaut *One Flew over the Cuckoo's Nest* (1975)—a job from which, though, as had happened on Francis Ford Coppola's *The Conversation* (1974), Wexler was fired (by producer Michael Douglas), but not before he shot a lot of it. (Wexler, who later admitted to meddling too much in director Milos Forman's production, shared the *Cuckoo's Nest* Oscar nomination with his replacement, Bill Butler.)

Moving, like Fonda, between mainstream Hollywood and hardcore activist pursuits during this period, Wexler also worked on yet another close-to-the-bone counterculture documentary, 1976's *Underground*, about militant activists Bernardine Dohrn and Bill Ayers, leaders of the Weather Underground, and their flight from the FBI. In Mark Wexler's 2004 documentary about his dad, *Tell Them Who You Are*, a paranoid Haskell Wexler theorizes that the FBI compelled the *Cuckoo's Nest* producers to fire him because of his association with fugitives Dohrn and Ayers.

"How long has it been since you've seen *Introduction to the Enemy*?" Fonda asks the elder Wexler in *Tell Them Who You Are*. A long time, Wexler answers, asking if she's seen it recently. Fonda, her chin lifted, says with what looks like pride: "Oh, I—*yeah*."

Introduction to the Enemy was the maiden production of IPC Films, an offshoot of the Indochina Peace Campaign formed by Hayden and Fonda, melding their activism (they also married in 1973, the year their son Troy Garity was born), beginning to branch out as the war ground down. According to contemporary reports, the movie's on-screen hosts were Fonda and Hayden, with little Troy in tow and Wexler wielding the camera, traveling from north to south across Vietnam, interviewing a range of citizens. The sixty-minute film was little seen and is now impossible to find; I've not laid eyes on it myself. It is such a rarity that the authoritative movie website IMDb does not even have a synopsis for it.

In the *Village Voice*, Molly Haskell described the movie's "ambitions" as "modest": "To introduce us to some people that we really should know better than we do—the people we have been fighting for over ten years."

"We feel like it's becoming possible now to start dealing with the Vietnamese as people," Fonda told Pacifica Radio as the film was screened briefly in New York, at noon and midnight for two days in a tiny cinema that Haskell described as "no bigger than a postage stamp." Added Fonda, "People seem to be surprised by the gentleness of the film; I guess they expect some firebrand kind of picture. But we really wanted to allow the Vietnamese to speak for themselves. . . . It's not a fast-moving film, because that's the rhythm of life there."

The New York screenings were in November 1974. Nixon had resigned three months earlier. The more expansive Vietnam documentary *Hearts and Minds* had debuted at the Cannes Film Festival in May; the following April, three weeks before the fall of Saigon, *Hearts and Minds* would win the 1975 Oscar for Best Documentary.

At a mere hour and fifty minutes, *Hearts and Minds* remains a comprehensive portrait of blundering, atrocity, and carnage. Rapidly it introduces the sight of US soldiers who have lost legs or arms, of soldiers frolicking in Saigon whorehouses, of soldiers lighting villagers' grass-roofed huts with Zippos as calmly as lighting candles; other times, flamethrowers are used for the job.

Repenting of the whole war debacle on camera in the film: Robert F. Kennedy, in a public statement, and LBJ secretary of defense Clark Clifford, succeeding Robert McNamara, in what looks like his cozy DC-area den. Standing firm: General William Westmoreland, interviewed outdoors and comparing Vietnam to a child.

When Pentagon Papers whistleblower Daniel Ellsberg is interviewed, he speaks to the phenomenon of five administrations lying about the war: "It's a tribute to the American public that their leaders perceived that they had to be lied to. It's no tribute to us that it was so easy to fool the public." A former GI bomber, after breaking down at the thought of napalm attacks on his own kids, answers the question "Do you think we've learned anything from all this?" by saying, "I think we're trying *not* to. . . . I think Americans have worked extremely hard not to see the criminality that their officials and their policy makers have exhibited."

Introduction to the Enemy, Fonda's baldest cinematic attempt to help Americans see what they might prefer not to, would vanish almost without a trace. But in these activist years Fonda had more than once controlled the means of film production, and in her own way began wrangling with the problems that animated *Tout Va Bien*. In the Paul McIsaac interview for Pacifica Radio as her documentary flickered and faded in New York, Fonda spoke of a Vietnamese actress she met in 1972 and again in 1974, a woman who modeled an art-activism nexus so basic Fonda simply called it *living*:

> I had made all kinds of changes in my life. I mean, I was living more simply, I had moved away from Beverly Hills—I really thought I had gone far. [*Fonda laughs at that.*] And here I am in North Vietnam—you're right, she was my counterpart. She is a movie star, she's very famous. To walk in the streets with her means to have people call her name—not whistle, by the way, at her, or objectify her, but respect her, because it is apparent that all of her work goes to try to portray the reality of the lives of the people that she represents. There was this woman who . . . [*Fonda pauses, takes a breath*] . . . defines success by how well she could inspire people, and how accurately she could portray their joys as well as their sorrows. And I saw—she didn't have to tell me, it was very apparent, by the way she lived, and when she wasn't working she was in the fields helping to repair the dikes with her hands—that she couldn't possibly do what she did unless her life was exactly the life of everyone else, to the degree to which someone who is famous can have a life just like everyone else. She lives very simply. There's no distinction between her—she has no particular privileges except those that she's deserved, like she's also in the Central Committee of the Women's Union in North Vietnam. And it really made me—it

just stopped me short. I came home and I realized that I hadn't even begun. I was not living the way most Americans live. Again, I never can completely because I'm Jane Fonda. But I live now, as much as I possibly can, like people I would like to make movies about live. [*Pause.*] That word that you used, *alienation*: having lived thirty-one years alienated, I can only say that particularly for an artist, but I think for anybody, you can't know what it means to be alive until you try to resolve those kind of contradictions and do away with alienation, you know? . . .

I was just on a television show and someone said, "Jane, what price have you had to pay" [*Fonda laughs briefly at this*] "for your political activity?" And I could say in all honesty, "The price I've paid is a loss of apathy, a loss of cynicism, and a loss of irrelevance." And I feel great about that.

8

FUN WITH *JANE* AND *JULIA*

Fun with Dick and Jane • A Doll's House • Julia

We're not interested in being protestors for the rest of our lives.

—Jane Fonda

February 1977 saw the first of ten substantial Hollywood features starring Jane Fonda, several of which she produced, all released over roughly five years. The next-to-worst would come first, though it was the flagbearer as Fonda charged back into the moviemaking fray with a purpose.

Fun with Dick and Jane (1977)

Meet Dick Harper.

Dick is an aeronautics engineer.

But the country is suffering through a recession. Dick's company is downsizing.

Uh-oh: Dick just got fired.

For the rest of the slight ninety-minute comedy *Fun with Dick and Jane*, Dick and his wife, Jane—characters borrowed from the stick figures of children's reading primers—navigate the flimsy American social safety net of welfare, food stamps, and job hunting before klutzily turning into Bonnie and Clyde. They even become folk heroes when they hold up the phone company, earning cheers from grumpy customers in line to pay bills.*

The movie's triumphant finish comes when Dick and Jane, now adept at theft, pull a heist on Dick's former boss, raiding the office where he keeps cash for bribing lawmakers. They crack the safe. Quietly, they blackmail the boss upstairs, away from the crowd during a swanky international gala. Then they swan out through the big shindig's front door. It's a clean getaway.

For Fonda, *Dick and Jane* was a chance to change the channel. "My 'she's back' film, proving to the studio heads that I was still a bankable star," she wrote.

Back, yes. But as what?

Jane Harper is a solid step up from Iris in *Steelyard Blues*: a headliner and narrative equal partner to her male costar, George Segal, and a housewife, not a prostitute, though that possibility comes up as Dick and Jane scramble for income options. Fonda's first close-up comes as Jane sits at the kitchen table, parrying with Dick, peering at Segal over clerk-like reading glasses. She has never worked, but, in a medium shot, she perkily lists her assets:

"I'm a college graduate. Reasonably intelligent. Not altogether unattractive."

"Yes. But," Segal needles, "will you be happy being a hooker?"

The camera cuts close. Fonda pauses, letting the insult sink in before jabbing back. "Interesting that the only two jobs you consider me qualified for are secretary and hooker," she says drily.

Segal, merrily: "You're not qualified to be a secretary."

Fonda, again in close-up, gives him the lemon face that will recur between them as a signifier of tetchy romance, squinching her eyes and pursing her lips.

* Regarding 1970s satires of corporate arrogance, see Ernestine, a popular pinched-faced telephone operator with a snorty laugh, played by Lily Tomlin and omnipresent on TV. Ernestine made an appearance when Tomlin hosted *Saturday Night Live* in 1976: "This phone system consists of a multibillion-dollar matrix of space age technology that is so sophisticated even *we* can't handle it. But that's your problem, isn't it? So, the next time you complain about your phone service, why don't you try using two Dixie cups with a string? We don't care. We don't have to. We're the Phone Company."

When Fonda briefly plays Jane as a rabble-rousing protestor, it's odd. She's dressed in a suburban version of working-class garb, with a blue denim jumpsuit, leather knee boots, and a poufy brown proletarian cap—half soccer mom, half Russian peasant. When Dick gets fired, the Harpers are in the midst not of a revolution but of a home renovation, and the landscapers repossess shrubs, trees, and sod as neighbors watch. Trying to save face, Jane acts like that's what she wants.

"Please remove this . . . tracheotomy, or whatever it's called," Fonda says with a flourish, like an indignant customer. The small crowd on the comfy California sidewalk cheers like they're at a rally. As a knowing joke deflating political Fonda, it's flat.

The picture is almost as sloppy as *Steelyard Blues*. Under the direction of Ted Kotcheff, of *The Apprenticeship of Duddy Kravitz* (1974), and later of *First Blood* (1982, Rambo's first rampage) and *Weekend at Bernie's* (1989), the filmmaking is just plain dull, rarely aspiring to be better than 1970s-grade TV. The screenplay is by David Giler, Jerry Belson, and Mordecai Richler, from a story by Gerald Gaiser, and it plays like committee work.

At least Fonda has a rock-solid comic sparring partner in Segal, whose career started at the same time as hers. Segal had industriously built a flexible brand, alternating adventures (*The Hot Rock*, *Russian Roulette*) and farces (*Where's Poppa?*, *The Black Bird*) with a reliable tide of romantic comedies. Between 1970 and 1975, the tireless Segal made a dozen movies, costarring with Eva Marie Saint (*Loving*), Barbra Streisand (*The Owl and the Pussycat*), Glenda Jackson (*A Touch of Class*), Susan Anspach (*Blume in Love*), and Goldie Hawn (*The Duchess and the Dirtwater Fox*). Segal and Fonda? Battle-of-the-sexes banter? Nothing easier.

Kotcheff's eye improves dramatically during the nighttime scenes, hitting a screwball stride as Fonda and Segal launch their crime spree. Fonda dons a rust-colored knit cap with matching scarf and lipstick that even blends with the color of the Harpers' station wagon. In the most glamorous shot of the picture, and with a one-liner ripe enough to tease in a movie trailer, Fonda, in close-up, fills the right side of the night-black frame as Segal tries to hotwire a car. Her arms folded, she says casually, "Oh, I think you can handle this one, Dick. The keys are in it."

Fun with Dick (George Segal) and Jane (Fonda).
© Columbia Pictures / Courtesy Everett Collection

There's nothing in the shot but Fonda. It's hardly a great line, yet suddenly it looks and sounds like upscale Hollywood comedy. Fonda and Segal smirk at each other. The adventure revs up. Segal blunders his way through the learning curve of stickups, with Fonda grinning at him from the passenger seat of their sporty stolen getaway car, even stifling a giggle as they evolve into droll suburban gangsters.

Jane Harper is the married adult emerging after Fonda's parade of ingenues and prostitutes. She's not like the scheming coed in *Tall Story*, nervous newlywed in *Period of Adjustment*, twenty-two-year-old virgin in *Sunday in New York*, anxious mistress in *Any Wednesday*, or, ending the run of Hollywood romantic comedies, newlywed Corie Bratter in Neil Simon's *Barefoot in the Park* (more about this last role in chapter 11). Nor is she like racy, spacey Barbarella, or operatically depressed Gloria, or flinty Bree, or smart-but-lost Iris. Fonda now is a very plain Jane, paying bills and raising kids.

There she is: mid-America.

If embarrassed Jane Harper's muffled *Get my lawn off!* protest is Fonda's activist moment, it feels like the world turned upside down—Hanoi Jane contained, safely embedded in the California 'burbs. But it's exactly what Fonda declared about the feet-on-the-ground Vietnamese actor she so admired. Knockabout as it is, the middle-class Dick and Jane, crusading in a station wagon, at last squarely placed Fonda where most Americans lived.

Not incidentally, the movie's politics aligned with the new real-world concerns of Fonda and Tom Hayden. Like the country, Fonda and Hayden were aging out of 1960s radicalism and maturing into the mainstream of America's democratic machinery. Hayden ran for one of California's US Senate seats in 1976; he lost, and then founded the Campaign for Economic Democracy, which would organize on behalf of progressive candidates and lobby for such issues as rent control.

Fonda, as always, raised money and kept up her income to support the causes. By 1982—in a disparity that privileged her politics over her art, which by then she was allowing to wither—Fonda's blockbuster workout business would be funding the CED at the rate of $30,000 a month.

The anticorporate *Fun with Dick and Jane* felt as innocuous as a sitcom, but it was a little too easily waved away by critics. Vincent Canby, in the *New York Times*, called it "a deceptively sunny, sometimes uproariously funny comedy about the bad taste, vulgarity, and awful aimlessness of a certain kind of middle-class American affluence." Pauline Kael wrote, "Jane Fonda looks radiant in it, but what does it say about an actress' judgement to look so relaxed and happy in this picture—a leftover from the Nixon era, another movie telling us we're all crooked and looking for a bigger piece of the pie?" Like Canby, Kael objected to the characters' "credit-card affluence": "Since this sour message represents the point at which the cynical right meets the idiot left, the film—for all its political stabs—means precisely nothing. It starts by saying America makes everybody corrupt, and then, having rationalized crookedness, makes the biggest crooks the heroes."

This reading is amiss. First: for Fonda, the Nixon era wasn't entirely over. The lawsuit she filed against the administration in 1973, claiming slander, harassment, and deprivation of constitutional rights after she learned of the file the FBI was keeping on her, wouldn't be settled for another two years; in 1979, the government admitted wrongdoing, and she then let go of her million-dollar claim.

Second, and more substantially, the movie does *not* start by saying "America makes everybody corrupt." It starts with a corrupt corporate culture making its own rules, as the drunken, portly, two-faced aeronautics executive played by Ed McMahon cavalierly lays off a bunch of unprotected workers. McMahon is soused in the morning, intoxicated with power, when he summons Segal.

"You're fired," he slurs.

What follows is a standard revenge fantasy, offering the frustrated working and middle classes a dream of reprisals against the corporate one percent.

Precisely the same wishes were stoked, of course, in the 2016 and 2020 campaigns by the crusading share-the-wealth candidacies of Bernie Sanders and Elizabeth Warren. Their opponent? The "You're fired" executive of *The Apprentice*, Donald Trump.

Fonda's *Dick and Jane* began closing the gap between what she wanted politically and what she played on-screen. The 2005 *Fun with Dick and Jane* remake with Jim Carrey and Téa Leoni shows how much more potent an activist vehicle this cute but distracted little story might have been.

The remake's inspiration—and its punch line—is Enron, the Houston-based energy/anything-goes corporate colossus that collapsed in 2000 under the weight of its labyrinthine business model and underhanded accounting practices. Offered "special thanks" atop the end credits are the fallen real-world figureheads of Enron, along with other scandal-smeared executives from the telecommunications giant Worldcom, the tainted accounting firm Arthur Andersen, Tyco International, Adelphia Communications Corp., HealthSouth, and the conglomerate Cendant. (The filmmakers left inside trader Martha Stewart alone, though Samuel Waksal of ImClone, the biopharmaceutical company Stewart was involved with, gets a shout-out.) The sweeping list of corporate collapses and disgraces demonstrated that the early 2000s suffered an epidemic of corruption.

The remake was as polished as a supermodel's fingernails, led by $20 million–per–picture actor Jim Carrey and updated to fit the go-go corporate culture. The movie gleams with office buildings of glinting glass, shiny metal, and buffed stone. Executives in designer suits drive BMWs and Mercedes-Benzes.

"We must never become a winner-take-all society," President George W. Bush is seen stating on TV, but the moviemakers believe that it obviously already is.*

The bad guy is Alec Baldwin, head of a corporate giant called Globodyne. Carrey's Dick Harper is a corporate climber glad to get promoted to Globodyne's communications VP. (In the original, of course, Dick's aeronautics job was more meaningful; "communications" neatly pokes at the mirage that Enron became.) In the remake's best scene, Dick gets shoved onto a cable news show patterned after the then-popular *Lou Dobbs Moneyline*.† The host grills Carrey's Dick Harper about Globodyne's bad practices. Carrey hasn't been briefed.

He vamps.

The market panics.

On a split screen, consumer advocate Ralph Nader, playing himself, chastises Harper and Globodyne. Hilariously, the TV shows the stock plummeting in real time, worsening the disaster with a graphic bursting into flames.

As a Globodyne executive, Richard Jenkins succinctly explains the catastrophe, slowly, drunkenly, with hand gestures. It's pure Enron—the "raptors" (shell companies of a sort) devised by real-life chief financial officer Andy Fastow: "We took our shifting losses and we put them into businesses that we actually owned," the Jenkins character says. "And in the balance sheet it showed profit. But actually, there was debt."

* "The most extreme winner-take-all economy in the history of the world," Democratic presidential candidate Andrew Yang said of America during a February 5, 2020, CNN town hall.

† In 2005 *Moneyline* inspired CNBC's *Mad Money,* hosted by Jim Cramer. After the nerve-racking 2008 global financial collapse, *The Daily Show* host Jon Stewart famously torqued what sounded like a sincere apology out of Cramer for his, what shall we call it? Irrational exuberance. Yet in 2024 and 2025, Cramer and CNBC hawked $399.99 subscriptions to his "Investing Club."

Jenkins laughs.

Unlike Fonda's Jane Harper, Téa Leoni's Jane has a job. But she quits once her husband gets his ritzy position, leaving them in the same tight spot as the 1977 Harpers when Globodyne goes belly-up. (Scrambling, this Jane becomes a fitness instructor, another potential Fonda in-joke that sadly gets no punch line.) As in the original, the story then blitzes through the fish-out-of-water business of White suburbanites struggling in an economically challenged America.

"We were good people, honest people," Dick says. "And we got screwed."

The movie's production notes make clear that this was Jim Carrey's project. Carrey brought the idea to producer Brian Grazer, who says it sounded funny and "torn from the headlines."* Director Dean Parisot, a TV stalwart whose few feature films include the affectionate *Star Trek* sendup *Galaxy Quest*, said, "I knew it would be terrific fun to watch Dick and Jane lose their minds and go after the corporate criminal who bankrupted them."

But Carrey, at the time the poster child for extraordinarily paid Hollywood stars, was less than ideal as the face for a populist comedy. As for Leoni, she was likable enough to star on TV for years and grave enough

* The headlines do indeed tell a story of the times:

- "U.S. Accuses Cendant of Fraud," by Floyd Norris, *New York Times*, March 1, 2001.
- "Accounting Firm [Arthur Andersen] to Pay a Big Fine," by Floyd Norris, *New York Times*, June 20, 2001.
- "Enron's Collapse: The Overview; Enron Corp. Files Largest U.S. Claim for Bankruptcy," by Richard A. Oppel Jr. and Andrew Ross Sorkin, *New York Times*, December 3, 2001.
- "Worldcom's Collapse: The Overview; Worldcom Files for Bankruptcy—Largest U.S. Case," by Simon Romero and Riva D. Atlas, *New York Times*, July 22, 2002.
- "SEC Charges Adelphia and Rigas Family with Massive Financial Fraud," Securities and Exchange Commission news release, July 24, 2002.
- "2 Top Tyco Executives Charged with $600 Million Fraud Scheme," by Andrew Ross Sorkin, *New York Times*, September 13, 2002.
- "S.E.C. Accuses HealthSouth and Chief of Accounting Fraud," by Kenneth N. Gilpin, *New York Times*, March 19, 2003.
- "Prosecuting Martha Stewart: The Overview; Martha Stewart Indicted by U.S. on Obstruction," by Constance L. Hayes, *New York Times*, June 5, 2003.

to do it playing a US secretary of state in *Madam Secretary*. In *Dick and Jane*, she got good notices simply for holding her own with the notoriously over-the-top Carrey, whose dramatic instincts had already been proven in *The Truman Show*, *Man on the Moon*, and *Eternal Sunshine of the Spotless Mind*, and whose Dick Harper turn is comparatively calm.

But the comedy, coming out the same year as Alex Gibney's documentary *Enron: The Smartest Guys in the Room*, lacked activist bona fides. It looked like a high-end corporate Hollywood product, and neither Leoni nor Carrey brought a political persona to bear. The slapstick project could have used a "Jane Fonda."

"It's nonsense to expect social commentary from a high-concept comedy," Manohla Dargis wrote in the *New York Times*, "especially one as self-congratulatory as this one (they care, they really, really care), but this is the rare studio comedy set in something like the real world. If the film never settles into a groove, zigging and zagging from belly laughs to pathos, it's because Enron remains raw as a wound."

Dargis also noted the surplus of writers, a higher pileup than on the original picture. The *Los Angeles Times* cited nine scribes as having had hands on the remake's script.

Testifying, though, to the rich activist potential of *Fun with Dick and Jane* is a strikingly thoughtful review from an actual pinko-commie rag, the *World Socialist Web Site*. In "Not So Much Fun with Dick and Jane," Joanne Laurier put the film in a broader social context. She liked what she saw.

"Currently, there is an unprecedented leveling of society under way," Laurier wrote, "an extreme polarization in which there is a tiny super-wealthy elite and then, more or less, everyone else. Significant layers of the middle class who have been dumped like so much garbage by corporate America have overnight become proletarianized." She went on:

> Actor Alec Baldwin speaks forcefully in the production notes about the modus operandi of corporate types, such as [Baldwin's character] Jack McCallister: "There is something fascinating about a guy who is paid a guaranteed salary of a couple of million dollars—or in his mind, a couple of lousy million—who has

> an expense account that is so lavish he doesn't ever spend any of his own money. He also gets an extraordinary stock option package. And then, on top of that, he decides it's necessary to steal an extra couple of hundred million from the company. They have this artificially inflated lifestyle and it seems all perspective is lost. When I saw that Dennis Kozlowski (former CEO of Tyco International) had a $6,000 umbrella stand, I knew we were going back to Roman times. It was just so vulgar." . . .
>
> There are rough edges and moments of exaggerated comic effort that do not come off. Nonetheless, it is honestly done and possesses a good deal of heart. Taking a look at the 1977 version, with George Segal and Jane Fonda, highlights some of the current film's strengths and sensibilities. Carrey and Leoni work well together (which is no small feat considering how overwhelming Carrey tends to be), although their performances never reach the depth and subtlety Segal and particularly Fonda bring to their roles. . . .
>
> Enron's demise involved not just the loss of jobs, as bad as that was, but the wiping out of pensions and life savings for thousands. It revealed, as well as those bankruptcies that followed, that what was at issue was not one bad apple but a system rotten to the core. As opposed to the 1977 film, significantly Dick and Jack in the new version concern themselves with all those shafted by McCallister and Globodyne, although their solution is hardly radical (or convincing).

That unconvincing solution: having Dick and Jane pilfer McCallister's account to fund severances and pensions for the affected workers. Convincing or not, this, too, was partially reality-based. In January 2003, the *New York Times* reported that Senator Chuck Schumer, among others, rerouted money that had been donated to him by tainted companies to the displaced workers who needed relief, and that the US Department of Justice likewise sent money collected from a plea agreement to the fund for Enron victims.

The risks and rewards of corporate capitalism accelerated between 1977 and the world of the 2005 remake; the discontents have only grown, as has the resistance to reform or regulation. In his 2020 State of the Union address, President Trump rebuked as "socialist" the calls for wealth taxes and single-payer health care looming on his left.* Belatedly joining the Democratic primary debates, former New York City mayor billionaire Mike Bloomberg, resorting to Red Scare tactics, used the word *communism* as he attacked Bernie Sanders. ("That's a cheap shot," Sanders replied.) That unresolved battle—calculatedly tempered in Kamala Harris's 2024 campaign—explains why Fonda, during her Fire Drill Fridays, pounced on each chance to call out major corporate malefactors. Twice she marched through downtown DC to occupy big banks.

A few years after her *Dick and Jane* fun, Fonda would muster her own production forces for a different shot at telling a deeper, more sweeping, more sinister Big Money tale, one that would signal the end of her extraordinary political moviemaking run.

Meantime, the new bottom line was clear. Fonda, still with something to say, was back in the Hollywood fold.

The comeback would be clinched by the 1977 drama *Julia*, based on an incident in playwright Lillian Hellman's memoirs that would soon blow up into a major literary controversy. But Fonda's bridge from *Tout Va Bien* and Hanoi to *Dick and Jane* and *Julia* was built by Norwegian playwright Henrik Ibsen.†

* After listening to the speech from her perch behind the president, House Speaker Nancy Pelosi tore in half her printed copy.

† Fonda made one other movie in this mid-1970s period: *The Blue Bird*, a forgotten fable notable for its all-star female cast and as an unusual Cold War collaboration between American and Soviet artists, shot largely in Russia, directed by George Cukor. Fonda is glamorous, treacherous Night, an archvillain trying to keep two questing children from unlocking cosmic secrets as they pursue the titular blue bird (of happiness) in playwright Maurice Maeterlinck's tale. Cukor's take on the kids' fantasy looks hopelessly stagy, with Cicely Tyson in a cat costume and Russian dancers as Water, Fire, and Milk. Elizabeth Taylor, though, is determinedly warm as the children's mother and as Light, the beneficent, almost absurdly glitzy figure in a sparkling white gown, diamonds dangling from her tiara and earrings. Luxury, a decadent figure in a sumptuous red dress, is played by Ava Gardner. Great cast and a little Cold War détente, but this difficult-to-find 1976 curio, which I fetched off eBay on DVD, is not worth seeking out.

A Doll's House (1973)

The adaptation of Ibsen's *A Doll's House* was not released in cinemas but was broadcast one December night on ABC; the entirety of what Fonda says about it in her memoir is "I'd done *A Doll's House* in Norway." But *A Doll's House* in 1973 starring Jane Fonda should have been a bigger deal.

The Equal Rights Amendment was blitzing ahead, with thirty states ratifying the constitutional ban on sex discrimination within a year of its March 1972 adoption by Congress.* The 1879 masterpiece about a blackmailed woman, with its famous women's rights manifesto as its heroine calmly shocked European audiences by walking out on her husband, gave majestic voice to a surging modern movement.

So perfect was Ibsen's play for the time that 1973 saw not one but two *Doll's House* films. The other featured Fonda's former costar in George Cukor's *The Chapman Report*, Claire Bloom. Like Fonda, Bloom had firsthand experience with marriage and its discontents. Bloom and novelist Philip Roth, her third husband, were married from 1990 to 1995, but the relationship dated back to the 1970s. The title of Bloom's 1996 memoir about living with Roth: *Leaving a Doll's House.*

The Bloom version is deeply English, with a plummy detachment of men surrounding Bloom's Nora Helmer—Anthony Hopkins as husband Torvald, Denholm Elliott as the blackmailer Krogstad, and Ralph Richardson, expert with muffled ardor as Nora's dying admirer Dr. Rank. Though Patrick Garland's direction is bookish and bland, the terror of Nora's plight snaps into focus once Hopkins, rippling with quiet menace, growls as she uses the word "petty." Bloom's sudden fright is pitiable. Hopkins's wrath is epic, and his elocution is devastating—arguably, though, pitched more for stage than camera.

Bloom, on the other hand, delivered a more lived-in performance. She had played Nora onstage in London, and in New York she was

* In 2020, Virginia became the thirty-eighth state to ratify the amendment—Nevada had passed it in 2017 and Illinois in 2018—meaning it had now had the approval of three-quarters of the states required to add it to the US Constitution. Supporters celebrated in Richmond. But the deadline for ratification was 1982, and over the years Nebraska, Tennessee, Idaho, South Dakota, and Kentucky had rescinded passage of the bill, though the legality of the rescissions was in doubt.

Nora while also headlining in rotating repertory as the title character in Ibsen's *Hedda Gabler*. (Once upon a time actors exercised remarkable muscles . . .)

"They're both rebels, frustrated by circumstance," Bloom told the *New York Times* as the 1971 rep of Nora and Hedda was announced. She added, "And all this was long before the women's liberation movement."

Was it? (See, for instance, the Seneca Falls Women's Rights Convention of 1848 . . .)

Bloom on-screen is a nimble, perceptive Nora. She does not overstate the compliant role-playing, and she deserved more than director Garland provided for the finish, when Ibsen finally strips away all the trappings of the era's formulaic "well-made" plays; it was highly radical at the time for Ibsen to sit husband and wife down at last for an honest talk about marriage and social justice before Nora famously walks out. Hopkins is thoroughly chastened. Bloom is suddenly sturdy. But Garland, for twelve minutes, has no directorial ideas. All he does is cut back and forth. It's Ibsen under glass.

Joseph Losey's *Doll House* is less reverent, and anything but housebound. Losey was a Hollywood blacklist victim whose sexually tense, prickly 1960s projects with English playwright and master of menace Harold Pinter were nicely perverse warmups for Ibsen. While *A Doll's House*'s action unfolds entirely in the Helmer home, Losey's film frolics in the actual wintry Norwegian village of Røros. Actors bundle under furs and ride horse-drawn sleighs through snow-covered streets. The indoor scenes look like real houses, with dark wood and gas lamps.

The picture opens on a skating pond eight years before the play's action starts—a substantial change from Ibsen's concentrated script, which plays out in just three tense days around Christmas. In Ibsen's original, characters *talk* about their long-ago past. At the start of this picture, we *see* their history. Unfortunately, screenwriter David Mercer's new scenes are inelegant. When we first meet Jane Fonda's Nora, she's younger than Ibsen ever depicted her, giddy with the prospect of marrying Torvald Helmer. Thus must Fonda gush with girlish joy.

She wears a knit cap and a cozy maroon dress. She busies herself with hot cocoa and pastries in a café where she's just skated with her old friend Kristine. The soundtrack's music, by cinema's prolific Michel

Legrand, of the ultra-sweet musical *The Umbrellas of Cherbourg* and so much more, toots holiday tunes. Fonda's keyed-up Nora rambles: "Kristine, we must write—we must write to each other. Every week. I love Torvald so much! He was—he was brilliant, the way he helped Pa-*pa* with his business difficulties. It's wonderful, Kristine, to love *and* admire a man. You shall admire him too."

Kristine, played with counterpoise by Delphine Seyrig, an icon of international cinema,* agrees that indeed she will.

Nora carries on: "Oh, look at the time! Oh, Kristine, I must rush. I must fly. Pa-*pa* will be waiting. Oh, but I wanted to spend this afternoon with you, Kristine. Dear Kristine!" Fonda's delight, glowing at Seyrig, eases this speech's bleating. But the movie's non-Ibsen dialogue is a pothole. Luckily, there isn't much of it after the opening moments.

Losey's long stage and screen experience gives the movie a comfortable visual style. He respects the play but is not handcuffed by it; he works confidently in the confined spaces, moving actors and the camera easily, rarely resorting to close-ups, preferring to observe multiple bodies in shared space. After the babbling opening he does a much better job framing Fonda—not, though, that he gives her the star treatment.

The movie would have been better if he had. Fonda delivers a subtly fascinating physical performance as Losey follows an assured Nora moving through the rooms of the Helmers' middle-class home, secure at last now that Torvald has been promoted to run the local bank. What you feel is Nora's pride at *owning* the place, knowing the role she played in saving it.

If the Bloom-Hopkins dynamic is regrettably stagy, Fonda's rapport with David Warner's Torvald is appealingly earthy. In a surprising bit of

* Seyrig broke into movies with Alain Resnais's influential 1961 New Wave tone poem *Last Year at Marienbad*, starred in Losey's 1967 film *Accident* (a Pinter project), and the same year played the title role in a French TV movie of Ibsen's *Hedda Gabler*. In 1975 she would anchor writer-director Chantal Ackerman's three-hour-and-twenty-two-minute drama *Jeanne Dielman, 23, quai de Commerce, 1080 Bruxelles*; Seyrig's brilliant embodiment of the routine-bound title character topped *Sight and Sound*'s once-a-decade poll of all-time best films in 2022. In 1975–76 Seyrig would film *Be Pretty and Shut Up* (*Sois belle et tais-toi!*), her documentary about the movie industry's poor attitude toward women in which Fonda would be among the actresses testifying.

business, Torvald guesses that he has tasted on her lips the macaroons that, as a pointless house rule, he has forbidden.

Fonda freezes for a second, then breezily role-plays. She puts on his glasses and enacts the prig: "Macaroons? What are macaroons?" She lifts her chin and puts on a stuffy accent: "Oh, you mean those little rowing boats for pixies?"

It's a demeaning thing for Nora to have to do, yet it's more lighthearted than many actors choose to be in that moment. Arguably, it's also more realistic, as a woman like Nora navigates the restrictions a man like Torvald imposes. Mocking him levels the field a bit and allows her to dance away from danger.

Warner's performance, too, keeps the marital dynamic from being so overbearing that you never buy the union. They talk together quietly and casually, and the affection seems genuine at the end of this scene: Warner seated, Fonda standing behind him, her hands on his shoulders as he reaches his hand up to hold hers. When, alone a moment later, Fonda's Nora twirls with optimism, the exuberance feels more earned than self-deceiving. Actresses playing Nora don't always find that note. (*A Doll's House* has lost none of its currency; playwright Lucas Hnath's puckishly imagined sequel of a Nora who comes back fifteen years later, *A Doll's House, Part 2*, earned Laurie Metcalf a 2017 Tony Award, and Jessica Chastain headlined an intensely lean production of Ibsen's original play on Broadway in 2023.)

Ibsen's plot, based on the sad but true experience of a woman named Laura Kieler, hinges on the fact that Nora forged her dying father's signature on a bank note. Why? Torvald was sick. They needed money to travel south for his health. They didn't have it. And banks would not lend to wives without husbands' signatures. Nora's ruse with Torvald (who *must not know!*) is that the money was given to her by her father. Losey shoots the scenes of Krogstad (Edward Fox) blackmailing Nora outdoors, on a snowy bridge over a rushing stream, and the cold seems to race straight up Fonda's back. The vise comes not only from Krogstad but from the discriminatory society.

"My father was dying," Nora says. Fonda, her voice urgent, sheds a single tear. "My husband's life was in danger. Surely the law takes account of such things."

> KROGSTAD: The law does not take account of motives in such matters.
> NORA: Then the law is wrong!
> KROGSTAD: The law will have its way. And if I show that paper to the police, you will be judged accordingly.

The movie's flaws are twofold. First, Fonda occasionally and jarringly tries to fit in with her European costars by resorting to British pronunciations—"chance" as "chonce" (rhymes with "ponce"). "She'd do delightful tricks if you'd gront her a wish," Fonda begs of Warner. "She'd donce in the moonlight, Torvald."

The slips are rare but annoying, and likely the reason certain critics carped that Fonda seemed out of place in the nineteenth century. But they must not have noticed how effortlessly, thus heartbreakingly, she says things like "Neither have I the courage" as her Nora and Fox's Krogstad confess that both, under pressure, thought of suicide.

More substantially, Losey demonstrated no vivid idea for how to handle the make-or-break final scene. Losey creates a sure sense of pace and a competent sense of narrative, but no sense of priority.

What is *A Doll's House* about, and why would it matter in 1973, or ever?

Kristine is the voice of reason in the story: the world-weary, level-headed, fact-facing model Nora must follow. Seyrig's performance ought to have been given more emphasis. Instead, in her pivotal scene about whether or not to reveal Nora's secret to Torvald, the camera largely stays *behind* her, instead giving us Fox's reaction as Krogstad.

Losey also declines to really zero in on Fonda during the climactic reckoning, which peters out with the wan line "Torvald, I don't believe in miracles anymore. We would have to change so much." That's merely the predicate of Nora's legendary exit; most translations finish, "So that our life together might truly be a marriage. Goodbye."

The picture ought to be about the two women abandoning illusions and taking charge of their lives. Their decisions guide the action. This focus is where Seyrig and Fonda disagreed with Losey.

"I had, as has become unfairly and unduly notorious, certain difficulties with Jane and Seyrig about the adaptation," the director said a few years later. But to complain, as Losey did, that somehow Fonda was performing the final scene "in an agit-prop way" seems to fly in the face of a) the inescapable sense of what *A Doll's House* is, notwithstanding even Ibsen's unfortunate rhetorical waltz contending that the drama is *humanist*, not actually *feminist*, and b) why Losey wanted Fonda in the first place.

"She's an absolutely electric person, and I like her complete honesty," Losey said. "What made me feel that she was right for Nora was her absolute conviction about the issues of women's rights, plus her background."

Nora walking out in 1879 was dubbed by George Bernard Shaw "the door slam heard around the world," striking an unexpected blow in the accelerating argument for allowing divorce while planting a game-changing flag for realism in the theater. Ibsen's plays of public reckonings, which also included *The Pillars of the Community*, *Ghosts*, and *An Enemy of the People* (a ruthless and evergreen dramatization of politics, science, journalism, and mob rule) startled audiences and critics and altered the tenor of Western drama.

As has often been observed, the line from the artistically solemn, politically sharp, personally irascible Henrik Ibsen to the artistically solemn, politically sharp, personally irascible Lillian Hellman could not be more direct.

Julia (1977)

The primary action of the 1977 film adaptation *Julia* is set in the 1930s, with Fonda as playwright Lillian Hellman in an excerpt from Hellman's memoir *Pentimento*. The story is Hellman's profile of a rich American childhood friend named Julia who grew up to be a Nazi resister in Europe, and how, for one bright, shining moment, the brave Julia—a child of immense privilege, yet an untamable social justice lion who loses her leg and then her life in the fight—guided the reticent but determined Lillian into resisting too.

Julia is not, strictly speaking, a 1970s activist film. In Fonda's context, it's uber-activist, abstracting its "fascists" four decades after they came to power in 1930s Europe to stand for *standing up*.

Not that there's much that isn't persuasively realistic in director Fred Zinnemann's picture, which leans heavily on his roots in 1930s documentaries and—especially striking for Fonda—silent film. The exquisitely made *Julia* marked her return at last to the classy form of *Klute*, and the role of "Lilly" stamped Fonda's purposeful template for the rest of the '70s.

In playing Hellman, whose first hit was the 1934 Broadway drama *The Children's Hour*, Fonda intersected with a literary lion who, late in life, was still feverishly etching her own profile in unambiguously heroic terms. By 1977, Hellman had aggressively repositioned herself as a memoirist in what became a highly dramatic second act. Her celebrity was so augmented by the acclaim for *An Unfinished Woman* (1969), *Pentimento* (1973), and *Scoundrel Time* (1976) that she was featured in ads for Blackglama furs, with the enviable tagline "What becomes a legend most?"

Scoundrel Time documents Joseph McCarthy's Communist witch hunts and Hellman's famous letter to the House Un-American Activities Committee prior to her 1952 appearance before them, where she declined to name names. The letter forged a durable, stinging quip in telling off the inquisitors: "I cannot and will not cut my conscience to fit this year's fashions."

Standing alone, the "cannot and will not" line is a game-ending stomp. In context, it's one flashy step in a complex tango:

> I am not willing, now or in the future, to bring bad trouble to people who, in my past association with them, were completely innocent of any talk or any action that was disloyal or subversive. I do not like subversion or disloyalty in any form and if I had ever seen any I would have considered it my duty to have reported it to the proper authorities. But to hurt innocent people whom I knew many years ago in order to save myself is, to me, inhuman and indecent and dishonorable. I cannot and will not cut my conscience to fit this year's fashions, even though I long ago came to the conclusion that I was not a political person and could have no comfortable place in any political group.

Neither her plays nor her life, of course, align with the phrase "not a political person." Among other bullet points, Hellman was pro-Soviet in the 1930s and '40s. In 1970, displeased with the surveillance and harassment the US government leveled at anti-Vietnam protestors, she spearheaded the Committee for Public Justice. Patricia Bosworth writes of a fundraiser for the campaign that Fonda attended: Hellman, nonplussed by the chatter rippling through the room as speakers soldiered through at the podium, grabbed the mic and scolded, "Shut up! Stop talking drivel and listen to something important!"

The memoirs in part reestablished just how political Hellman *was*, and the McCarthy moment was indeed a high-water mark. Victor Navasky, in his review of Alice Kessler-Harris's 2012 book *A Difficult Woman: The Challenging Life and Times of Lillian Hellman*, noted that Hellman's HUAC testimony "served the larger political purpose of resisting unjust authority and also had an educational function for the citizenry at large. It took courage and literary elegance to pull off, yes, but more important, it was inspirational to a mostly cowed generation."

No surprise, then, that *Julia* is congenitally political, even if Zinnemann told Fonda's costar Vanessa Redgrave it wasn't. Like *Scoundrel Time*, *Pentimento*'s sketch of Julia casts Hellman heroically as she labors to walk in the immaculate activist footsteps of this childhood friend. In the Hollywood treatment, Redgrave—herself born into theatrical royalty yet an untamable social justice lion—was destined to play the inspirational Julia. The adaptation's Lilly is a maturing artist whose blossoming career gets sidetracked by a shattering mission resisting the war. No more natural choice existed to play this figure than Jane Fonda.

Any account of Fonda as an actor must reckon with this sterling, sturdy work, which conveys not only Hellman's notorious combination of grandeur and dudgeon but also Fonda's own ease gliding through this international epic with Hollywood aplomb. Zinnemann's picture has often been characterized as a throwback to "classic" style, and what that meant for Fonda was carrying large chunks of the story in nonverbal close-up, especially once the plot hits its second hour and bathes in intrigue.

Lilly, coaxed by a mysterious messenger from her now-underground pal Julia, nervously agrees to ferry $50,000 from Vienna to Nazi-controlled Warsaw. The journey, by train, commands twenty minutes of screen time, with few words, no musical underscoring, and a feathery touch as Zinnemann efficiently dispenses cinematic information. The sound design bustles with track clatter and hissing steam. When a stranger hands Lilly a candy box and says, "This is your birthday present from Miss Julia," a train whistle screams faintly in the distance.

The tension is Hitchcockian as Fonda's Hellman—the newly famous playwright of *The Children's Hour* somehow gliding under the Nazi radar, flying by the seat of her pants, knowing nobody on this potentially fatal operation—labors to keep cool while anxiously reading the signals from two strangers in her cabin. Fonda orchestrates her confusion and brave cover-ups with delicate strokes, even as Lilly breaks into such a nauseous sweat that she excuses herself from the dining car and heads for a washroom—where the walls, in one of the movie's many deft design touches, are bile green.

The women in Hellman's cabin say cryptic things like "You would put on?" about a fancy hat she has been given. That is followed, more pointedly, by the declarative "You would put on." Fonda's exploring hand squeezes the hat's lining and pauses, letting us know where the money is.

Questions and answers ripple across Fonda's expressive face, an ideal canvas for Zinnemann's trademark inquiry into private conscience and public action. Viewers in 1977 noted similarities between *Julia* and previous Zinnemann works like *High Noon* (1952), *From Here to Eternity* (1953), *The Nun's Story* (1959), and *A Man for All Seasons* (1966), all rational, coolly grounded, and intimate yet attaining a grand scale. As Fonda freezes and the train chugs, you feel Lilly's heart race. This train sequence, in particular, is a remarkable profile of a woman who, to use the words Fonda repeated often during her Fire Drill Fridays, was discovering the courage, politically, to put her body on the line.

The second half of *Julia* becomes such an exercise in cloak-and-dagger that when Maximilian Schell arrives as the furtive go-between, he actually wears a fedora and a trench coat. Schell immediately establishes his oppressed, fundamentally decent character by smiling and politely murmuring the divine line "Do you think I could have an egg, a hot milk, and a roll? I could not pay for it, however," two evocative, characteristically terse sentences drawn almost exactly from Hellman's memoir sketch.

In the opulent, empty hotel dining room, Zinnemann shoots Schell in profile while we watch Fonda straight on, discreetly disapproving as he finishes his breakfast and mops his brow. It's a flicker, but it lands: Fonda's impression of Hellman as a mean-spirited elitist. At times, the flicker erupts into spectacle: a fair portion of Fonda's haughty, chin-up performance is hot temper and clenched teeth. She bellows at Dashiell Hammett (Jason Robards), impulsively throws a typewriter out the window of their Cape Cod cottage, and knocks a drunken, salacious old friend (John Glover) to a barroom floor. Lilly Hellman is badass.

Hellman wrote herself that way, so the brusqueness is a badge that Fonda doesn't need to clean up as she rudely barks on the phone at an incompetent stranger, "I want somebody better than you!"* Lilly isn't *nice*. But she's learning, professionally and personally, to be *good*. Conscience is what's in play throughout the film, whether Lilly is laboring to write something with meaning or to right the world's wrongs.

Fonda's eyes dart as she calculates. She sucks on cigarettes like a punishment for not yet having worked it out.

"Will you help us?" Schell asks on the park bench in the Tuileries.

"I, uh," Fonda begins. She looks at him and quickly glances away. "I need a few hours," she says back to him, decisively. "To think it through, I need to think it through."

Fonda's spontaneity and economy make this response complex but not belabored. "I always find questions of conscience photogenic," Zinnemann once said. "That kind of interior drama is to me very, very interesting." Film historian Jennifer Smyth quoted *Julia* editor Walter Murch describing movies as a "theater of thought."

* It's worth remembering that Hellman was hovering around the edges of this adaptation, dashing notes to Zinnemann and screenwriter Alvin Sargent. The gap between star and subject was collapsed entirely at the 1977 Academy Awards, before *Julia* was released, as Hellman, riding high on the success of *Scoundrel Time*, presented the documentary awards, where she was introduced in glowing terms by Fonda. "It is with great pride that I introduce to you my friend Lillian Hellman," Fonda said after a recap of Hellman's HUAC stand. The ovation for Hellman lasted more than forty seconds, with the crowd eventually on its feet, and with Hellman ever so briefly touching the corner of her dry right eye.

"Do you understand?" Julia asks Lilly repeatedly, as Lilly concentrates so hard that Zinnemann has to give her not one but two stretches walking alone, head down, with Fonda, viewed at a distance, isolated in the wider world, adopting a slow, contemplative gait, pondering weighty things. (On the Cape Cod beach she wrestles with the script for her play. Through the Tuileries she decides about the mission.) Fonda would never get a more sustained, more shrewdly calibrated workout in this mode of conscience-riddled acting.

That nothing in the picture feels cliché owes much to Zinnemann's ruthless eye for authenticity. Zinnemann, who apprenticed with famed early documentarian Robert Flaherty (*Nanook of the North*, *Man of Aran*), was such a stickler for history on *Julia* that he hired three separate production designers to capture the looks of different nationalities, and to keep track of period details as Alvin Sargent's screenplay weaves back and forth through time. Conjuring Hitler's rise, Zinnemann uses an instantly recognizable news photo of the Nuremberg Rallies, transitioning to street unrest in Paris late one night as Lilly, alone, watches from her hotel window.

That authenticity somehow was not compromised by the movie's astonishingly luxurious look. Cinematographer Douglas Slocombe filtered the light to blur the ages of Zinnemann's leading ladies, who would need to look right whether playing twenty or forty. "The picture depended on that," Zinnemann later wrote. Every glint of light sparkles—eyeglass frames, candle flames, earrings, champagne flutes. It added an almost distracting level of glamour and nostalgia to a memory play that Hellman claimed was real.

The controversy about Hellman's Julia grew after the movie's release, yet another example of Fonda's on-screen accomplishment getting blotted out by ancillary events. The closer people looked, the more it seemed that Hellman made up her story of a childhood friend in the resistance. A related literary feud between Hellman and Mary McCarthy detonated in 1980 when McCarthy remarked to Dick Cavett on his PBS TV show, "I said once in some interview that every word she writes is a lie, including *and* and *the*." In 1983, psychoanalyst Muriel Gardiner wrote a memoir of her own World War II antifascist experiences, which paralleled those of Hellman's Julia; her story was compelling, and though she'd never met Hellman, she declined to squabble with her about whether she was the inspiration for the story of Hellman's supposed long-dead friend. "I cannot prove that I am or that I am not," the eighty-two-year-old Gardiner told the *Washington Post* that same year.

Hellman, imperious as ever, stubbornly refused to identify who Julia really was, which made her look shifty. She died in 1984, her legend flecked by the dustups. "It's beginning to appear that, for winning public attention, the woman herself is pulling ahead of her plays," biographer William Wright wrote in 1996, but that had already been true. "Researching my book was a three-year struggle to distinguish the real turtle soup from the mock."

It does not matter to *Julia*, though, whether or not Julia was real. The story of an elite American woman wading fully into Europe's antifascist fight was true enough for Zinnemann, an Austrian refugee whose parents were killed in the Holocaust. Hellman's activist role as depicted in *Julia* stands little scrutiny; the tale feels awfully tall as the newly famous Jewish American author of *The Children's Hour* ditches her traveling companions, Dorothy Parker* and Parker's husband Alan Campbell, to risk her life sneaking across Nazi Germany. It is harder still to swallow the story's strange, unprovable footnote about Julia's baby, named Lillian, whom Lilly looks for in France but cannot find after Julia is killed.

Again, though, for Zinnemann, even that facet of the story would have been more than true enough. One of his first full feature films was the devoutly humanitarian project *The Search* (1948), chronicling the plight of WWII's child refugees, shot in postwar Munich and Nuremberg, developed in coordination with the United Nations Relief and Rehabilitation Administration, researched at displaced persons camps. The calm, methodical movie is a striking document, with Montgomery Clift as a heart-of-gold army engineer taking in a street waif played by Ivan Jandl, and with Jarmila Novotna as the searching mother (Garbo-esque of face and kindly with the huge clusters of orphans). Rubble is

* The great American writer Dorothy Parker is barely a blip in the picture; she's played by Rosemary Murphy, who was the wife of Jason Robards's philandering executive in Fonda's 1966 romantic comedy *Any Wednesday*.

everywhere in the picture, and so are orphaned children—by the trainload, herded onto trucks and into dorms and schoolrooms to be cleaned up, fed, taught, then relocated, many of them to Palestine. The sheer volume of lost kids is part of the message, and Zinnemann's black-and-white captures the worried faces. The story has the kids running away when they're guided toward the refugee workers' trucks; to the traumatized children, everything looks sinister, like a route to a concentration camp. They are hard-bitten, wary, in tattered clothes, quiet, orderly, gray. The sentimentality of the main plot—one orphan, one mother, reunited in postwar Europe against the odds—in no way erases the immediacy of wave upon wave of these decidedly non-Hollywood children.

"Preconceived ideas were out of the question," Zinnemann later wrote of *The Search*. "These children had to been seen; they could not be imagined."

Fonda, too, had seen war orphans in Vietnam, and like her character Lilly, she was a privileged American artist who had placed herself perilously close to the front lines. Whether Hellman had actually been through what she said she had been through was as immaterial to Fonda's work as it was to Zinnemann's.

Lending still more activist élan was Redgrave as Julia, who would cement the reputation of *Julia* as a lightning rod for controversy with her Best Supporting Actress acceptance speech at the 1978 Academy Awards. Redgrave then was living the artistic-political life to the hilt. She had intersected a bit with Fonda during the Vietnam years, and both women, in their memoirs, write that Fonda's daughter Vanessa Vadim got her name from Redgrave (though *Newsweek*'s 1977 cover story showcasing *Julia* claimed parenthetically that Vanessa was "not named after Redgrave," perhaps due to Redgrave's extreme leftism and Fonda's centrist pivot).

Like Fonda, Redgrave had very recently starred in a Henrik Ibsen drama about a married woman yearning for more freedom; a 1976 production of *The Lady from the Sea* was her Broadway debut. Redgrave was already a member of the Workers Revolutionary Party and had stood for the UK Parliament in a losing effort. During the *Julia* shoot in Paris, Redgrave lodged with a young Palestinian couple. After filming, she sold two houses to finance a documentary about the plight of

Palestinian refugees at the Tal al-Zaatar camp in Beirut, a flashpoint for the Lebanese Civil War.

"What had happened at Tal al-Zaatar was so hideous that I immediately wanted to do something to assist the situation," Redgrave later wrote, "so I suggested to Gerry Healy [the head of the Workers Revolutionary Party] that I should go to Lebanon, as Jane Fonda had gone to Vietnam, with a camera team and make a documentary about the Palestinians." Between wrapping *Julia* and the 1978 Academy Awards, Redgrave completed *The Palestinian* and tried to muster industry support.

The alignment of the headlining stars did not go unnoticed at the time. Two Feisty Feminists Filming Hellman's "Pentimento," announced a 1976 *New York Times* article by Judith Weinraub, dateline London. The lead paragraph illustrated what the actors were really about: "Vanessa Redgrave is stalking the studio canteen, trying to get a young electrician to join the Workers Revolutionary Party. Jane Fonda is at a rally in Birmingham, urging a consumer boycott of California red grapes."

On-screen, Redgrave and Fonda did not disappoint. Their climactic eleven-minute scene in *Julia* remains thrilling, a classic encounter between canny screen actors at the top of their games. It's the end of Lilly's clandestine mission; stepping off the train, more strangers bustle her in the direction of a small café. Surprisingly, there is Julia, unseen by Lilly since Julia vanished from a Vienna hospital, badly beaten by fascists and bandaged like a mummy.

Zinnemann works in two-shots and close-ups, still without music to underscore emotion, instead filling the soundtrack with accurate ambient noise. As the old friends, now underground operatives, carefully govern what they say and how they behave in the café, raw feeling radiates between the actresses.

Redgrave's Julia, garbed in rough proletarian gray, smiles and says with deep affection, "Fine, *fine*."

Fonda's Lilly, swathed in a classy gown and an elegant fur, gushes tears at the sight of weathered Julia and her wooden leg, a prosthetic earned by charging into a mob of thugs. "I want you to know that you've been better than a good friend to me," Julia says, quietly showering much-wanted praise on her ever-questing friend. "You've done something important. We can save five hundred people, maybe a thousand if we can bargain right."

Lilly Hellman (Fonda) reunites with her childhood friend (Vanessa Redgrave) in *Julia*. *Collection Christophel / Alamy*

The scene proceeds in two keys: clandestine tones as the operation continues to play out (Lilly will now discreetly slip Julia the money-loaded hat), and playful yet melancholy moods as the friends race to catch up during their brief encounter. Redgrave's voice as the older Julia is soft and soothing, even though life has been cripplingly hard. Fonda's betrays tremors as the always younger friend.

"You still look like nobody else," Fonda's Lilly blurts through tears and a smile, and it's true; the natural wildness of Redgrave's wavy red hair and the steadiness of her blue eyes are usefully striking. Redgrave has a singular offhand, laserlike quality that erases almost all hints of performance,* and her assured calm and acute awareness in the midst

* Having bought a ticket in 1991 to see the "great" Redgrave on the London stage as Isadora Duncan in Martin Sherman's *When She Danced*, I waited for the star's appearance, and realized after several moments that the completely absorbing, casual, hardly larger-than-life figure I'd been watching was indeed Redgrave. I was young(er) then, yet the actors I'd seen onstage at that point included Judi Dench, Peter O'Toole, Ian McKellen, Zoe Caldwell, Christopher Walken, Rex Harrison, Diana Rigg, and Angela

of danger is Julia's superpower. It's how Fonda's edgy Lilly would like to be, *strives* to be, as she beams at her mentor. That dynamic also defines her relationship with the ultracool Hammett played by Jason Robards.

Fonda, whose Lilly has been guarded though much of the picture, finally emotes freely, as if the stress of the journey and the joy at seeing Julia can't help at last but blow. They share conspiratorial grins as Redgrave's Julia, always giving guidance, tells Lilly, "I like your anger."

Fonda answers wryly: "You're the only one who does then."

Incandescent, inspirational anger is an essential part of *Julia*'s legacy.* The synchronicity of characters, performances, and personae could not have been more resonant.

Years later Zinnemann laughed when asked if he was surprised to see Fonda weep so much in the scene. "Jane is technically superb," he said. "I was pleased to see how well she and Vanessa did it. . . . These two were one hundred twenty per cent, way beyond what I thought could be accomplished. They shared a triumph, I thought."

"I think that Jane Fonda and I have done the best work of our lives," Redgrave said as she accepted her Oscar, "and I also think it's in part due to our director, Fred Zinnemann, and I also think it's in part because we believed and we believe in what we were expressing—two out of the millions who gave their lives and were prepared to sacrifice everything in the fight against fascist and racist Nazi Germany."

Next, Redgrave's speech called out the opponents of her politics and her largely unseen movie *The Palestinian* as "Zionist hoodlums,"

Lansbury, among others with notable presence. Redgrave's fluid ease and understated command were, as Lilly put it, like no one else.

* "Don't you let anybody talk you out of it," Julia counsels Lilly. "I am angry and I own it," Democratic presidential hopeful Elizabeth Warren was compelled to write in a November 2019 e-mail to supporters; the issue would flare again after her surgical takedown of Mike Bloomberg in his first debate appearance three months later. "Over and over we are told that women are not allowed to be angry. It makes us unattractive to powerful men who want us to be quiet." The "anger" accusations echo Trump's "nasty woman" jab at Hillary Clinton in 2016, and typically function as a distraction to avoid reckoning with what the anger is *about*. The strategic, palatable (though not victorious) watchword of Kamala Harris's 2024 presidential campaign: *Joy*.

which turned the cheers for her performance into boos for her politics.* *Network* screenwriter Paddy Chayefsky took the Ricky Gervais route and denounced her from the podium, saying, "Personal opinion, of course, that I am sick and tired of people exploiting the occasion of the Academy Awards"—this part drew sustained applause—"for the propagation of their own personal political propaganda," he concluded, with the response beginning to be mixed.

It was, a *New York Times* headline decided in 2019, The Most Political Ceremony in Academy History.

"I often feel that only drama, or fiction, can be deeply trusted," Vanessa Redgrave would write years later. "In drama, which we know as 'fiction,' you hear the ring of the soul. Be it ever so slightly cracked or faulty, we all hear the pitch." Hellman biographer Carl Rollyson wrote, "What makes Julia such a satisfying wish-fulfilling character is that she represents everything Hellman"—and Fonda, and certainly Redgrave—"was looking for: a person who would take personal responsibility for healing the world." The absence of specificity, the convenient historical remove of fighting fascists and questing after a lost child, made it unassailable.

Yet it is difficult to imagine *Julia* being as compelling as it is without the forcefully lived activist experiences of these two particular actors, plus Zinnemann, grounding their exacting work.

Zinnemann believed Fonda's performance was worthy of an Oscar, but the actress trophy went to Best Picture winner *Annie Hall*'s star Diane Keaton; perhaps, not unreasonably, the Academy felt they had seen something like the impeccable *Julia* before but never anything quite like *Annie Hall.*† Fonda is entirely overlooked in Steve Vineberg's chapter on Zinnemann's actors in the 1999 book *The Films of Fred Zinnemann*, as he valorizes Deborah Kerr, Burt Lancaster, Audrey Hepburn, and others. Yet *Julia* is inarguably among Fonda's finest

* Two months later, a Beverly Hills theater was bombed because *The Palestinian* was scheduled for a screening there.

† In an early taste of Hollywood's blockbuster revolution, the cinematography and costume Oscars were scooped up by Vilmos Zsigmond and John Mollo for, respectively, *Close Encounters of the Third Kind* and *Star Wars*.

performances—mature, subtle, acute with dialogue and easy to read in silence, carrying the sweeping story without dominating it. And amplifying the *Klute* breakthrough, *Jane Fonda* was totally on brand, successfully melding high (if generic) political purpose with refined art.

With this serious new aspect freshening her persona, hitting screens shortly after the lark of *Dick and Jane*, a *Newsweek* cover story announced her as the frontrunner of a new cinematic pack, heralding a "swarm" of movies (*The Turning Point*; *An Unmarried Woman*; *Looking for Mr. Goodbar*; *The Goodbye Girl*; *A Night Full of Rain*; *One Sings, the Other Doesn't*) that were expanding the ways women were framed:

> She is likely to be the most important figure in this latest, uncertain cycle in a notoriously cycle-happy industry. . . . She's a fine actress whose very behavior seems to mean something to us even before we connect it with the role she's playing. And despite her sometimes strident radicalizing that angered many Americans in a divided time she's an image in the American grain—direct, clear, appealing, with the resilience of the old American optimism, good faith, and high spirits in her movements and her voice.

Pauline Kael, though, resisted *Julia* for what she saw as Hellman's reductive sense of right and wrong, lingering on the unexploited tragic complexities suggested by Fonda's layered performance.

But right and wrong—hard, clear choices—are what activists are about.

Hellman knew this as she penned the myth, clawing for the highest imaginable moral ground. It's worth noting that the rigid, flat prose Hellman used, and the stingy storytelling style she so clearly borrowed from Hemingway and Hammett, left wide-open spaces in the narrative for the interpretive artists to fill. "She pares away her life until it resembles a fable," Rollyson observed of Hellman's memoirs.

Hellman wrote like that in part because the unembellished style felt *important*. That's the gist of Lilly's scenes with her romantic partner, the detective novelist Hammett; Jason Robards plays him as a sequel to his growly turn the previous year as *Washington Post* editor Ben Bradlee in *All the President's Men*, and won Oscars for both roles. Sexuality is almost entirely beside the point in *Julia*. Lilly's relationship with Hammett, not unlike her relationship with Julia, is defined by her emergence, under his guidance, as a writer of significance.

"I'm in trouble with my goddamn play and you don't care?!" she yells across the nighttime beach at him in the movie's opening moments. Zinnemann literally lets her drift away into the dark, unseen as she talks: she is going to have to find herself. The art matters a lot, and Robards grumbles back with bite: "It's not as if you've written anything before, you know. Nobody'll miss you. It's a perfect time to change jobs."

Hammett's lessons are pivotal. As he critiques a draft of *The Children's Hour*, he murmurs sagely, "You'd better tear that up. Not that it's bad. It's just not good enough. Not for you."

Zinnemann gives Fonda a full ten seconds to take in this criticism, which she does thoughtfully, with the pain of a wounded ego barely kept in check. You sense a burgeoning understanding, a hard-boiled code that the character gradually absorbs from Hammett, and from Julia—a code of commitment. High standards. The right kind of work.

"She was hard on herself, but she knew how to be understanding of others," Roger Vadim wrote of Fonda in *Bardot, Deneuve, Fonda*. "Her goals were higher, more ambitious and less egotistical. She made a cult of hard work."

"It is very important to make movies about women who grow and become ideological human beings and totally committed people," Fonda told the *New York Times* during the *Julia* shoot. "We have to begin to put that image into the mass culture."

9

A FAREWELL TO ARMS

Coming Home

> SUE: *Where are all the wonderful women that were in the movies in the old days? Bette Davis? Katharine Hepburn? Joan Crawford?*
> JEANETTE: *Where are all the women?*
> ERICA: *Well, we've got, uh . . . Jane Fonda.*
> JEANETTE: *Oh, please.*
>
> —*An Unmarried Woman* (1978)

BY 1978 THE PROTESTING *BRAS D'HONNEUR* of *F.T.A.* became the peacemaking, helping hands of *Coming Home*.

For four tense minutes during *Coming Home*'s climactic showdown, Fonda stands practically still, utterly distraught but reaching out, elbows at her sides, open palms in front of her. She's gesturing toward Bruce Dern, playing her marine captain husband Bob Hyde, just home from Vietnam in 1968.

Bob is freaking out in their living room, in uniform, commanding the scene at the point of his rifle's bayonet. He's forcing a marital showdown with his wife and her paraplegic Vietnam vet lover Luke, played by Jon Voight. Bob has become radically unglued by the war.

The sexual politics of the triangle were essential to Fonda. So were the military politics. Both hit the boiling point in the scene. Bruce Dern, a lean, tall actor with a menacing edge (revisit his brief, threatening work as Bonnie Bedelia's husband in *They Shoot Horses, Don't They?*), is like a live grenade.

"The enemy is this fucking war," says Voight, long-haired and easy-going as cool-handed Luke, finally finding the words that help Bob stand down.

With that, Fonda relaxes her arms. That long-held pose, practically a statue, deserves a title: "Soldier, We Love You," after Rita Martinson's ballad from *F.T.A.*

Coming Home (1978)

Technically, *Coming Home* was a lesser acting accomplishment for Fonda than *Julia* had been. *Julia* demanded that she carry the picture in Bette Davis style, charisma ablaze, holding the screen through everything but the youngest flashback scenes. In *Coming Home* she does much less. She plays only her part in an ensemble picture, often in reaction to characters who are more directly in the thick of things. The story is so balanced that four actors earned Oscar nominations.

The focus alights on Fonda's Sally for two high-impact moments in the movie's middle. The first is the famous groundbreaking love scene with Voight's Luke, who is paralyzed from the waist down. The second comes when Fonda sits on Voight's lap on the Southern California beach—idyllic scenery, sea breeze tousling the gorgeous heroes' 1960s hair—as they fret about the likely end of the affair.

Cinematographer Haskell Wexler's camera startlingly pulls back a hundred yards to reveal that the FBI is surveilling them; Luke has emerged as a war protestor, and of course Fonda, an enemy of Nixon's, had firsthand experience with the kind of government attention that could bring. As the camera recedes, Fonda's role retreats. Her husband Bob is coming home, and he will eat up most of the rest of the story, along with Voight's Luke, who talks Bob down and then sums it all up. Fonda hangs out at the edge. There's a half hour of movie left.

Even so, *Coming Home* would earn Fonda her second Oscar for Best Actress. Voight would win too—one of only seven times, as of 2025,

Best Actor / Best Actress Oscar winners Jane Fonda and Jon Voight in *Coming Home*. *© United Artists / Courtesy Everett Collection*

that the Best Actor / Best Actress awards have gone to performances from the same film.*

But Fonda by now was more than her acting, and *Coming Home* became by far the most complete articulation of *Jane Fonda* that she would ever make as a Hollywood feature. It is adamantly against the "fucking war," though not a frame of it takes place in Vietnam. We only glimpse Vietnam on TV sets; sensibly, the picture never places Hanoi Jane closer to Vietnam than Hong Kong, where she is a dutiful wife with a husband on R&R.

Like *Winter Soldier* and *F.T.A.*, it is aggressively pro-veteran, casting actual wounded soldiers wheeled in chairs and on gurneys to medical

* Three years later, another Jane Fonda joint, *On Golden Pond*, would join that rarefied club (Jane herself was nominated for Supporting Actress). Perhaps illustrating an understudied balance in the New Hollywood years, four of those seven movies came from 1975–81, with the Fonda films following *One Flew over the Cuckoo's Nest* and *Network* as Actor-Actress champs.

appointments and riffing on their experiences; part of the shoot was embedded in a Los Angeles VA hospital. And Fonda's character is a middle-American military wife who grows an antiwar conscience. Sally Hyde witnesses how permanently combat—especially a wrongful combat, inhumane on the ground, blatantly unwinnable, vastly unpopular—crushes hearts and minds.

Fonda's new production company, IPC (don't call it Indochina Peace Campaign!) Films, was not identified in the credits. But IPC's Bruce Gilbert—a newcomer to movies, and a Fonda acquaintance from his days working in a Bay Area day care where Fonda's daughter Vanessa was enrolled—was listed as an associate producer. And it was no secret that this was *the Jane Fonda Vietnam movie*, distinct from the upcoming Robert De Niro vehicle *The Deer Hunter* and Francis Ford Coppola's much-anticipated *Apocalypse Now*.

Ascribing writing credit on *Coming Home* is as complicated as it was with *The Chase*. "Even though I'm Jane Fonda, even though I have things to say," she said at the time, "it's still very difficult to find screenwriters who can combine the political and the emotional."

The project started with Fonda encountering disabled vet Ron Kovic at a speaking engagement. Kovic, whose memoir *Born on the Fourth of July* was published in 1976, is nowhere mentioned in the credits. But, inspired by his story, Fonda/IPC commissioned a script from Nancy Dowd, an *FTA Show* writer and Fonda pal; Bosworth writes that Dowd went with Fonda to Norway for *A Doll's House*. A UCLA screenwriting alum, Dowd earned major Hollywood credibility with the salty 1977 Paul Newman comedy *Slap Shot*, about a minor league hockey team struggling through rusting American industrial towns.

But the story Dowd handed IPC wasn't quite what Fonda was after, and before *Coming Home* opened Dowd was already calling Fonda an "ex-friend" in *Newsweek*.

Waldo Salt, a formerly blacklisted screenwriter who won an Oscar for *Midnight Cowboy*, tackled a rewrite, then suffered a heart attack. Robert C. Jones—a longtime editor and occasional writer who would not get credit for his writing on director Hal Ashby's next picture, *Being There*—further reworked the script.

The war vets hired as extras spoke off the cuff on-screen and gave Voight, in particular, lots of material to build on. The Strasburg-trained Voight, Dern, and Fonda improvised dialogue. Ashby gave Wexler a free hand to frame and pan as he imbued certain scenes—notably the opening—with documentary's uncertain, in-the-moment dynamism. Elsewhere, Ashby and Wexler devised compositions.

All of these people "wrote" *Coming Home*, knowing it was fundamentally Jane's mosaic. "Am I too bossy?" Fonda once asked Voight between takes, fretting about her producorial touch.

All of it was animated by conviction.

"*Coming Home* was made by people mostly who were against the Vietnam War," cinematographer Wexler says in the DVD commentary. "Being against the Vietnam War was not being against or derisive of our citizens, many of whom were drafted, many of whom were deceived. We wanted to make a human statement . . . that war makes paraplegics. War destroys people's logic."

"It was certainly the most improvised movie that I had ever done," Fonda said in *Hal*, the 2018 documentary about Ashby. "A lot of what was told to me by wives and by soldiers are actually lines in the movie. And the character of Sally was based on the women that I met—and partly on me, because the Vietnam War changed me very much."*

Coming Home signaled Hollywood's belated reckoning with Vietnam—"The first important movie on the subject," critic Jack Kroll wrote in *Newsweek*—and Hollywood saluted. The picture racked up eight Oscar nominations, including supporting nods for Dern and for

* Aaron Hunter's book *Authoring Hal Ashby* explores the complexities of film "authorship," detailing some of the variety of contributions to *Coming Home* and citing Alan Lovell and Gianluca Sergi's *Making Films in Contemporary Hollywood* on the "ten individual roles with the potential to contribute to the authorial collective: producers, screenwriters, directors, production designers, cinematographers, editors, visual effects artists, sound designers, composers, and actors, particularly stars." Hunter concludes with a case study on Ashby's *Being There*: novelist Jerzy Kosiński's screenplay was substantially rewritten by the uncredited Robert C. Jones; Ashby dreamed up the magical final sequence with Peter Sellers's Chance walking on water; and Sellers improvised the capper to the visual joke, lowering his umbrella like a dipstick into the lake.

Penelope Milford as Sally's friend Vi, for director Ashby, for Best Picture, and for sound design.

In addition to Fonda and Voight's lead acting wins, the movie notched a third win for its screenplay.

The ratification of this *story*, combined with her own Best Actress win over Ingrid Bergman in *Autumn Sonata*, Ellen Burstyn in *Same Time, Next Year*, Jill Clayburgh in *An Unmarried Woman*, and Geraldine Page in *Interiors*,* indicated that in the wild Fonda 1970s—which started with the lurch from *Barbarella* to *Klute* to Hanoi and had now evolved into a hip, crafty, glossy, heartbreaking Vietnam War statement that hit America where it lived—her peers could not help but admire her.

For Sally Hyde, as for *Julia*'s Lilly Hellman, the moral arc of life's lessons bends toward activism.

The source of Sally's political awakening is an irrational war's brutal toll on American soldiers, and it's established in the first shot. Real disabled vets shoot pool and talk about whether they'd re-up for another tour. *No*, goes the winning argument. The only rationale for anyone saying they'd go back is that if the war wasn't *worth it*, it would be psychologically impossible to cope with being "crippled for the rest of their fuckin' life."

Wexler films the scene in *The Bus / Medium Cool, Winter Soldier / Introduction to the Enemy* verité style, with the camera following a group's improvised dialogue around the room. As the last argument sinks in, Wexler and Ashby zoom in on Voight, on a gurney, on his belly, head down, pensive. The slow zoom gives us Voight as our subject, and it magnifies his crisis of conscience.

Fonda doesn't appear until more than seven minutes in, meeting Dern at the officers' club. Her Sally Hyde, hair and pantsuit both ironed stiff, is styled as conservatively as Anita Bryant. (Bryant was a culturally central figure at the time for the wrong reasons: her unabashed

* Oddity: Page's was one of two nominated turns that year, along with Dern's, that ended with the character tragically walking into the surf.

homophobia, which she detailed in, among other venues, a May 1978 *Playboy* interview.) Sally is the dutiful, loyal military wife, and Fonda does not subvert the character. Sally's affection for Bob feels real, if not passionate.

Still, Fonda shows early hairline fissures in Sally that will grow into structural cracks. She is lightly sarcastic at the prospect of Bob being promoted to major. "I'll have to get my skirts lengthened for that one," she jokes quietly in the officers' club.

More telling is her *Klute*-like conjugal sendoff. Underneath Dern, she is distracted by worry, not erotically moved. An understated joke: Dern's murmured foreplay song is "The Marines' Hymn" ("*From the Halls of Montezuma . . .*"). Instead of glancing at her watch like Bree, Sally nervously twirls her fingers in the dog tags that have spun around to Bob's back.

The Bob and Sally marriage is straight out of *A Doll's House*. "I *am* afraid," Sally tells Bob in the car as she drops him off at night for his overseas deployment, surprising him with the gift of a ring. "But I'm proud of you." Sally's role is strictly support, and it's going to be tough: Ashby, whose films often dazzlingly pulse with the music of their era, throttles the Beatles' consoling "Hey Jude" extremely low under the scene. When the men get on the bus bound for war, the song revs at full volume into its clanging, screaming climax.

Jittery about being alone, Sally asks Vi, the girlfriend of Bob's sidekick Dink, if she'd like to get a drink. They go to Vi's, a funky loft that's alien to Fonda's straitlaced Sally. When Vi moves to switch off the TV as the station signs off for the night with "The Star-Spangled Banner," Sally asks to keep it on through the end of the song. "Tonight especially, I sort of felt superstitious. . . . It's the way I was brought up," Sally explains, and Vi agrees. No flag-burning radicals here!

Wanting to be useful, Sally heads to the hospital for one of the grossest "meet cutes" in movie history. Voight's Luke, still belly-down on a gurney, poles himself through the VA ward like a prone cross-country skier. He needs an aide to empty his urine bag.

"You better watch it before you pop your melon," a fellow patient says.

That's what happens when he crashes into Sally coming around a corner, humiliated as the loaded bag shoots a stream all over her dress.

Voight milks the indignity for all it's worth, slamming everything in sight with his cane and swearing at the orderlies, going so phenomenally berserk that the cast's real vets, as extras, can be seen cracking up at the edges of the frame.

Our rooting interest in Luke is clinched in a brilliant single take, a scene with his hands strapped down as his nemesis, an orderly he calls Pee Wee (inverting "Big Nurse" Ratched in Ken Kesey's *One Flew over the Cuckoo's Nest*), feeds Luke against his will. The camera slowly pans from left to right behind Pee Wee's head. We watch Luke calmly saying that being spoon-fed is unnecessary, *ridiculous.* He makes a joke of it. Ultimately he protests in silence.

"I'm not eating," he says plainly.

Pee Wee pushes the egg into his lips anyway. It dribbles into Luke's beard. That Voight keeps his dignity is a small early triumph.

This gives Fonda's new hospital volunteer Sally a chance to clean Luke up. Turns out they knew each other in high school, and Voight begins the transition from wrath to charm.

Still, cranky Luke pointlessly insults prim Sally the next time they meet.

Sally chases him down the hall. She grabs the back of his gurney, lifts it, and slams it. "Why do you have to be such a bastard?" she asks, the hurt fracking Fonda's voice and face. She stomps away, not knowing she's won his respect.

The inadequate care for the vets turns Sally activist. Dressed in a white-and-navy tennis outfit accessorized with chunky white beads, she proposes that the ladies' auxiliary write an article in the newsletter. "There's not enough beds," she says politely but firmly (Sally is not *Jane Fonda*). "There's not enough staff. It's really crowded. The guys have to wait in line, and they are just not prepared for the number of wounded guys that are being sent back."

The ladies demur.

"I want to say that I'm really shocked," Sally says. "I'm just shocked that you'd rather write about a goddamn home run than about what's going on in this hospital. I mean, you wouldn't feel that way if they were your husbands."

Sally, in tune with her evolving conscience, stops straightening her naturally frizzy hair; like Fonda's actual shag at the beginning of the decade, it's a small but vivid declaration of independence. (So is Sally's declining to move in with Bob's mother; instead, Sally rents her own tiny house near the beach.) The bearded Voight looks a little like Ashby did at the time, and you see Ashby's hair streaming in the wind too, in a long-shot cameo—he's the hippie zipping past in the matching sportscar next to Fonda's on a freeway, flashing the peace sign, intercut in the closing montage with Voight's climactic speech to high school kids and Dern's doomed vet beginning to strip on the beach.

Hair was no minor point in the 1960s, from *Hair* the musical to David Crosby's song "Almost Cut My Hair." Warren Beatty's working title for *Shampoo*, set in 1968 and released in 1975, first dreamed up after his *Bonnie and Clyde* success, was *Hair*. When Sally goes to Hong Kong to see Bob for R&R—before she sleeps with Luke—she restraightens her hair and wraps it in a scarf. When Bob comes home for good, his first words, on the tarmac are confused, not delighted: "What the hell did you do to your hair?"

Sally's changes respond to a dramatic subplot involving Luke and Billy (Robert Carradine), Vi's brother, who is back from the war with heavy trauma. As Billy breaks down during a picnic, it's Luke who soothes him. Sally is moved.

Luke's healing gesture sets the table for their first nervous dinner date at Sally's. Voight, whose Luke is a *no bullshit* straight shooter, turns on a laid-back surfer allure. Ashby chooses "Follow," a slow, tactful Richie Havens song, to quietly underscore the scene.

Voight asks if it's "have a gimp over for dinner" night: "You're not one of *those* weirdos?"

Fonda gives him a long look. "No, I'm not," she finally says, with simple sincerity.

"I know you're not," Voight replies. The tension dissolves. They begin to behave more like friends. "I'm just very happy to be here."

"I think people have a real hard time seeing who other people really are," Fonda's Sally says outdoors at night after dinner. "People don't see me like I really am." Luke and Sally have that in common.

It is lucky for *Coming Home* that Ashby landed the gig after John Schlesinger (*Midnight Cowboy, Sunday Bloody Sunday, Marathon Man*) didn't work out. Ashby's New Hollywood pictures from 1970 to 1979 form an exceptional time capsule, more purely and perceptively in an American tune than any director of those imposing years can claim: *The Landlord, Harold and Maude, The Last Detail, Shampoo, Bound for Glory, Coming Home*, and *Being There.*

In *Authoring Hal Ashby*, Aaron Hunter notes that Ashby's grounding as an editor on movies like Norman Jewison's *The Russians Are Coming the Russians Are Coming* and *In the Heat of the Night* marked him:

> This propensity for making popular films that tackled political themes in a thoughtful albeit sometimes comical manner would stay with Ashby throughout his career and would become a marker of noticeable difference from many of his 1970s peers. Few Americans of the decade (if any) so consistently addressed political topics—both in the broad sense of governmental and institutional decision-making and in the quieter, "personal is political" sense—as Ashby would in each of his films.

Ashby's *Shampoo* was a culture-summing hit generated, like *Coming Home*, by a massive activist star. Warren Beatty had been an inside player in the 1972 presidential campaign of Nixon challenger George McGovern, and he not only produced and starred in *Shampoo* but also cowrote the script (for years) with Robert Towne. The story makes sophisticated use of William Wycherley's Restoration farce *The Country Wife*, in which a man poses as a eunuch so husbands will trust him with their wives.

Shampoo updates the premise to 1968 L.A., with Beatty as hairdresser George, whom fat cat Lester (Jack Warden) assumes must be a "fairy," while Beatty sleeps with Warden's mistress (Julie Christie), daughter (Carrie Fisher), and wife (Lee Grant, winning a Best Supporting Actress Oscar). The movie is set on the eve of the 1968 election and on election night, and during these two days Beatty somehow manages *not* to sleep with his girlfriend, Goldie Hawn.

Vietnam is hardly mentioned, and the campaign's issues are barely heard in the background. Instead, the politics are implied. Morally, George meanders; he eventually connects as well with the thuggish Lester as he does with anyone else, and he may end up in business with him. The country is having a big election. George is bumbling around with a battery of self-inflicted wounds.

Literally, you can hear Ashby's *Shampoo* in *Coming Home*. Jimi Hendrix's "Manic Depression" drives the *Shampoo* climax at a massive Playboy Mansion–style party, with Beatty and Christie being discovered in flagrante delicto by Warden and Hawn, and you hear that Hendrix jam again during Luke's first protest in *Coming Home*, chaining himself to the gates of a military base. You can also see Ashby's vision of 1968 romantic leads in the look that both Beatty and Fonda sport when they are most themselves: broken-in jeans, white peasant shirts, arrestingly thick manes of brunet hair. As Ashby displays them, they could nearly be twins.

Bound for Glory came after *Shampoo*, sharpening the politics in a story about folk singer Woody Guthrie finding his activist voice in a *Grapes of Wrath* migration from Dust Bowl Oklahoma to California. Haskell Wexler would win an Oscar for his dirt-tinged cinematography, which included the first Steadicam shot in a Hollywood feature—a stunner, slowly following David Carradine's Guthrie into a sea of disappointed migrants who have once again failed to get a day's work.

Pauline Kael wrote a long, deeply mixed *Bound for Glory* review (an example of her peerless knack for observation and style), and her view of that movie applies to how *Coming Home* works:

> It's filled with woozy generalities about Woody Guthrie as a man who fought the good fight against greed, and about radicalization's being the same thing as finding himself as an artist. It's about being in touch with the people—not just people but the people. Ashby's open approach led him to imbue the movie with the sort of mythologized idealism that stirs people when they listen to political folk and rock music—the generalized piousness and good will of youth. This is nothing terrible, but since it's the glue that holds the picture together, *Bound for Glory* is like a

> dreamy, druggy young kid's view of hard times. It's so beautiful you can get a high from the dust.

Coming Home, likewise, is about fighting the good fight. Luke and Sally make common cause as activists, and as lovers. It's beautiful too, partly because of the warmth it builds for its characters—an affection deeper than the admiration and awe inspired by the towering moral heroes of Zinnemann's *Julia*, and more relatable than the sexually opportunistic L.A. high flyers of *Shampoo* and Guthrie's Dust Bowl victims.

Audiences in 1978 would certainly relate to *Coming Home*'s 1968 characters, perhaps to none more easily than the hip Vi as lightly played by Penelope Milford.* Pivotally, Milford's down-to-earth style—a hallmark of so many figures in Ashby films—rubs off on Fonda's character. Hippie Vi, suffering through her brother's crack-up, is everything the officers' uptight wives are not. Vi helps Sally thaw.

But unlike *Shampoo* and *Bound for Glory*—and unlike the swoony yet severe *Julia* and Fonda's next signature activist picture, *The China Syndrome*—*Coming Home* is an unapologetic romance.

Fonda wanted the love story between Sally and Luke to be revolutionary, and it is. It follows the *Julia* template of bonding through political commitment: after Billy, with "Sympathy for the Devil" beating its sinister rhythm on the soundtrack, spectacularly kills himself in front of his pals in the VA ward, Luke gets himself on TV by chaining himself to the military base gates. Sally sees the newscast and picks him up from jail.

"I'm not a very nice person," he tells her.

"You are to me," she says. After a pause she delivers the bombshell, confirming how sexy the direct action/protest gesture is: "I want to spend the night with you."

* During *Julia*, Fonda, in producing mode, thought of young Meryl Streep for Vi, as Streep had made such an impression in brief *Julia* scenes as a society snot. But Streep as Vi is hard to picture. Streep was already in demand; she would soon appear as Woody Allen's ex-wife in *Manhattan* and nab her first Oscar in 1979's *Kramer vs. Kramer*. She was so arresting as the love interest of both Christopher Walken and Robert De Niro in *The Deer Hunter* that Kael wrote of her "heroic resources as a mime." Vi, a blue-collar woman who works in the hospital kitchen, would not benefit from a striking turn. Though her movie career did not take off, Milford was perfect.

The bedroom scene, another variation on the "Soldier, We Love You" theme, is famed for showing Voight easing out of his wheelchair and thrilling Sally erotically. We see her wedding ring as she caresses him during long, wandering takes (with a body double for Fonda).

"Oh, softly," Sally whispers.

Fonda's eyes shut tight, then open wide as Sally not only experiences the climax but ponders it. Luke, unlike Bob, gets eagerly held and kissed.

"That's never happened to me before," she says.

In Fonda's *My Life So Far*, her ungainly synopsis goes like this:

> Our story has a Marine, my husband, with full use of his body (including his penis), who wanted above all to prove his manhood by being a "hero." But because he was neither sensitive nor spontaneous, he was not a good lover. The paraplegic I met in the VA hospital, on the other hand, did *not* have a functioning penis, and all he wanted was to be human. His willingness to examine long held beliefs, along with his physical incapacity, made him sensitive to another's needs. His pleasure came through giving pleasure—at least that was my intention, and thus the film could potentially illuminate a sexuality beyond genitalia.

There are accounts of Ashby urging Fonda to "ride him" and Fonda resisting. "From the evidence on the screen I would say that Fonda won the battle," scholar Linda Williams writes in *Screening Sex*. What's onscreen fits Fonda's clinical description but also holds up as tasteful and intimate. As with practically everything else in the picture, the scene was grounded in research and experience, as Kirk Honeycutt reported in the *New York Times*:

> Dr. Joshua Golden, director of the Sexual Dysfunction Clinic at U.C.L.A., and his wife, Peggy, a sex therapist, supplied them with information regarding the sexual abilities of the disabled, as well as providing access to many patients and therapists. Mr. Voight, however, received a more colorful education in these matters. "Five hundred guys were telling me how they did it. Every time I turned around somebody would say, 'You know what I do?' or, 'Want to make it really terrific?'"

In the postcoital scene on the beach, Sally joins Luke in the wheelchair, nestling in his lap, contemplating Bob's return. The close-up is tight. The camera wanders, frequently catching Sally's rings.

"It's very scary for me," Sally says, as Fonda pauses for a beat. "To think that maybe it's not going to work out with him."

"I know," Luke says. Voight radiates understanding. Luke makes no demands.

"Because we've been together for so long," she continues, talking it out. "It's going to be very hard for him. He's not going to like the fact that I've changed. And I have changed. You know that I've never been on my own before?"

That's the extent of her big speech, in Fonda's second Oscar-winning performance.

Fonda in *Coming Home* is understated, practically pulling off a sneak attack on the audience's feelings. The work accrues without bravura moments, never reaching for the kind of camera-gripping acting that electrifies the endings of *They Shoot Horses*, *Klute*, and *The China Syndrome*, or that makes the second hour of *Julia* so delectably tense. Sally's part, pitched toward the kind of "honesty" that Peter Fonda believed he'd achieved with *Easy Rider*, hinges on two scenes and two plaintive signature lines, testaments to a pro-feminist, antiwar evolution: "That never happened to me before," and "I've changed." Gone are the tears of *Julia*; Voight, on the DVD commentary, says he was prepared for heavy emotion, but that Fonda wanted a drier approach.

"She wanted to protect from getting too maudlin," he says. "She had that ability to make a scene very clean. She was very direct."

If *Coming Home* lapses into "woozy generalities," it's in the depictions of the vets—Billy and Bob. Both are doomed thanks to the straitjacket of traditional masculinity (in Bob's case) and the horrors of war (both cases). The war took a far greater psychological toll than Americans were used to after World War II: the suicide rate among servicemembers rose during the Vietnam War and actually peaked in 1975, as the conflict was ending and the movie was made. (The rate has been substantially worse in the twenty-first century.)

Yet neither Billy's lethal self-injection via an elephant-sized hypodermic needle nor Bob's turgid Norman Maine surge into the surf ring true. Critics have rightly been dissatisfied by these fates. It's worth considering, though, that Fonda and Ashby were not only wrestling with statements about the cost to servicemen of a bad war. They also had in common, during their adolescence, a parent who died by suicide.

The movie seems entitled to an over-the-edge portrait of Billy *or* Bob, but not both. Bob seems the more shortchanged.

When Luke turns antiwar, the government puts him on its watch list. When Bob gets home, agents ask what he knows about the subversive paraplegic they've been tailing. They show Bob pictures of Luke with Sally. Bob has already been diminished by his war injury. The implication of his "accident" story is that he shot himself in the calf on the way to the bathroom (or perhaps got fragged, though that's a harder conclusion to draw). Being cuckolded by a hippie paraplegic is too much salt in the wound.

Early drafts apparently had Bob taking hostages in the Hollywood Hills, which sounds too gonzo by miles. Yet in the final film, his sneaky jungle-style entrance into the beach cottage to confront Sally is also too much. It's arguably the heaviest moment in Ashby's 1970s canon, going toe to toe with Louis Gossett Jr.'s similar, more terrifying flip-out in *The Landlord* as the Black activist who just caught his girlfriend (Diana Sands) sleeping with their new White landlord (Beau Bridges).

The *Coming Home* arc doesn't wash. Bob, whom Sally has discovered sleeping with a pistol under his pillow, enters not only with a gun but with a *long* gun, and not just a long gun but a rifle *lengthened by a bayonet*. He's the ultra-phallic man about to get his manhood bobbed.

Soldier, we love you, say Fonda's outstretched hands.

But the scenario, the mise-en-scène, and the Chambers Brothers' bombastic "Time Has Come Today" on the soundtrack add, *The guns have got to go.*

The movie's clincher belongs to Voight, riffing in front of high school kids in a Ron Kovic–like speech about putting your body on the line for the wrong things. Ashby crosscuts the speech with Bob formally taking off his Marine uniform and wedding ring and charging into the waves; Tim Buckley's folksy ballad "Once I Was" ("*Once I was a soldier / And I fought on foreign sands for you . . .*") is the mournful track.

In Luke's anti-recruitment speech, Voight hushes the room, absorbingly frank, breaking down about his tragic mistake: "And I'm telling you it ain't like it's in the movies; that's all I want to tell you. . . . And there's a lot of shit that I did over there . . . that I find fucking hard to live with. And I don't want to see people like you, man, coming back, and having to face the rest of your lives with that kind of shit."

The emotion gets thick. He pulls it back together.

"I don't feel sorry for myself. I'm a lot fucking smarter now than when I went." Voight again pushes aside a surge of feeling. He makes the rational case. Ashby's camera tracks from the back of the school auditorium, around the audience, slowly toward Voight, finally giving us a close look from the side, a sinuous move that puts us fully in the room and tight with Luke.

"And I'm just telling you," Luke concludes, "that there's a choice to be made here."

Who doesn't like to hate political art? Inevitably, critics protested.

"As romantic as John Wayne in 'The Green Berets,'" Jack Kroll wrote in *Newsweek*, calling Voight "Robert Redford on wheels." "The ideology is the opposite of Wayne's, but there's more to truth than ideology. 'Coming Home' stacks the cards in a good cause; nevertheless, the cards are stacked."

"Jane Fonda isn't playing a character in *Coming Home*," Kael began her review, "she's playing an abstraction—a woman being radicalized." A woman being radicalized was hardly abstract to Fonda, of course. It was the reality of her life, the structure of her days, and now, at last, the clay of her art. Kael was intensely mixed, finally skewing negative and unable to resist a quippy walkoff: "Are liberals really such great lovers?"

Even Tom Hayden apparently scoffed to his wife, "Nice try," after screening the film.

The charges of didacticism are accurate, because *Coming Home* is an activist picture, with an activist agenda. Voight's closing argument is indeed as blatant as a public service announcement—or, to put it in twenty-first-century vernacular, it's an Aaron Sorkin speech. It's also rock-solid lyrical moviemaking, the way Ashby put the final sequence together, and the kind of thing Ron Kovic said he wished he'd heard when he was in high school instead of the gung-ho stuff that bandwagoned on the Hollywood images of glory and war.

"It was like the day the Marine recruiters came," Kovic wrote in *Born on the Fourth of July*. "What if I had seen someone like me that day, a guy in a wheelchair, just sitting there in front of the senior class not saying a word?"

The circle of influence goes all the way round: Kovic also writes of seeing Donald Sutherland at a rally, reading *Johnny Got His Gun*, which Sutherland did during *The FTA Show*.

"Something I will never forget swept over me . . ." Kovic wrote. "There were tears in my eyes. Just before Sutherland finished I found myself pushing my chair toward the stage and telling them that I wanted to be lifted up the steps. 'I have a poem,' I told them. 'I have a poem about the vets who threw away their medals and I want to read it.'"

There *is* a choice to be made, *always*. The value of having Fonda's alt-recruiting movie in Hollywood's war archive is immeasurably high.

The immediate comparison was with *The Deer Hunter*, an action picture bristling with doom and machismo, a sordid buddy tale with very little to say about the actual war beyond the cryptic "Fuck it" uttered by an unidentified Green Beret (Paul D'Amato), drinking alone at the bar during the movie's long wedding scene. Instead, director Michael Cimino, who cowrote the story with Louis Garfinkle, Quinn K. Redeker, and writer of the screenplay Deric Washburn, uses Vietnam as a staging ground, a plausible setting for depraved behavior and for whipsawing viewers' emotions.

The Deer Hunter is a blast of testosterone, beginning with an immersive, hour-long depiction of poor yet idealized Rust Belt life. Its rituals are manly: working with strapping vigor amid the heat and noise of a steel mill, unwinding with beers and insults around the local tavern's pool table, uniting with the whole community for a buddy's wedding in a lovely Russian Orthodox church, reveling for hours at the reception—"Cimino is big on hubbub," Kael would write in her review of his next colossus, *Heaven's Gate*—and finally piling into a station wagon for one of the fraternity's sacred deer hunting trips, amid mountains so heavenly that clouds kiss the trees and angels sing on the soundtrack.

Cimino shreds this American heartland fabric the instant he cuts to his vision of brief, anarchic Vietnam carnage. A North Vietnamese soldier casually kills a bunker full of women and children, then in turn gets wasted by a flamethrower operated by our hero, the taciturn, ultra-competent, Hemingwayesque Michael (Robert De Niro). Corpses blaze. Wild hogs feast.

And then, with calculated sadism, we are plunged into a bamboo cage, half-submerged in a rat-infested river, where the Vietnamese force Michael and his fellow prisoners to take part in the first of the Russian roulette scenes upon which Cimino's brutal exercise utterly depends.

The roulette was a metaphor, some thought, for the inevitable self-destruction of America's crapshoot military intervention. "More about the mind of the America that fought the war than the Vietnam War itself," Vincent Canby wrote of *Deer Hunter* several years later, reflecting on Oliver Stone's decidedly war-specific *Platoon*.

The problem is how sloppily Cimino sets up any sort of antiwar critique. (Though, to be fair, the lone Green Beret does say "Fuck it" a second time, gnomically and acidly, to De Niro and his offended pals, all of them geeked up for deployment. The year is 1968.) Cimino, in the movie's production notes, said the war was not top of mind: "The war is really incidental to the development of the characters and their story. It's part of their lives and just that, nothing more." His movie loves *the guys*. It sanctifies their mill valley home, be it ever so humble.

The roulette scenes, on the other hand, come off as lazy and racist, more potent as shock value than as politics. The politics are rancid; the Vietnamese are unindividuated killing machines, leading Kael to observe that the picture played into General William Westmoreland's contention, documented as he spoke in *Hearts and Minds*, that "The

Oriental doesn't put the same high price on life as does a Westerner. Life is plentiful. Life is cheap in the Orient."

The Deer Hunter takes that as a premise for its pulp fiction, veering toward Graham Greene territory by giving us a dissolute expat Frenchman idling in a dark alley, poised like a spider to ensnare Michael's truest pal Nicky (Christopher Walken) for the picture's second roulette scene, still presided over by rabid Vietnamese, only now pried away from the prisoner scenario and practiced as pure sport—a human cockfight, with avid, sweaty gamblers screaming around the edges. Having escaped the river cage, Walken's Nicky has clearly snapped like Billy in *Coming Home* and De Niro's Travis Bickle in *Taxi Driver*, as Hollywood begins molding an image of vets turning psycho. Walken, en route to an Oscar for his creepy, action-packed tragic turn, electrifies this underground gathering. He cold-bloodedly grabs the gun. He presses it to his head. He presses it to another player's head. Both times he clicks the trigger and gets away with it, his face as mischievous as the devil's. The sordid room goes bananas. A sicko myth is born. Walken strides like a zombie into the misty nighttime streets.

Cimino isn't interested in the actual war. He's interested in emotion—the ride from innocence and loyalty to ruination, rendered in shocking terms and closing, freeze frame, with the friends loyally raising a glass to country and to Nick, who finally died across the Asian roulette table from Michael. It's not a picture you'd double feature with *Introduction to the Enemy*, unless you were being "biliously ironic," which is how Richard Brody reads the movie's ending as De Niro and the survivors sing a subdued "God Bless America." Ironic is the only way an audience could take the anthem after such a horror show. The ending was received as troublingly enigmatic, if not an outright cop-out.*

"Slips into the wildest sort of melodrama," Canby wrote in the *New York Times*, after crediting the film with aiming to be "nothing less than an appraisal of American life in the second half of the 20th century." In 1979, *The Deer Hunter* split the Oscar prestige with *Coming Home*,

* Cimino, like (more pleasurably and more plausibly) Elaine May of *Ishtar*, are "cinematic heroes and martyrs of critical obliviousness," Brody asserted.

winning Best Picture and, for Cimino, Best Director.* The sweep and intensity were irresistible, at least on a primal level.

And the stage was set for the rightist tilt of Hollywood's 1980s Vietnam pictures.

At least the metaphor was more alluring in *Apocalypse Now*, which cohered enough to the contours of its source material, Joseph Conrad's 1899 novella *Heart of Darkness*, for the narrative mission to make sense. The movie emerged as instantly quotable, phantasmagorical myth from cinematic godfathers Francis Ford Coppola and Marlon Brando. Its monumental frenzy, with Martin Sheen terminating Brando's Kurtz ("with extreme prejudice") to the brain-exploding strains of the Doors' "The End," added to the Woodstock/*In the Year of the Pig* inventory of Vietnam as America's long, bad, nobody's-in-charge trip.

In *Inventing Vietnam: The War in Film and Television*, Michael Anderegg noted:

> Precisely when film ceased to be the primary form of mass entertainment it came to be recognized as perhaps the dominant art form of the twentieth century. Filmmakers were now expected to go beyond the superficialities of a mass cultural form and to "say something," to comment significantly on the subjects they treated. In this context, *The Deer Hunter* and *Apocalypse Now*, when released in the late seventies, were received not simply as movies but as important cultural events, as intellectually respectable statements, however "right" or "wrong" they might be, about the war.

As *Apocalypse Now* was released in August 1979, a flurry of letters to the *New York Times* editor included this from a writer who was "in country" in 1974:

> The U.S. genre of Vietnam films that I've seen—*The Boys in Company C, Coming Home, The Deer Hunter*, and *Apocalypse*

* Cimino is typically, if too simply, credited with wrecking United Artists and putting a full stop to the golden age of New Hollywood auteurs with the excesses of his next film, *Heaven's Gate*.

> *Now*—all have one thing in common: they are made by Americans and they focus on the American point of view. There's nothing wrong with that. But I'm wondering if any American film on the subject of Vietnam will take the time to humanize our perceptions of the Vietnamese.

Fonda, then, had not been alone in thinking that somehow a camera should capture some sort of genuine introduction to the enemy.

It wouldn't happen soon in Hollywood, though, especially not once the revisionist blockbusters took hold. That era was inaugurated by *First Blood*, from, of all people, *Fun with Dick and Jane* director Ted Kotcheff. The 1982 crudity involved reactionary small-town sheriff Brian Dennehy hassling introverted vet Sylvester Stallone, whom Dennehy takes for a hippie. *First Blood* is fast food, sizzled down to ninety-three minutes. As John Rambo, Stallone has to do a lot and say very little. He talks mainly in his last agonized speech, wailing about the horrible treatment of soldiers, especially when they returned from Vietnam.*

"There *are* no friendly civilians!" Stallone blurts to Richard Crenna, the Green Beret who trained him in his extraordinary battle skills; the early 1980s, according to Jerry Lembcke in *The Spitting Image* and *Hanoi Jane*, is when the myth of protestors spitting on veterans began to spread. *First Blood*'s single-handed heroism made it a massive Reagan-era hit: one man against a messed-up world, wreaking cathartic, cartoonish havoc as he eludes capture by burrowing through a local mine, outmaneuvering two hundred assorted law enforcement personnel to blow up the town.

The success of *First Blood* spawned Rambo as a pop franchise (five movies through 2019's *Rambo: Last Blood*), quickly copied by martial artist Chuck Norris in the *Missing in Action* series. "In addition to liking Mr. Norris, the Rivoli [Theatre] audience also showed enthusiasm for the film's attitude toward Vietnamese soldiers and officials, who

* Gaylyn Studlar and David Desser noted in 1990 how the 1980s revisionist films slickly changed the subject: "'Were we right to fight in Vietnam?' has been replaced (displaced) by the question 'What is our obligation to the veterans of the war?' Responsibility to and validation of the veterans is not the same as validating our participation in the first place. Yet answering the second question mythically rewrites the answer to the first."

are depicted as no less unequivocally shifty, villainous, and deceitful as their stereotyped Japanese counterparts were in B-movies about World War II," *New York Times* critic Janet Maslin noted when the first *MIA* picture arrived in 1984.

Closer to reality, 1987's *The Hanoi Hilton* showed POWs enduring torture in the notorious North Vietnamese prison that held John McCain and others for years. But writer-director Lionel Chetwynd's picture includes this brief bit of right-wing red meat: a caricature of a female star, plainly a Fonda stand-in, cooperating with North Vietnamese officials and their propaganda goals.

"What had been virtually forgotten by the end of the seventies came back with a vengeance by the end of the eighties," Anderegg writes. "Vietnam films intent on justifying the war—*Rambo* (1985), *Hamburger Hill* (1987), *Hanoi Hilton* (1987), and the like—portrayed anti-war protest of any kind as little more than collaboration with the enemy."

Major directors would take more nuanced, prestigious shots at Vietnam through the decade—Stanley Kubrick in *Full Metal Jacket* (1987), Brian De Palma in *Casualties of War* (1989)—but nobody claimed the territory with more authority than Oliver Stone. In Stone's *Born on the Fourth of July* (1989), Ron Kovic tells his own story of serving in Vietnam, being wounded and paralyzed for life from the mid-chest down, and finally protesting the God-awful folly in full voice. Kovic cowrote the screenplay with director Stone, amplifying Kovic's 1976 memoir, an easy-to-gobble book that reads like it was written in a single angry afternoon.

Reversing the form of *Coming Home*, *Born on the Fourth of July* is more visceral than articulate—a wounded scream, not a persuasive journey. It's on the same mission as *Coming Home*, but its story is even more personal than Fonda's. It's literally Kovic's life. Kovic's antiwar position climaxes at the 1972 Republican National Convention in Miami, where he spoke his piece on national TV.

The movie is incredibly romantic as Tom Cruise, playing Kovic, sprints through the rain to dance with Kyra Sedgwick at the high school prom, and in beautifully silhouetted shots of soldiers in combat on the beach in Vietnam. (John Williams did the original music; the movie shares "My Girl" with the *Coming Home* soundtrack, though Ashby uses the craggy Rolling Stones version, while Stone opts for the silkier original by the Temptations.) Its testimony includes the squalor of the rat-infested Bronx VA hospital and, once Kovic moves back in with his parents, inebriated, the vulgar midnight shouting contests ("Penis! *Penis!*" Cruise screeches, agonized that his no longer works) disrupting the Kovics' otherwise quiet Long Island home.

The big set piece is the grotesque grappling in the Mexican desert between Tom Cruise's Kovic and cynical Willem Dafoe, a fellow Vietnam vet who is now lord of a Mexican tequila-and-hookers den. Dafoe grins an alligator smile at Cruise. He goads the younger veteran: "You ever have to kill a baby?"

These brooding, bitter expats have been kicked out of a taxi in the desert because of Dafoe's relentless rants. Dafoe and Cruise pry each other out of their wheelchairs and into the sand. Cruise says something about how their lives have catapulted way beyond anything *normal.*

Kovic has a guilty secret: he accidentally shot a fellow soldier. It happened in the immediate aftermath of an atrocity where his unit riddled a hut with bullets and killed an unarmed family. Stone contrasts slow-motion imagery of idyllic American flag–strewn parades with Kovic's punishing reality. His love scene is harrowing, not like *Coming Home.* It's a furious movie, enraged at the country's profound military misdirection. You cannot miss the point.

Like Fonda, Stone earned himself a platform and used it to make issue-oriented feature films that became cultural "talkers." His fertile run of must-see pictures stretched from *Salvador* in 1986 to *Nixon* in 1995, with *Wall Street*, *Talk Radio*, *JFK*, and *Natural Born Killers* among the ten fevered movies he directed that decade. Stone, like Michael Cimino, nursed a sensationalist streak; he picked up a screenwriting Oscar for the grueling American-guy-in-a-Turkish-prison drama *Midnight Express* during the year of *Coming Home* and *The Deer Hunter*, then cowrote *Conan the Barbarian* and penned *Scarface.* In 1985 he intersected with Cimino as a writer on Cimino's seething *Year of the Dragon*, with Mickey Rourke as a Dirty Harry cleaning up Chinatown.*

* The sensationalism extended to Stone's third Vietnam movie, 1993's *Heaven & Earth*, based on the story of Le Ly Hayslip. "This is a tale of extraordinarily melodramatic

Cinematically, though, Stone became a pundit, which is different from being an activist. His paranoid pictures were about interpretation, thriving on conspiratorial points of view. Fonda, decisively less polarizing during her late 1970s run, was about movements.

Stone's political bona fides began with *Salvador*, a small-scale, Vietnam-y look at American intervention in Central America. With *Platoon* only months later in 1986, Stone drew from his own tour in Vietnam. An infantryman (Charlie Sheen) is torn between two high-contrast sergeants, one a typical military brute (Tom Berenger), the other Christ-like and beneficent (Willem Dafoe). Stone's movie is knowing, realistic, and grand; swirling camerawork and Samuel Barber's elegiac Adagio for Strings ennoble the suffering. Inarguably, it was a major new entry in Hollywood's Vietnam gallery.

"What 'Platoon' does—better than I've ever seen before—is to show what it was like *being there*. What those men went through," Fonda told the *Los Angeles Times* in 1987. (She was careful, as usual, to express solidarity with vets while dutifully apologizing yet again for her Hanoi debacle.) She theorized that *Platoon* could be the middle part of a Vietnam trilogy, with *Coming Home* as the end, and who-knows-what as the beginning. "I'm still waiting for a movie that explains why we were there at all—why it all happened," she said.

Well: in 1998, Fonda would be one of the prime forces behind the HBO film adaptation of reporter Neil Sheehan's Pulitzer-winning Vietnam chronicle *A Bright Shining Lie*.

"John, the war's not about warriors anymore," says that movie's fictionalized journalist to John Paul Vann, the real-life subject of Sheehan's book. That comes near the movie's climax, as we grasp how early and acutely Vann saw where the American mistakes were. His tragedy—America's tragedy—was that he still couldn't resist trying, militarily, to get it right. "It's about children and women and rice paddies," says

---

hardship, involving rape, torture, disgrace, prostitution and a disastrous marriage to an American G.I., all heightened by the despoliation of the heroine's homeland," Canby noted on the picture's release. "His best direction is volatile, angry and muscular in ways that Ms. Hayslip's story, that of a resilient, long-suffering victim, simply cannot accommodate."

the journalist, sounding like the Fonda who made *Introduction to the Enemy*. "You know who told me that? *You* did."

The movie's closing text informs us that Vann was not counted among America's nearly sixty thousand fatalities, because his helicopter went down in a rainstorm. The last words on the screen report the estimate that over one million Vietnamese died in the war.

The acceptance of *Coming Home* did not decommission "Hanoi Jane." Reagan-era patriot fervor wedged it back open, and the Internet stokes the *traitor bitch* embers forever.

Still, *Coming Home* wrapped Fonda's decade of hazards, closing the Vietnam circle mournfully and triumphantly. Her definitive statement had been crafted at last. The activist artist was validated for good.

She shifted her focus to the present.

10

STAR, POWER

The China Syndrome

Why aren't we prepared?

—Gillian Steinberg, March 2020

Michael Douglas, producer and star of *The China Syndrome*, loved the thrust of the film for its menacing "monster" character: a malfunctioning nuclear power plant. Yet nuclear power is not the actual target of the taut muckraking drama.

Sure, the movie helped galvanize an international protest movement as the Three Mile Island accident panicked central Pennsylvania just two weeks after the jarringly timely movie opened in March 1979. And yes, the exhaustive tick-tock of the real-life accident's five crazed days, swiftly reconstructed by B. Drummond Ayres Jr. for the front page of the April 16 *New York Times*, "Three Mile Island: Notes from a Nightmare," still reads like an apocalyptic thriller:

> Inside the reactor, the fuel rods crack and bend severely as the heat builds higher and higher. It is 3:59 A.M. The unthinkable is beginning to happen in the bowels of one of this country's 72 nuclear reactors and no one realizes it. . . .
>
> Whether the officials are attempting at this point to put an optimistic face on the accident or whether they are simply telling all they know is to become a matter of considerable dispute. In

coming days, the company will release few details of the early hours of the crisis.

The Governor, Dick Thornburgh, is informed of the accident at 7:50 A.M. "I can't make much sense out of what Met Ed is reporting," he tells aides. "You can't make decisions about people's lives without solid facts. See if we can't get more information."

The aides try in vain. In the interim, civil defense officials begin, as best they can, to work up evacuation plans for the million or so people living within a 20-mile radius of Three Mile Island. Tentatively, they decide to rely on interstate routes, blocking off incoming lanes and feeding evacuees out to distant shopping malls, armories, and sports arenas.

There is not a great deal of confidence in the plans. A single wreck can seal off an escape route. The civil defense officials are dealing with an emergency that most never contemplated. . . .

Antinuclear protests break out in many United States cities, as well as in cities in Europe and Asia. Demonstrators play dead in front of a utility office in San Francisco. In Hanover, West Germany, 35,000 protestors chant, "We all live in Pennsylvania." Some supermarkets in Middle Atlantic cities post signs that say, "We don't sell Pennsylvania milk." . . .

Optimism is premature. In mid-afternoon, Met Ed workers are forced to dump thousands of gallons of mildly radioactive wastewater into the river to make room for overflow from the accident. The reactor is not cooling down as it should. . . .

At 11:15, President Carter calls the Governor. He has become deeply concerned about all the confusion and the inability of Federal officials to get solid information about what is happening. . . .

Perhaps 100,000 people have fled. Entire blocks are empty in Middletown and the police are under instructions to shoot any looters—who never materialize. In Goldsboro, 500 yards across the Susquehanna from the reactor, only a mongrel wanders Main Street. "It's a ghost town," says Mayor Kenneth Myers.

Twenty miles away, at an evacuation center in Hershey, 6-year-old Abby Baumbach is confused. "Something's wrong with the air," she says. "My mommy told me it could kill me."

In the decade of the disaster movie—your *Airports*, *Hindenburgs*, and *Poseidon Adventures*, your *Hurricanes*, *Earthquakes*, and *Towering Infernos*—worst-case scenarios are popcorn lures, and *The China Syndrome* surely aims to scare. Director James Bridges's style is studiously realistic, so when he plunges audiences into the blackout darkness and red emergency lights of a power plant going bad, Klaxons blaring, it's alarming. The threat's scale swells when a scientist pivots toward maverick cameraman Richard Adams (Michael Douglas) and L.A. TV personality Kimberly Wells (Jane Fonda). Painting a doomsday picture, the scientist explains what the term "China syndrome" means, summed up in yet another frightful word for the Cold War / Atomic Age / mutually assured destruction generation: *meltdown*.

Again, though, *The China Syndrome* does *not* say *No nukes!* What the plot says is *No lies*. Even though Fonda and costar Jack Lemmon were firmly anti-nuke, their movie does not assert that nuclear power is inherently unsafe. Instead, it argues that *profit-minded corporate executives cannot be trusted*.

That also goes, the movie adds, for the ratings whores running newsrooms.

Spring 2020 delivered another invisible, fast-moving public health threat, and it hardly seems accidental that on April 4, 2020, forty-one years after Three Mile Island and with the country locked down hard because "something's wrong with the air," Washington, DC's PBS channel chose to broadcast *The China Syndrome*.*

It remains an essential movie to see at any time—a lean, clean tension machine. And it boasts Jane Fonda, in her Hollywood story-driving prime, an on-the-mark Cassandra delivering her definitive, clarion *Jane Fonda* acting turn.

* The following Saturday night the station offered another Fonda's Atomic Age apocalypse: *Fail Safe*, the sober side of *Dr. Strangelove*. Henry Fonda is the American president in Sidney Lumet's stark 1964 picture (delayed and released months after *Strangelove* due to a lawsuit by *Strangelove* director Stanley Kubrick); after US bombers follow an errant code and attack Moscow, Fonda, grim with tragedy in this spartan black-and-white exercise, chooses to destroy New York City to prevent all-out nuclear war. Such was the dreadful spring 2020 pandemic mood.

The China Syndrome (1979)

Fonda and her IPC right arm Bruce Gilbert wanted to develop a film about Karen Silkwood, the whistleblowing employee of a nuclear fuel rods plant who was killed in a suspicious 1974 car crash. But they couldn't get the rights.

Michael Douglas, by 1976 an Oscar-winning producer for *One Flew over the Cuckoo's Nest*, had a script by Mike Gray about a nuclear plant crisis. Douglas and IPC joined forces, under the aegis of Columbia Pictures (Roz Heller was credited with officially making the match), and there is an evocative scene with Fonda and Douglas, viewed in a two-shot, sitting across the table from the powerful news executives, begging to be allowed to air the story of the nuclear accident they've just caught on film.

The execs fret about being sued for possessing unauthorized footage from inside the plant. "Bullshit!" the shaggy-haired, bearded Douglas bellows; he's a handsome rebel. Kimberly nonverbally urges diplomacy with their bosses. "Don't kick me under the table!" Richard snaps at her, then continues: "It was an accident, and we could have been killed!"

The irony: Fonda and Douglas did not have to beg to tell the story of this film. They were emerging as formidable players, both descended from the final generation of old studio system stars. Michael's dad was Kirk Douglas, maybe best known for the 1960 Stanley Kubrick epic *Spartacus*, and Kirk produced the first film Michael starred in, 1971's *Summertree*, a small anti-Vietnam war picture that follows Michael's *Graduate*-like character as he falls through the cracks of student deferment, gets drafted, and is almost immediately killed in battle. (That appealingly understated adaptation, with an upbeat, lively young Michael reprising his off-Broadway performance, is from a 1967 Pulitzer-nominated play by Ron Cowen, who would go on to develop the Emmy-winning AIDS drama *An Early Frost* and the Showtime series *Queer as Folk*.) *China Syndrome* writing credit would eventually be shared by Mike Gray, T. S. Cook—an emerging screenwriter with a background in tech writing—and director James Bridges, as Bridges made the most disciplined movie of a career that included *The Paper Chase* (1973) and *Urban Cowboy* (1980). But Hollywood scions Douglas and Fonda were calling the shots.

"Jane was one of the first to edit out any heavy statements that crept into the script," Bridges told the *New York Times*. "We all agreed the picture should be, first of all, an entertainment, to reach the biggest audience possible. I'd write shrill preachy things, like a dream one character had of a nuclear holocaust with all the birds dying, and Jane would chop them out."

In the same article, Douglas admitted that getting backing for the picture was a chore. "Awfully talky and awfully technical," the moneymen told him. Yet the realistic talk and patient technical explanations are the movie's core strengths, enlightening viewers while driving suspense. Even more than *Coming Home*, the information-rich *China Syndrome* immediately feels *purposeful.*

A careful, detailed fifteen-minute set piece at the power station is precision-engineered as a routine tour gets shaken up. It starts casually, when the movie is only in its seventh minute. "This is a rare opportunity to see inside a nuclear power plant," Kimberly says to the TV camera,

Fonda's Kimberly Wells reports from inside a nuclear power plant in *The China Syndrome*. *Album / Alamy*

abuzz with the "scoop"; the guided tour on an ordinary day is another in her line of puff pieces. She's standing in front of jumbo pipes, speaking above the heavy turbine thrum, sounding impressed as she delivers statistics fed to her about how the facility can power a city of three-quarters of a million people.

Bridges catches everything in the process—the TV camera, the soundman, Kimberly, and the smiling company PR flack guiding the tour, with everyone in hard hats. The long sequence accurately portrays the genial, canned quality of this sort of reporting via supervised access. Douglas rings true—loose and snarky as the freelance cameraman with a built-in suspicion of nukes. So does Fonda, personable yet guarded as Kimberly. Kimberly is the face of the TV station, at once nervously responsible and gingerly ambitious. She's careful not to step out of line.

Then the visit becomes an adventure, with the building quaking and the engineers freaking out behind glass. The accident lasts for eight minutes of screen time, with Kimberly and Richard locked in an observation area over the control room. Equipment and procedures are diplomatically explained to the TV team, but we hear things they don't hear when Bridges swings through the control room to Jack Lemmon, playing shift supervisor Jack Godell.

Godell will emerge as the pivotal whistleblower; the story is actually about him. The movie needs Kimberly, though, to broadcast it.

Bridges keeps his camera moving through the incident, tracking and panning, never edgy or jumpy. He is watchful, instructive, showing how the complex works, stoking curiosity. The production designer is George Jenkins, who worked with director Alan J. Pakula and cinematographer Gordon Willis on their sinister *Klute–The Parallax View–All the President's Men* "paranoia trilogy"; for research, Douglas got access to the Trojan nuclear facility in Oregon, and Jenkins built an imposing-looking control room based on Trojan and other online plants around the United States. Bridges shoots the control room with lots of wide and medium shots, eyeing the gauges and the flashing monitors—they're called "enunciators," the PR flack tells Kimberly and Richard—and watching the engineers flail through the crisis.

Equally critical to the movie's high-tech ambience, and established right off the bat, is the fat-free dialogue and the mission-driven acting.

Characters are their *jobs*, period. Just as Fonda and Douglas are energetic, cynical newspeople, Lemmon and the folksy Wilford Brimley are long-experienced engineers. Both actors are believable as unpretentious workingmen; Lemmon and Brimley (in his first major role) are fluent with the tech as they tinker under an extraordinary hood. Their rapport is no-nonsense. We read the depth of the predicament through them. So do Kimberly and Richard.

Lemmon prays for a water level indicator to rise over the reactor's overheating core. "Please, God, cover it," Lemmon murmurs, his face in full close-up, sweating. "*Cover it!*" Bridges watches for seventy-five seconds without another word. The soundtrack thrums low, punctuated by high beeps. Helplessly, hopefully, viewers hang on each tremor of the life-or-death gauges and dials.

Robert Redford apparently turned down the part of Godell, which makes sense. At the beginning and at the end of the movie, Lemmon's agitation as the plant acts up is more apoplectic than anything you can imagine from Redford.

Back in 1971, Lemmon had narrated the first TV documentary on nuclear plant safety, called *Powers That Be*. Eight years of litigation followed between California's Pacific Gas and Electric and the L.A. TV station KNBC. By 1979, Lemmon's Emmy and duPont Award–winning friend and colleague Don Widener, the writer and producer of the documentary, long mired in the lawsuits, told the *Washington Post* that he had been blacklisted ever since. So Lemmon, in addition to his suspicion of nuclear safety, maybe had an axe to grind.

Fonda, in a featurette on the DVD, described Lemmon's position as "feeling this was an unforgiving technology, and we have to do everything we can to expose the dangers of it." That is where Lemmon's deep, troubled performance is pitched. For Fonda, working with the anti-nuke Lemmon—drawing on bone-deep conviction and lived experience through the PG&E suit that buried his documentary—was like acting in *Julia* with the antiwar Redgrave.

Middle-American anxiety is one of Lemmon's gifts: think of him stammering through the deceptions of *The Apartment*, sprinting bandy-legged in a dress through *Some Like It Hot*, jabbering through Neil Simon comedies and winning the Best Actor Oscar as the addled businessman in *Save the Tiger* (1973). His performance as the rational, scientific Godell includes physical eruptions, and in the soundless film that Douglas's cameraman records on the sly, Lemmon's control room freak-out is wild. Trying to prevent a catastrophe, he's terrified, and it shows.

That makes Redford impossible to picture as Godell. Redford displays concern but keeps his cool. Lemmon lets go. He melts down.

"The best role he [Lemmon] has had in a long time," Vincent Canby would note in his admiring *New York Times* review.

As in *Tout Va Bien*, Fonda plays a reporter—a redhead, her tribute to the iconic comic strip character Brenda Starr, but also a response to a TV trend that she and IPC producer Bruce Gilbert examined. Market studies prompted TV stations to package "personalities" in ratings-friendly combinations, with styled-up women like Fonda's Kimberly Wells relegated to petty tasks: lite featurettes, "happy talk." At the time, Fonda noted that most women at L.A. TV news desks dyed their hair, guided toward—or ordered about—how they "ought" to look by male honchos.

"Red hair was a good idea," we hear the off-camera male producers murmuring as they watch Kimberly prepare for a sprightly stand-up spot about singing telegrams. "We talked about cutting it. . . . She'll do what we tell her."

This pad-your-bra, break-your-jaw nonsense was what Fonda encountered the moment she broke into Hollywood almost twenty years earlier. "These were personal issues to me," Fonda wrote in *My Life So Far*.

TV news is the movie's frame; Bridges begins and ends with a shot of two TV monitors and Fonda's Kimberly on camera, drawing adrenaline from the deadlines and live performances. The first four minutes are an almost real-time stand-up of Fonda's Kimberly: she takes her on-camera position, microphone in hand, then she preps the spot, shoots the spot, and hustles off to the next location.

The movie also sends up the medium's inanity, the babble of voices on camera and off. "Pete, what did you do the last time someone had a birthday?" Kimberly begins the singing telegram segment, fielding the toss from oily anchorman Pete Martin (Stan Bohrman). On another monitor we see Pete leering at a birthday belly-dance-gram. In the control room we see executives pleased by the sappy show.

It's not the wild, savage satire of Paddy Chayefsky's 1976 "I'm as mad as hell and I'm not going to take this anymore" film *Network*; the tone is too realistic for that. The super-sober *China Syndrome* even forgoes music almost entirely (in high contrast to *Coming Home* and its wall-to-wall rock 'n' roll). Again, this about people at work. The soundtrack growls softly with the workplace noises of news hubbub and nuke rumble.

Bridges and Fonda, who developed the Kimberly Wells character together, capture the cadence of daily reporting, the fleet vitality and agreeable, flexible personality. More than once we see Fonda zipping through halls and toward company cars with her arms full of notes, bags, a cup of coffee, and a bite of food. Her high-octane metabolism is on the mark.

Fonda also takes care to illustrate the challenge of a woman fighting her way out of commercials, onto TV news, toward the respectability of serious reporting—all while accepting that her looks are an inescapable factor.

"What are you going to do with the film?" Kimberly asks station head Don Jacovich (Peter Donat). They are at a party, on a couch, by a cozy fire. (More on fires in a moment.)

"Not to worry your pretty head about," Jacovich condescends.

Jacovich tells Kimberly she's good for ratings. Fonda leans in, purses her lips, and puts a purr in her voice.

"So Don," Kimberly flirts. "Let me do some hard news."

He declines, keeping her in her supposed lane.

The encounter does not feel like it will get sexual; despite his jock-itch name, Jacovich is not skeevy Pete Martin, the anchor who waves a vegetable at Kimberly and makes a lewd remark. But this dialogue is on the edge, and Kimberly plainly feels compelled to please in a "feminine" way. The Jacovich dictums illustrate a demeaning standard that's still in play a half century later, as pointedly explored in the 2019 docudrama *Bombshell.* "Nobody wants to watch a middle-aged woman sweat her way through menopause!" Fox News chairman and CEO Roger Ailes (John Lithgow) snaps at on-air host Gretchen Carlson (Nicole Kidman). Carlson has just broadcast a segment about makeup while not wearing makeup on camera, making a point about objectification. Beginning with the notorious 2015 Republican debate exchange between Fox's Megyn Kelly and loose cannon candidate Donald Trump, with Kelly calling out Trump's systematic misogyny (and Trump griping the next day about Kelly's tough questions, with "blood coming out of her eyes, blood coming out of her wherever"), *Bombshell* spotlights the Fox News culture of exploiting women's bared legs and bottled blondeness.

"It's a visual medium," Ailes murmurs as he asks women to "twirl" for him in his office.

"There's a reason for clear desks," Charlize Theron, as Kelly, says directly to us, narrating the workplace hazards. Ailes commands a female reporter, "We need you in a shorter dress," and he barks in the control room, "Wide shot. Wider! I want to see her goddamn legs! Why the fuck do you think I hired her?"

By 2016, Ailes was removed from the network, denounced at last for longstanding sexual harassment. In *Bombshell*'s coda, Kidman's Gretchen Carlson—who initiated the decisive legal action against Ailes—narrates one of the movie's takeaways. "Roger always said everyone in television only has one real job: to be likable," Carlson says. "Well, I don't care if you like me. Only that you believe me."

That's the transition that Fonda's carefully drawn Wells makes—no thanks to the Jacoviches above her.

Fonda shows Wells maturing as the "greatness" of high-impact reporting is thrust upon her. Trying to track down cameraman Richard, who has stolen back his contraband footage from the skittish station, Kimberly instead bumps into Lemmon's Godell in a bar near the reactor. Godell mistrusts reporters. Journalists, he says, seem to think "the only good news is bad news, and oh God, they give our industry a very, very rough time."

Kimberly pursues it: "Don't you think that reporters serve a public function? Woodward, Bernstein?"

"Well why don't you ask me a public function question and I'll tell you whether I do or I don't."

It's like watching someone try on a new jacket, the way Fonda shows Kimberly venturing into a serious new role. Kimberly doesn't yet trust her own credibility; the whole bar has already toasted her as a lite celebrity. Acting in tentative stages, she risks the word "accident."

"I'm using that word very deliberately," Kimberly explains, "because I think a good investigative reporter would do that."

Godell explains that nuclear plants are designed for all eventualities: "Why, hell, we've got a quality control that's only equaled by NASA. . . . Every single thing is checked, is double checked, is rechecked. Everything."

Kimberly presses: "You haven't answered the question."

Godell is taken aback. Fonda's Kimberly purses her lips slightly, professionally pleased with herself.

As in *Coming Home*, Fonda recedes as the plot tightens on:

- Godell, alarmed as he learns about faked inspections.
- Experts vetting Richard's accident footage, with an engineer saying gravely, "I may be wrong, but I would say you're probably lucky to be alive. For that matter, I think we might say the same for the rest of Southern California."
- Hector the soundman getting rammed off the highway en route to a public safety hearing; he was delivering evidence of the plant's safety cover-up (faked radiograph inspections of the pump support structure's faulty welding). Hector's crash intentionally evokes the circumstances of Karen Silkwood's death.
- Godell again, also chased on the highway, taking refuge at the plant, grabbing a security guard's gun, clearing the control room and demanding a live TV interview to explain why the reactor needs to be shut down *now*.*

As an interviewer, Kimberly still isn't nimble enough to control the frantic Godell on live TV. He rambles, too complicated to make sense

* It is a weakness, a narrative tic, that this is the second straight Fonda joint that crests via a wild man wielding a gun. It plays much better the second time around.

to viewers needing clarity. But after a SWAT team breaks in and shoots Jack dead right in front of her, Kimberly's focus crystallizes.

Most of the remaining minutes are Fonda's, and they are bravura—flinching at the cold-blooded PR spin, fighting to the front of the reporter scrum, demanding answers, refusing to allow a lie to take root. Kimberly is like Lilly in *Julia*: conscience-driven but in over her head, then forced, under extreme pressure, to sink or swim. (Sally in *Coming Home* is not as required to act, which is why she freezes in a helping/helpless position at that film's gunpoint climax.)

Fonda does not let Kimberly get bigger than she actually is. The movie never says whether Kimberly ever actually trained as a journalist; all we hear is her throwaway comment about previously shooting commercials. With the long red Brenda Starr hair, she looks like a shampoo commercial. But Kimberly refines her craft—her very *self*, in this movie of workers and core truths—on the fly.

And there she is, fully her actor-activist self at last in a big, mission-driven Hollywood picture: *Jane Fonda*.

Fonda's newly ferocious Kimberly elbows to the front of the scrum, fights through tears, and fires off a dozen questions in less than a minute, each on point, dominating a live TV close-up filled with the faces of the plant's tragedy. It's a theatrical and activist tour de force.

"Why was he killed?" "Who ordered the SWAT squad into the control room?" "Was Jack Godell emotionally disturbed?" Kimberly knows Godell isn't nuts; her knowledge is power. Fonda's face is a ribbon of sorrow and rage. Godell's murder must be explained.

Her authoritative questions, posed with passion, command silence from the throng. Kimberly presses her advantage. "Mr. Gibson [the PR flack] said he was drinking. Is it true?" "What did he say to you, Mr. Spindler?" "Do you agree with that? Should it be shut down?"

Brimley's Spindler mumbles that it's not his place to say.

Citizen Jane spanks the truth into view. "If it's not your place, Mr. Spindler, whose is it?" Kimberly insists. "Mr. Gibson, if there's nothing to hide, *let him speak*." Brimley's Spindler defends Godell and implicates the plant, beginning Brimley's fruitful feature career as a BS-free teller of earthy truths.* The focus swings back to Fonda for the finale, and Bridges shows her on dual monitors, still airing live in real time, with brief cut-ins of "Come on, Kimberly," watching her process the moment, calm her emotions, and compose her report. Brushing tears from her eyes, she delivers.

"I met Jack Godell two days ago, and I'm convinced that what happened tonight was not the act of a drunk or a crazy man. Jack Godell was about to present evidence that he believed showed that this plant should be shut down." The voice quavers: "I'm sorry I'm not very objective." The subjectivity is OK. It's *honest.*

Kimberly's conclusion is the activist picture's grace note: "Let's just hope it doesn't end here."

"Not the least bit fair-minded about nuclear power," Richard Schickel wrote in *Time*, and that almost seems true.

The power company execs are deceptive and sinister, only wanting to make the problem go away so they don't lose half a million dollars per day. We see them in a leisurely early scene, post-accident, sitting around a large round conference table after hours, a jumbo chandelier glowing overhead and the L.A. skyline twinkling beyond a giant plate glass window. (Bridges is mischievously sensitive to energy sources throughout the picture; Kimberly's tête-à-têtes with Jacovich and Godell both take place next to small indoor fires, and the corrupt inspector tosses Godell's incriminating radiographs into a small barrel fire.)

Yet the film never contradicts Godell when he insists to Kimberly and to Richard, "The system works." Nuclear technology is not the villain. What drives Godell to act are the corporate cover-ups.

* See the climax of another journalism flick, the savvy *Absence of Malice* (1981): Brimley strolls in near the end, untangling frame-ups and hijacking the Paul Newman–Sally Field picture for ten juicy minutes. Brimley's ethos was so formidable that Quaker Oats hired him as the spokesman who immortalized the line "The right thing to do, and a tasty way to do it."

"Basically, the movie's intended as an attack on greed, not on nuclear energy," Fonda said before the picture's release. "If I intended to attack nuclear energy, I would have made a documentary." That sounds disingenuous, of course. Inarguably, the picture rings a frightening bell, and in the coming months, Fonda would headline No Nukes rallies.

Still, in the *Times*, Canby had no trouble reading the bottom line. "*The China Syndrome* is less about laws of physics than about public and private ethics," he wrote. "The film isn't only concerned with safety procedures, but also with the ethics of a certain kind of journalism that packages news that won't offend." He judged it to be a "smashingly effective, very stylish suspense melodrama."

Pauline Kael had complained that Fonda hammed it up in *California Suite*, released three months before *China Syndrome*: "So tensely eager to act that she puts out too much." But that wing-flapping Neil Simon–Herbert Ross farce—a brand extension of Simon's Manhattan-set 1968 play / 1971 movie *Plaza Suite* and hands down the least satisfying Hollywood picture Fonda made in the late '70s—made nearly everyone in its all-star cast look bad: Walter Matthau as a mild-mannered husband caught by wife Elaine May with a young prostitute in his bed, Bill Cosby and Richard Pryor as bickering buddies, and Fonda as a frosty New York–based *Newsweek* editor vying with the soulful, L.A.-based Alan Alda as divorcées debating where their teenage daughter should live. (As an anxious Oscar-nominated actress and her blithe bisexual husband, Maggie Smith and Michael Caine brought off a Noël Coward routine with enough acerbic flair that Smith won an actual Supporting Actress Oscar.)* The unsatisfying crux of Fonda's character: both professionally and in her relationship with Alda, she is troublingly withholding, hard, *masculine*. (Alda calls her "Sir.") As a mother, she is humane and vulnerable; the insinuation is *feminine*.

To say that much about this role is to say more than Fonda said about it in her 579-page *My Life So Far*. To quote what she wrote, in its entirety: "I had to get into shape for my next movie, *California Suite*, in which I had to appear in a bikini."

* Smith topped Penelope Milford in *Coming Home*, Meryl Streep in *The Deer Hunter*, Maureen Stapleton in *Interiors*, and Dyan Cannon in *Heaven Can Wait*.

Kael was right to gripe about Simon's brittle writing, but in fact Fonda's acting was continuing to deepen. In her first two IPC projects, her performances benefited from real-world experience, from hard information, and from her larger sense of purpose. "I've learned how hard it is to put movies together," Fonda said in 1978. But at forty, she already sensed the window closing:

> I will only be in a position of power in Hollywood—a position where I can do the kind of films that I want to do—for a while longer. Then it will be over, essentially. I can become a character actress, but I'm not going to have clout. So I want to use this period of time to do as much as possible. I want to milk it, I really do.

The quotes come from a book called *Creative Difference: Profiles of Hollywood Dissidents*, written by members of a short-lived (1974–77) Hollywood collective called the Socialist Media Group. Fonda and Haskell Wexler were portrayed as role models, because their films were examples of how progressive content could be channeled into mainstream moviemaking. For Fonda, acting and activism were finally proving to be a rich two-way street.

"The three stars are splendid," Canby wrote to cap his review of *The China Syndrome*, "but maybe Miss Fonda is just a bit more than that. Her performance is not that of an actress in a star's role, but that of an actress creating a character that happens to be major within the film. She keeps getting better and better."

In *Newsweek*, David Ansen—who complained that "the political drama is outrageously black and white"—almost exactly echoed Canby. "There's a new simplicity in her acting that impresses all the more because it isn't calculated to impress," Ansen declared. "It's a pleasure to watch a superb actress continually refining her art."

Karen Silkwood's story got made as a 1983 movie directed by Mike Nichols, his style sanded down to a flat, workmanlike finish when compared to his high-moxie late 1960s breakthroughs *Who's Afraid of Virginia Woolf?*, *The Graduate*, and *Catch-22. Silkwood* is defined by Nichols's dry, respectful eye for rural Oklahoma life at home and work. Nothing stands out except for the harsh decontamination showers at the plant . . . and Meryl Streep.

Streep is hyperactive as the mischievous/antic/scattered Karen Silkwood, whose personality steals the show. The movie doesn't lean into the issue of worker protection at the Kerr-McGee fuel rod pellet plant where Silkwood works until seventy-nine minutes in; *Harlan County U.S.A.* this is not. (Barbara Kopple's cinema verité 1976 Best Documentary winner ran only 103 minutes chronicling a long, violent labor standoff in Kentucky coal country.) Nor is it the determined pro-union *Norma Rae* (1979), though Silkwood has a fling with a labor organizer played by Ron Silver (as did *Norma Rae*'s worker Sally Field with labor organizer Ron Leibman). Because Nichols and Streep focus on a warts-and-all portrait of Silkwood, and since shifty, complicated acting was Streep's hallmark in these *Holocaust* / *Kramer vs. Kramer* / *The French Lieutenant's Woman* / *Sophie's Choice* years (Molly Haskell would write that Streep was quickly stereotyped as the actor who can't be stereotyped), attention is lavished on the roller coasters of Karen's relationships with beau Kurt Russell and lesbian housemate Cher, and on Karen's relationships with coworkers as, for instance, she pinballs around the workplace break room, shrugging her shoulders with showy boredom, annoyingly pinching bites from everyone's lunches.

In *China Syndrome*, nobody has a personal life. "I love that plant," Godell tells Kimberly and Richard. "That's my whole life." We believe him: He's home. He lives alone.

Kimberly's apartment is empty too, except for her giant pet turtle and bulky answering machine. Richard, of course, is his cause and his camera. The characters are their social-professional function, period. Only Spindler has a spouse, briefly seen; she's with him at the bar near the plant, and they scurry off together when Godell starts talking to the reporter. Spindler doesn't understand his civic responsibility until after Godell gets killed.

"*Whose place is it?*" Kimberly demands in the aftermath.

The worker's duty, the citizen's duty—this gets thrust upon Streep's Silkwood too, reluctantly. But where *The China Syndrome* detonates, *Silkwood* sputters. Its ending is cautiously legalistic.

Mark Harris, in his Nichols biography, notes the rarity at the time of actually naming a company such as Kerr-McGee in a movie and the hassles of fighting off its legal challenges. In the finale, Karen glances with alarm at headlights in her rearview mirror, then we see the wrecked car. On-screen text then declares that nobody knows for sure what happened.

The admirable movie certainly doesn't feel as ambiguous as that. Silkwood, who died in 1974, was well fixed in the public mind as a martyr to the anti-nuke cause.* Yet unlike *The China Syndrome*, the psychologically subtle *Silkwood* rarely acts like a social justice project.

Even so, it added to the radioactive image of nuclear power as a threat. Is that portrait unfair? The *New York Times* fact-checked *China Syndrome* with scientists even *before* Three Mile Island. It largely passed muster, and the story noted that the industry was already reeling because of "growing political opposition."

The author of the article, headlined Nuclear Experts Debate "The China Syndrome," was David Burnham—the same journalist Karen Silkwood was driving to meet when she died.

The climate crisis has prompted a reconsideration of nuclear power as a clean, sustainable energy source for a planet on the brink. Representative Alexandria Ocasio-Cortez (D-NY) and Senator Bernie Sanders (I-VT), champions of the Green New Deal, have tempered stances that used to be automatic on the left, stopping short of a full No Nukes policy. Scientists and engineers increasingly advocate for nuclear power, refuting the old scare tactics of activists and filmmakers.

* Newsman Pete Hamill, reviewing a Silkwood biography in 1981, called her story "a vivid case of life imitating bad art: soap opera in its early scenes, melodrama for the finale," while Nichols wrote a letter to the *New York Times* after an editorial questioned whether his feature film of her recent history somehow amounted to reckless journalism.

"It's often said that with climate change, those who know the most are the most frightened," psychologist Steven Pinker wrote, "but with nuclear power, those who know the most are the least frightened."

In 2007, *Freakonomics* authors Stephen J. Dubner and Steven D. Levitt wrote a *New York Times* op-ed headlined THE JANE FONDA EFFECT, even-handedly suggesting that the pop success of *The China Syndrome* chilled nuclear power to the public's detriment, chucking the energy industry backward into dirty, expensive coal. Despite that lingering black eye, Dubner and Levitt contended that nukes were poised to make a comeback.

"But," they concluded, "it may all depend on what kind of thrillers Hollywood has in the pipeline."

The China Syndrome would not have been so industry-chilling, of course, without the disturbing reality of Three Mile Island. And what was in the *industry* pipeline, just four years after the Dubner-Levitt op-ed, was a devastating tsunami washing into Japan and the catastrophe at the Fukushima Daiichi nuclear plant.

In April 2019, Pinker teamed up with political scientist Joshua S. Goldstein and nuclear engineer Staffan A. Qvist—authors of the 2019 book *A Bright Future: How Some Countries Have Solved Climate Change and the Rest Can Follow*—for the *Times* op-ed "Nuclear Power Can Save the World." The argument:

> In 60 years of nuclear power, only three accidents have raised public alarm: Three Mile Island in 1979, which killed no one; Fukushima in 2011, which killed no one (many deaths resulted from the tsunami and some from a panicked evacuation near the plant); and Chernobyl in 1986, the result of extraordinary Soviet bungling, which killed 31 in the accident and perhaps several thousand from cancer, around the same number killed by coal emissions *every day*. (Even if we accepted recent claims that Soviet and international authorities covered up tens of thousands of Chernobyl deaths, the death toll from 60 years of nuclear power would still equal about one month of coal-related deaths.)
>
> Nuclear power plants cannot explode like nuclear bombs, and they have not contributed to weapons proliferation, thanks

> to robust international controls: 24 countries have nuclear power but not weapons, while Israel and North Korea have nuclear weapons but not power. . . .
>
> Opinions are also driven by our cultural and political tribes. Since the late 1970s, when No Nukes became a signature cause of the Green movement, sympathy to nuclear power became, among many environmentalists, a sign of disloyalty if not treason.
>
> Despite these challenges, psychology and politics can change quickly. As the enormity of the climate crisis sinks in and the hoped-for carbon savings from renewables don't add up, nuclear can become the new green. Protecting the environment and lifting the developing world out of poverty are progressive causes. And the millennials and Gen Z's might rethink the sacred values their boomer parents have left unexamined since the Doobie Brothers sang at the 1979 No Nukes concert.

Weeks later, though, the alarming 2019 HBO miniseries *Chernobyl* told the story of the 1986 USSR disaster, piling onto the dominant image of nuclear accident as the ultimate horror show, the last word in man-made nightmares.

The massive-scaled production looks radioactive: the dominant color is noxious bile green, lit by dim light from weak fluorescent fixtures or dead gray sky. We see the consequences of exposure to radioactivity in "cooked" faces, sudden rampant bleeding, projectile vomiting, and skinless patients decaying alive. The miniseries starts with the accident and becomes a procedural about containing damage as radioactivity spews widely. (Almost four decades later Chernobyl is a thousand-square-mile "exclusion zone," still largely de-peopled; tours were available, disrupted by the 2020s war with Russia but as of 2025 still a facet of Ukraine's economic hopes.)

Only in its final hour does *Chernobyl* get to the trial, finally exposing the cause of the bizarre explosion that blew the roof off Reactor 4. As in *The China Syndrome*, it was not the science that went wrong, it was the management. Flaws discovered in the 1970s—namely, that graphite-tipped boron control rods initially accelerate fission rather than slowing it down—were concealed. That hidden fact magnified the mistakes of a pigheaded manager, one of several who made ruinous decisions under bureaucratic pressure. The Soviet Communist regime was as corrupt in its way as *The China Syndrome*—basing its plot points on verifiable incidents to that date—showed capitalist managers to be in theirs.

Capitalists lie to hide cheap, risky choices. Communists lied for the same reason, and to promote a propagandistic image of infallible greatness. Among other qualities, *Chernobyl* draws a stark portrait of the Cold War–era USSR's inflexible power structure, dependent upon a national identity of satisfying its people's needs reliably and competently, in all circumstances.

"What you're proposing," Boris Shcherbina (the real-life bureaucrat tasked with managing the Chernobyl disaster) says to Ulana Khomyuk (a composite figure based on numerous scientists who hurled themselves into the crisis), "is that Legasov"—Valery Legasov, the real-life Soviet scientist who emerged as a whistleblower—"humiliate a nation that is obsessed with not being humiliated."

Cover-ups, the weary comrades acknowledge among themselves, are a way of life. *The way the world works*, goes their refrain.

And so, by the end of 2019, Carolyn Kormann studied Fukushima eight years after its disaster and asked in a *New Yorker* headline, Is Nuclear Power Worth the Risk? Kormann adds up the pluses and minuses but concludes with a quote that starkly echoes Fonda's paraphrase of Jack Lemmon's view, that nuclear power is "an unforgiving technology": "As Eric Schlosser, a journalist who has written extensively about nuclear weapons and risk, told me, ultimately, with a technology that complicated and powerful, 'We don't know what the fuck we are doing.'"

Can nuclear power sceptics really be expected to change their tune when corporate and political leaders keep lying? *The China Syndrome* in the age of coronavirus amplified the question.

"I don't feel confident in our politicians to know, or listen to, the right answers," quarantined Bronx high school teacher Gillian Steinberg wrote in the March 29, 2020, *Washington Post Magazine*, in a first-person essay about coping with the sudden global pandemic. "So much of the political response seems haphazard and uncertain; we saw this coming, so why aren't we prepared?"

The *Washington Post* front-page headlines of April 5—a typical day that ghastly spring—added wood to her outcry's fire: Warlike Efforts from Ford, GM May Come Too Late; Once Again, Government Is Caught Unprepared; and—the banner—70 Days of Denial, Delays and Dysfunction.

The following day came another front-page headline about a Chicago anesthesiologist reporting from a hospital: "You're Basically Right Next to the Nuclear Reactor."

"I don't take responsibility at all," President Trump declared in March 2020, speaking not in his arena-rattling Huey P. Long roar, for public gatherings of any size were *over* in America and most of the world, but instead intoning in his camera-practiced Don Corleone *You're fired* murmur.

Fonda, in her iconic moment from Aaron Sorkin's HBO drama *The Newsroom*, portrays responsibility differently. Fonda plays Leona Lansing, a media mogul in the mold of Fonda's ex-husband, CNN founder Ted Turner, and toward the end of season 2 her network has to retract a story about US military abuses in Pakistan because the lead journalist "cooked" an interview—fudged an unnamed military leader's quote. The network president (played by Sam Waterston) feels he must resign, along with the *News Night* executive producer (Emily Mortimer) and anchor (Jeff Daniels).

But that's pro forma, *performative*. Leona won't have it. Her staff did *right*. She will *defend* them. The rogue journalist who cooked the interview: *He* will go down. *He's* the one who cheated.

It's a diva performance from Fonda, flipped from Kimberly Wells, now atop the news power pyramid, swanning in from a gala screening of the latest James Bond movie wearing a formfitting black gown, sheer at the shoulders with fancy black tendrils snaking toward her neck and sparkly earrings dangling like chandeliers. Leona prowls the conference room like a lion. Her subordinates freeze. Chin lifted, hands on hips, flippant, outraged, defiant, this titan of industry nobly speechifies (in an un–*China Syndrome* way) about how the network loses money but makes her *proud*.*

* Sidebar on speeches: Sorkin, whose triumphs include repurposing Harper Lee's American classic *To Kill a Mockingbird* for Broadway in 2018 with Jeff Daniels as Atticus

Waterston tries to snap her into the bleak reality of the moment: "Leona! We don't have the trust of the public anymore!"

Fonda's pause is brief. Then she roars that command:

"Get it back!"

The screen goes black. The imperative resonates. It's the last word.

In the too-real world of pandemics and nuclear accidents, the stakes are unforgiving. Fonda's *China Syndrome* was adamant: There is no alternative for those in power. Get trust back.

Finch, has made a living writing idealistic speeches. But critics somehow love to hate a nicely scripted speech.

"Even today, the Big Speech, pounding in the message with a sledgehammer, often spoils political movies," Terry Christensen asserted in his *Reel Politics: American Political Movies from Birth of a Nation to Platoon*. "Film is still a visual medium, and wordiness still defeats it."

On the contrary, "wordiness" is often the stuff of inspiration, and certainly the stuff of thought. "Stop making speeches, Andrew," the imperious Lady Britomart says to her husband, the munitions magnate Andrew Undershaft, in George Bernard Shaw's *Major Barbara*.

"My dear," Undershaft replies, "I have no other means of conveying my ideas."

Henry Fonda endures in the imagination as *Henry Fonda* in part, at least, because of Big Speeches like the one he delivers as Tom Joad at the end of *The Grapes of Wrath*. Speeches remind the public of its ideals, potential, and capabilities.

In the pandemic spring of 2020, America could have used a resonant, reassuring, galvanizing speech.

11

SIDE TRACKS: HORSES FOR COURSES

The Electric Horseman • Barefoot in the Park • Cat Ballou • Comes a Horseman

The public doesn't want to see films that they think are good for them. . . . The first question they ask themselves is, are they going to be entertained and have a good time.

—Jane Fonda's producer Bruce Gilbert, 1979

NOT EVERYTHING FONDA did in her bountiful late 1970s career came from her art-activist IPC. The difference was telling as she saddled up for two watchable Hollywood westerns, *The Electric Horseman* and *Comes a Horseman.*

The Electric Horseman (1979) / *Barefoot in the Park* (1967)

The Electric Horseman, a bigger box office hit than *Comes a Horseman*, was Fonda's third movie with Robert Redford and her second with director Sydney Pollack. All three filmmakers were Hollywood high fliers by Christmas 1979, when this right-minded bauble came out.

Pollack and Redford, though, were working together for the fifth time, after *This Property Is Condemned* (1966), *Jeremiah Johnson* (1972), *The Way We Were* (1973), and *Three Days of the Condor* (1975), and this project is undeniably Redford's. He plays Sonny Steele, a worn-out five-time world-champion cowboy reduced to heavy drinking, promoting breakfast cereal, and appearing briefly at local rodeos, a has-been decked out in a suit trimmed with electric lights. Glen Campbell's song "Rhinestone Cowboy" had been a massive hit single in 1975, so the public was primed for this blinking American vision.

The movie's best sequence is the set piece in which Steele, at the end of his tether, rides a doped-up $12 million former champion horse onto a stage at Caesar's Palace in Las Vegas, filled with hot-pants-clad women dancing in front of an oil pump. Sonny steers the mistreated stallion—like the rider, disgracefully trimmed with lightbulbs—through the delighted audience, who reckon the spectacle is standard at the glitzy casino. Down they ride along the glittering Vegas Strip and off into the Nevada night. The music segues from blipping disco to Willie Nelson crooning the outlaw anthem "Midnight Rider."

That hijack is a lovely, wicked sight. It targets a lot of ills that Redford and Fonda were against: animal cruelty, corporate cheats, even the venalities of showbiz.

The film also takes a shot at celebrity journalism with Fonda's character, Hallie Martin—yet Hallie is in a horse race with the editor she played in *California Suite* (who speaks with some dimension about her own life) for the least interesting of the six reporter/writer/editor figures Fonda played in the 1970s, from herself in *Introduction to the Enemy* (in Vietnam, holding the mic, asking the questions) to Suzanne in *Tout Va Bien* and Kimberly in *The China Syndrome*. It's never satisfyingly clear what Hallie is doing in Vegas at a corporate convention, where the washed-up Steele is barely an afterthought.

"I work for television," she says generically, though she looks and acts like she's from a magazine like *People* or *Rolling Stone*.

In the lead-up to Sonny's horse-napping, the corporate jerks who own the valuable thoroughbred drug him with steroids and tranquilizers as they show him off. Sonny can't stand that abuse.

Meanwhile, a business merger is afoot, which mirrors 1960s–70s Hollywood itself, with studios gobbled up by conglomerates. Mel Brooks made a joke of it in his 1976 spoof *Silent Movie*, which, he writes in his memoir, was a tough sell with producer Paramount, at the time a subsidiary of the conglomerate Gulf + Western: in the movie he's Mel Funn, trying to get backing from the conglomerate Engulf & Devour. All of these profiteers are ready-made villains. What could conglomerate heads possibly know about movies? Or stallions?

Yet the merger doesn't have Hallie's attention. And Sonny Steele, a cowpoke on the ropes, isn't on her radar until she hears, in an elevator, that his corporate handlers are happy to tout his endorsement of their Ranch Breakfast cereal but aim to keep him away from the press. "So they don't want us to talk to the cowboy," Hallie mutters. She sniffs blood.

When Steele wobbles late into a press conference, she aggressively puts him on the spot. The interrogation is meant to embarrass him: "Why were you forty-five minutes late?" "Do you in fact eat Ranch Breakfast for breakfast?"

Such hard questions! Sonny is pissed, and the movie's purpose is sparked. Their beef is tinder for romantic comedy.

The Electric Horseman aimed to rekindle the Fonda-Redford chemistry of their 1967 hit, playwright Neil Simon's comedy *Barefoot in the Park*. There, the young actors were ideal, sweetly and skillfully investing the one-liners with exasperation and wit. And for the first time, Fonda was matched with a suitable star. From the moment Fonda and Redford's newlyweds arrive kissing in a carriage that's alighting at Manhattan's Plaza Hotel, their affection feels real. Fonda's eyes are alive; she delightedly gobbles him up. Redford smiles with his mouth agape, amazed and amused by her exuberance.

Barefoot in the Park was directed by Gene Saks, who would also direct *The Odd Couple*, several more Simon movies, and most of Simon's serious later plays. Saks gives Fonda space to ground Corie, her cheery character, as she takes in the couple's run-down Manhattan apartment. Energetic romantic that Corie is, she falls in love with the little place. She dashes through rooms and sprints like a rabbit up the five flights of stairs (six, including the formidable stoop) that exhaust everyone else. She adroitly follows their flirty upstairs neighbor (Charles Boyer) when he glides in through the front door, slides familiarly through the bedroom, and climbs out the window toward his rooftop flat.

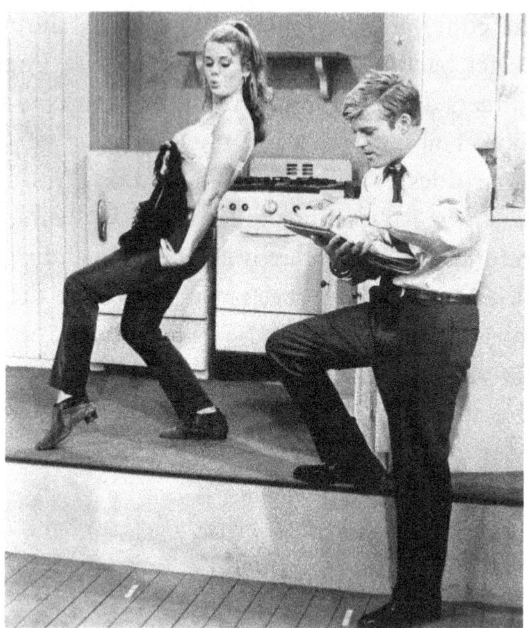

Fonda's first film with Robert Redford, *Barefoot in the Park*.
Courtesy Everett Collection

Boyer's smiling, shrugging European is a life force inspiring the straitlaced characters. Ethel, Corie's widowed mother, is acted with middle-class conventionality that blooms into savoir faire by Mildred Natwick, illustrating what's possible with an open mind. You've got to be a little crazy in life, the movie says. On an icy morning, you've got to walk barefoot in the park.

Those quirky supporting figures are a little much for Redford's Paul. Fonda, as Corie, dives in. "Well, here goes!" she grins; the line could be her slogan. She pops into her mouth an Albanian-cooked eel.

It makes her starchy husband blanch. "I have a bad arm," Redford says, declining to pop one himself.

Corie is a "doer," she tells her stuffed-shirt husband, while he is a "watcher." They argue in front of a bullfight poster by their tiny bathroom. Fonda's Corie is plainly the charging bull. Redford's Paul is the stationary matador.

Redford clowns beautifully, refining the performance he developed in the 1963 Broadway stage version directed by Mike Nichols and costarring Elizabeth Ashley. He enters breathlessly after scaling the apartment's stairs, and his angry, crab-angled stomp across the small living room toward the bar causes a phone repairman caught in a domestic squabble to flinch hilariously.

Redford also snaps off sarcastic lines while retaining a "proper and dignified" aura, which becomes Corie's complaint as she gets tired of his gripes.

She accuses him: "You're very nearly perfect."

He's hurt: "That's a rotten thing to say!"

Neil Simon was in his prime—*The Odd Couple* flowed next from his pen—and this is pro comedy. One-liners fly; recurring gags top themselves.

Ah, but the *lesson*: Mother Ethel advises Corie that the wife's job is submission. So Fonda has to hear it again, just as she did in the Manhattan apartment of *Any Wednesday* the previous year, with Dorothy—wife of the older man Fonda's character was sleeping with, let's recall—telling the younger woman to fight in the living room and make peace in the bedroom.

Regardless, Fonda shines. Corie dances freely through a loopy night on the town, soaking up life. Redford beholds her, in the end aglow with adoration.

Sydney Pollack later said he felt Fonda and Redford "joined the big leagues" with their *Electric Horseman* chemistry. But his film takes an unequal interest in the stars.

Sonny is the subject, period, even though the movie's ad campaign basically trumpeted three words: REDFORD. FONDA. ELECTRIC. In the poster, they are wrestling, or something. He is bent at the knees, holding her in the air, waist-high, like a bale of hay. She is folded upside down. We don't see her face. We barely see his. We mainly see his hair and her rump.

Like Bubber in *The Chase*, Sonny is the righteous American fugitive. Like Luke in *Coming Home*, Sonny is full of virtue. He will open Hallie's eyes and change her priorities.

Unlike Sonny Steele or Sally Hyde or Kimberly Wells, Hallie gets no backstory or context. Costumed in fancy glasses, designer jeans, and a beret, she is a superficial city slicker. Her role is to validate the authentic cowboy and his Redford-y renunciation of an America that is fallen, right down to its soggy breakfasts. Through most of the movie's second hour she *learns* from him, trailing in her too-fashionable boots through the gorgeous western wilderness where Sonny aims to release the $12 million horse.

The smartest, truest thing Hallie says on her own—not under Sonny's influence, or parroting him—is correcting the cowboy when she tracks him down in the desert. He loftily announces, "I've just retired from public life." Like Godell in *The China Syndrome*, Sonny dislikes journalists, so she has to work to build trust. He doesn't want to be anybody's story.

For once, Hallie's knowing attitude adds up. "Did you think we wouldn't notice?" she chides the high-end horse thief. "You're a story, all right."

But Hallie's questions are inane, and her pitch is limp. "I'm just trying to earn an honest buck, tell an honest tale," Hallie says, following Sonny and the stallion through the desert night. She only wants to tell "the truth about the great American cowboy and the world-champion horse riding together into the sunset."

He tips his hat. "Boy, are you full of shit," he says. "With all due respect." (Redford, who acts like he wants to say this in a lot of his movies, is splendid as the soul-weary Sonny.)

Hallie fudges a report for TV, declaring on air that "We talked together for many hours." As the *China Syndrome* nuke honchos smeared whistleblower Godell ("He was drinking"), so do these conglomerate heads smear Sonny ("A long history of alcoholism and drug abuse"). Counterpunching, Sonny phones Hallie and offers her an exclusive if she can meet him alone in the desert. She does, and while he thinks she's setting up her camera, he rants about the maltreatment of the horse in such a basic, honest way that she is moved. Without telling him, she films it (shades of Michael Douglas's secret taping in *China Syndrome*; what is it about the 1970s and clandestine tapes? Oh, right—Nixon). His speech wins her.

It also wins the public. He's an instant folk hero.

Romantically, this is *Coming Home* all over again. Activism is sexy. Righteous Sonny liberates the horse and wins Hallie's love.

After Sonny has spontaneously explained it all to her, he prepares, like Godell in the *China Syndrome* control room, to talk more formally (awkwardly, unnaturally) to the public. He asks if he and the horse are adequately framed.

"I can see everything," Fonda's Hallie says warmly, the line bulbously pregnant.

Hiking toward the remote canyon where Sonny will free the horse, Hallie and Sonny bond, even learning each other's real names: Alice and Norman. The seduction comes when he discovers her awake in the wee hours.

"I don't sleep," she says with a city slicker's anxiety. "Not in front of people I don't know."*

The dialogue is bad, with at least five hands on the writing, several uncredited, their efforts guided by Pollack. After Kimberly in *China Syndrome*, it's maddening to see Fonda in such a flimsy role, especially because by then she knew so much about the press. Lazily, the movie only shows its journalist banging around on her own or occasionally on the phone with a faceless, voiceless producer, and briefly at a broadcast news desk near the end.

So Fonda is edgy and urban, Redford is reticent and outdoorsy, and the two cynics—worlds removed from the puppy-love kids of *Barefoot in the Park*—ease into their moral Venn overlap. As a romance, this is nowhere near Pollack's smart, swoony *The Way We Were* with Redford and Barbra Streisand. *Horseman*, Pollack figured, was far lighter, in a Hepburn-Tracy vein.

"I still pinch and bite," the feisty Hallie tells Sonny before they kiss, a tetchy Katharine Hepburn–esque warning.

"OK," Sonny says, a stoic Spencer Tracy response.

* Delightfully, this will be turned on its head in the actors' 2017 reunion *Our Souls at Night*, from the Kent Haruf novel about aging neighbors Addie (Fonda) and Louis (Redford) who decide, at Addie's suggestion, to spend nights together. It's a chaste offer; she can't sleep well alone. The roles suit the stars' types: Fonda twinkles at the prospect of companionship and intimacy. Redford considers, coolly, before saying, without elaboration, *Sure*.

Fonda with Redford again for *The Electric Horseman*.
Photo 12 / Alamy

Pollack gives in to a moony montage that saturates Hallie in the simple goodness of Sonny's world and his quest. Traveling by foot, unplugged, off the grid, she has to slow down and *see*. But as far as we can tell, Hallie the *gotcha* reporter never really *looked*.

Maybe, in the end, this was all that Fonda wanted to show. *The Electric Horseman* was never going to be a layered portrait of a journalist.

At least the movie pays lip service to Hallie's professional capability. "You are good," Sonny declares, pointing out that nobody else tracked him down.

But the purple story notes she reads to Sonny undercut his praise. "'I feel I'm seeing this country for the first time,'" she reads to him, "'not looking down from a jet thirty thousand feet up but from the low angle of a special man who means to cross it on foot, leading a thoroughbred stallion to a secret destination, to a private goal, to a fairness that he intends to find in these valleys.' They're just my notes. I'm embarrassed."

"Nice," he says.

"It's hype," she replies, accurately, too late. *His Girl Friday* this ain't.

As the romantic leads part at the end of the movie, horse headed for the heaven of a free range, corporate nitwits outdueled for a day, Hallie tells Sonny she is assigned to Paris to cover the French election. Really? It sounds like an odd inside joke, a *Tout Va Bien* reference nobody would get.

Hallie, we hardly knew ye.

Cat Ballou (1965)

Fourteen years earlier, Fonda had a key Hollywood breakthrough with another western, *Cat Ballou*, a comedy so antic that during the opening credits (with a ballad sung by Nat King Cole and Stubby Kaye) the familiar Columbia Pictures logo statue turns into an animated cartoon.

Fonda's Cat is an aspiring schoolteacher turned outlaw. Lee Marvin is Kid Shelleen, wiggling into a corset so he can fit into his purty ol' black 'n' silver rhinestone cowboy gunfighter getup. Marvin's Shelleen is such a drunk that he sways like wheat in the breeze, so soused he's usually three-quarters off his galloping horse.

Marvin also plays Shelleen's brother Strawn, the strongman with a fake silver nose strapped to his face because "his [real] nose was bit off in a fight." Strawn is such a snake that the soundtrack rattles with a shaking tambourine whenever he appears. Marvin hams it up, and his sidewinding Strawn plus his sashaying Shelleen equaled Best Actor, topping Oscar nominees Richard Burton, Oskar Werner, Rod Steiger, and Laurence Olivier.

Keeping up, Fonda is hyper from the moment she gets stuck on a train with a) a drunk priest, and b) a handsome convict on the lam. Her 1890s Wild West accent is over the top: "I didn't mean to scream but he came out of *no-whayre*. And that nose—who *is* he, Poppa?"

He, the startling Strawn, is a hired gun for the powerful industrialists invading Wolf City, Wyoming. "They want your daddy's water rights," Cat is told.

But there is no issue here, no activist flag to wave, even after Poppa gets killed by Strawn. It's madcap adventure, with plain bad lyrics in the intermittent ballad:

It took a crafty female brain
To stage the holdup of a train . . .

Before it's done, young Jane, as Cat, leads her Hole in the Wall Gang out of Butch Cassidy's hideout. (This Cassidy, played by the deeply seasoned westerns actor Arthur Hunnicutt, is a quiet retiree pouring drinks to nobodies and has-beens.) Clowning, Fonda ends up outwitting the big industrialist via seduction. "Oh," she says, removing a thin shawl and revealing her décolletage as the industrialist coos and fawns, "you like our wide-open spaces."

The jumpy *Cat* rubs the wrong way. Chalk it up as Fonda's first rodeo.

Comes a Horseman (1978)

"Stardom is defined by intuition," Stuart Rosenberg, director of Paul Newman's 1967 prison drama *Cool Hand Luke* and Redford's 1980 prison reform picture *Brubaker*, told Redford biographer Michael Feeney Callan. "Stars are not 'directed.' They possess an intuition for the audience response that is beyond the likes of me, or anyone else who calls themselves a director. They have some hotline to a greater intelligence, however you attribute that."

Fonda had it and knew how to display it for directors who could frame it. In *Comes a Horseman*, released between *Coming Home* and *California Suite* in her three-picture 1978, Alan J. Pakula trusted that the Fonda qualities that had worked for him in *Klute* would work again, almost exactly.

Midway through the movie, cinematographer Gordon Willis locks the camera down to one side of Fonda's glowering Ella Connors, watching her work in the gloom of a small prairie cabin. It's the 1940s, and Ella is busy with short lengths of rope; as a single woman running a ranch, her tasks never stop. Gradually she confides something deeply troubling to Frank (James Caan), the working partner she's hired to help her hang on to her struggling business: years ago, when she was young, her nemesis (a menacing, stone-faced Jason Robards) sexually assaulted her.

Pakula cuts briefly to Caan a couple times, sitting still, listening; Caan, once an actual rodeo competitor, is believable as a knowledgeable ranch hand with no more than two or three dozen words in him per day. But the scene belongs to Fonda, dressed in worn brown work clothes, positioned in the deep browns and blacks of the lantern-lit cabin—the Willis palette, with George Jenkins of the "paranoia trilogy" and *The China Syndrome* as production designer.

Fonda is fierce, quiet. The eyes burn. The mouth is taut, downturned. The words are few and clipped. Her determination blazes. "I *hate* him," she finally hisses, repeating it in whispered rage. "I *hate* him."

If this is a star at work, it's also a conscientious actor building on previous experience—namely the high-octane tragedy of Gloria in *They Shoot Horses, Don't They?* and the defensive wariness of Bree at the climax of *Klute*, practically reprised in this scene.

This grim *Comes a Horseman* moment has a jarring echo—arguably a smudge—in *The Electric Horseman*: When Hallie first sneaks up on Sonny in the desert, he tackles Hallie and swats her. After a split second, Hallie defiantly says she won't stand being hit. Later, no longer an adversary, she confesses she told her producer where Sonny planned to take the horse. She expects Sonny to be angry about it . . . *and she asks Sonny why he doesn't hit her*. As with much else regarding Hallie, it doesn't seem thought through.

Fonda's efforts to stop violence against women have been substantial; she has long been part of the international V-Day movement founded by playwright V (formerly Eve Ensler). The movement blossomed from V's 1990s interview-derived stage piece *The Vagina Monologues*. But violence against women is not what either of these westerns is about. The matter is so glancing in *The Electric Horseman* that the troubling incidents could be lifted out and not be missed.

In *Comes a Horseman*, however, there is a painful aura of repression about Ella, explained by her confession to Frank. It helps drive Fonda's clenched-teeth performance, even when the picture meanders down its dusty *protect the ranch* path.

A threat stems from an oil agent (George Grizzard) who dynamites the green valley. Accidentally and unforgivably, that blast kills Dodger (Richard Farnsworth), Ella's longtime hired hand and beloved family friend. The bigger villain, though, is Robards as J. W. Ewing, a madman obsessed with dynasty.* In the George Jenkins design, western melodrama meets Greek tragedy: the vast, dark interior of Ewing's estate features a grand staircase like the steps of a temple, carpeted bloodred. In a climactic scene, Pakula even resorts to something like the *ekkyklema* of ancient Greek theater—a rolling cart revealing slain characters, because in Greek tragedy, the violence is done offstage. Near the end of *Horseman*, the director has a door slowly swing open, revealing a bloody corpse hung on a hook. Westerns lend themselves to rich formal images, and Pakula's compositional classicism is museum grade.

If Ella had power, as Ewing does, her fury would be wrath. Instead, it is rage, largely internalized but detonating now and then. When Ewing brings his cattle across Frank's land, Ella begs Frank not to allow it. "He tried to do this to my dad!" she yells. "He's pissing on you!" When Frank is slow to respond, Ella gallops in and scatters Ewing's herd herself.

As in *Cat Ballou*, it's mildly progressive for the western to focus on a female protagonist, and the industrious Ella feels authentic. The problem is that her enemy is a rote villain, so stereotypical that Robards plays it with little more than a scowl and a low baritone sounding like the mouth of hell. The dialogue is ludicrous, once you strip it of the gravitas applied by the formidable cast.

"Down to the two of us now," Robards's Ewing murmurs as the picture begins. "Just us." He's on her porch. She's fifty feet away, nature behind her. (Willis's picturesque cinematography is already capturing grassy expanses, snow-dusted peaks, slate-gray skies.) The showdown looks like a gunfight. But they're just talking.

Actually, he does all the talking—monologuing, as *The Incredibles* calls it when villains start to gloat. Moving close, he intones, "I don't want to have to ruin you, Ella."

She stares back, then walks past. Robards, gray and grizzled, well established on Broadway as America's great Eugene O'Neill actor, frowns, his face a primal mask.

* Earlier in 1978, the TV melodrama *Dallas* debuted, focusing on the villainous oil man J. R. Ewing—weirdly similar but unrelated to *Comes a Horseman*. Soon after came the *Dallas* imitation *Dynasty*, about a Colorado oilman.

Fonda's face is sun kissed and windburned. Listening to Robards, she looks hunted.

The rest of the movie is Ella working like a Trojan and squirming to stay free. To play Ella, Fonda dusted off her riding skills while learning roping, herding, and branding. Her acting, laden with business, is built on ranch work: Fonda loads pack horses, gallops after stampeding cattle, and totes an orphaned foal into the barn, moving from chore to chore.

Yet *Comes a Horseman* isn't taut and real; it's arty. Ewing obsessively stares at a vast oil canvas hanging in his den, a painting of a lone man overlooking the same mountain-rimmed green valley Ewing angles to control as his forefathers once did. The mesmerizing outdoor scenery is volatile, stormy. Lightning seems triggered by Fonda's relentless black mood.

"What in the hell is the matter with you?" Caan's Frank eventually has to ask Ella, generally.

The ire is epic—Fonda at Medea pitch, scaled to the majestic setting. The parts are impressive; the whole is beautiful. But it doesn't amount to much more than horsing around.

12

ON TARGET

9 to 5

[ARTHUR PENN]: Jane can do some really remarkable work, though she hasn't always done it.
[ROBIN WOOD]: Her career has been very unsatisfactory into the '80s. Even the things she's tried to develop herself, like Nine to Five, *have been so compromised.*
[PENN]: And schematic rather than organic. They're not made out of passion, rather, "Let's talk about the working woman" . . .
[RICHARD LIPPE]: . . . "but not offend anybody very much."

—Arthur Penn interview, 1986

BY THE END OF 1980 a complacent new decade was underway. Ronald Reagan was elected president. New Hollywood was over. A blockbuster mentality began to dominate. Runaway box office champ *The Empire Strikes Back* zoomed into the zeitgeist, heralding the movies' future.

Still high on the political agenda, though—and divisive enough to keep fighting about—was gender equality. Women's participation rate in the workforce topped 50 percent for the first time as the 1970s ended, having climbed sharply since the mid-1950s. Yet by the dawn of the Reagan era, women still made only 59 percent of what men earned, while often enduring sexual harassment, nonexistent job descriptions, and no chance of advancement.

The Equal Rights Amendment, passed by Congress in 1972, stood tantalizingly close to ratification by the required thirty-eight states. When momentum stalled after Indiana brought the total to thirty-five in 1977, Congress granted a deadline extension from 1979 to June 1982.

That was the climate into which Fonda's *9 to 5* merrily sailed, a pop hit powered by the trio of Fonda, Lily Tomlin, and Dolly Parton as ill-treated office workers finally getting the best of their sexist boss.

9 to 5 (1980)

Fonda and Bruce Gilbert developed the project for IPC Films with "the help and encouragement of Working Women, the National Association of Office Workers," as the movie's closing credits acknowledge. Working Women had been formed by Fonda's friend Karen Nussbaum—they met as antiwar protestors—and the first organization Nussbaum formed, at Harvard in 1973, was called 9 to 5; founding member Ellen Cassedy's 2022 book *Working 9 to 5: A Women's Movement, a Labor Union, and the Iconic Movie* catalogs the horror stories shared with the organizers by office workers, keenly repurposed in the comedy. As the movie came out, Nussbaum, then thirty, was merging Working Women with the Service Employees International Union to create a new union: District 925. When Fonda and Gilbert hired screenwriter Patricia Resnick to work up a story and screenplay, and then added Colin Higgins as cowriter-director, they made sure the project was rooted in the reality of office work and workplace discrimination—and largely along gender lines.

The result was an antic farce with political force.

The challenge, Fonda explained to a *9 to 5* audience in 2005 (the occasion was the Labor Film Festival at the American Film Institute's branch in Silver Spring, Maryland), was how to translate the issues "into a cultural statement. And it became an anthem for a movement."

9 to 5 lodged deeply. The 2020 documentary *9to5: The Story of a Movement* illustrates the longstanding American realities undergirding the picture; a 2022 documentary, *Still Working 9 to 5*, shows the sustained relevance of both the movement and the movie. Reboots are routinely rumored: Jada Pinkett Smith was working on one as Fonda talked with the AFI crowd; in 2017–18 the original stars were reportedly developing a new revival idea; on ABC-TV's *The View* a week before writer-director Paul Weitz's *Moving On* was released in March 2023, Tomlin and Fonda gabbed off the cuff about approaching Weitz for a reboot; by 2024 the notion was a Jennifer Aniston production to be written by Diablo Cody. During Elizabeth Warren's 2019–20 run for president, Parton's catchy, chart-topping *9 to 5* title tune was the candidate's walk-out music.

Coming Home was the capstone statement Fonda needed to make about her Vietnam years. *The China Syndrome* perfectly vectored her actor-activist planes. The frothy *9 to 5* would be vastly lighter in tone, and hardly without its faults—among them allowing Fonda the Activist again to almost totally eclipse Fonda the Actor.

The activist never expressed regret, though. Of all her movies, *9 to 5* generated the largest, most lasting waves.

---

9 to 5 would not need Fonda's Oscar-winning prowess. One of her biggest contributions was offscreen, in the casting: handpicking Tomlin and Parton as costars, stepping back, letting them shine.

It was Parton's first movie, and she is present from the first shot as the credits roll over a montage of faceless workers hitting the alarm clock and striding to work. Pointedly, it's *women* striding to work, in knee-length skirts and office-appropriate heels. Parton's title song has a strut in its step; the tempo is a caffeinated piano pulse, ultimately releasing into a gleeful swing and a Nashville chorus. The title sequence even includes a shot of three metronomes in a storefront, swaying with the beat. The movie is bright and colorful and fun even before it gets started. Almost all of that can be chalked up to Dolly.

Parton claimed she was not much of an actress, but she was already a veteran performer—not just as a musician but as a TV regular going back to *The Porter Wagoner Show* from 1967 to 1974. (Feeling she owed Wagoner something when she departed the country and western variety telecast, she wrote and recorded "I Will Always Love You" in his honor.) Parton did not have to stretch for the film; Fonda had her two stars in mind before the script was written, so both Resnick and Higgins tailored the characters to their personae. As Doralee Rhodes, the cheerful secretary to the sexist boss Franklin Hart (Dabney Coleman), Parton could play a figure that already fit the public's imagination of her—straightforward, friendly, and country tough.

Her signature moment comes when she learns the whole office thinks she's "screwin' the boss," as Doralee angrily puts it—having an affair with Coleman's dapper, disgusting Hart, whom we have already seen pushing a pencil holder off his desk so he can get on the floor with Doralee. The outraged Doralee gives Hart an earful, ultimately backing him down into his faulty office chair. Parton looms over Coleman and wraps up her juicy *tell him off* speech.

"If you ever say another word about me or make another indecent proposal I'm gonna get that gun o' mine, and I'm gonna change you from a rooster to a hen with one shot," she snarls. Walking out, she twangs angrily: "Don't thank I can't do it!"

The writing is so nifty and the performance is so lively that critic Roger Ebert raved mainly about Parton in his review. The character is convincingly Doralee and easily Dolly Parton, from the tangy warmth of her dialogue to the top of her poufy white hairdo and the fringe of her cowgirl outfit.

Doralee's rant comes hot on the heels of Tomlin's tirade as Violet Newstead, the office manager of the generically named conglomerate Consolidated. Violet long ago bumped up against the glass ceiling. She trained the weasel Hart for the job he now holds.

Tomlin, like Parton, was already a star: she'd been on TV going back to 1969 with regular stints on *Laugh-In*, and onstage in the 1977 Broadway show *Appearing Nitely*, when she made the cover of *Time* magazine as New Queen of Comedy Lily Tomlin. In movies, Tomlin was featured in Robert Altman's ensemble epic *Nashville* (1975), costarred as a 1970s kook opposite Art Carney's aging 1940s-style detective in writer-director Robert Benton's *The Late Show* (1977), and starred opposite John Travolta in the underappreciated romance *Moment by Moment* (1978), written and directed by Tomlin's longtime partner, Jane Wagner. (Tomlin and Wagner married in 2013.) In Violet Newstead, Tomlin could seamlessly slip into the role of a brainy, humorous efficiency whiz passed over by the sexist system. Her wry delivery suited the movie's relatable tone of weariness at the daily injustice of office life, especially for women.

When Doralee comes into Hart's office, Violet has already called "bullshit" (literally) as Hart passes her over yet again for a promotion, just because the "company," he contends, "needs a man in this position." As Doralee watches, Violet revolts. "I am your *employee*," Tomlin seethes in close-up, her cool voice full of intensity. She lifts her fists, adding an edge of ferocity and an extra decibel: "And as such I expect to be treated equally, with a *little* dignity and a *little respect*."

Tomlin was renowned for quirky comic characters ranging from the congested tot Edith Ann to the snooty phone company operator Ernestine. With her fertile imagination and knack for sketch work, Tomlin stood out as nimble, versatile, ultracompetent. The levelheaded, hyperorganized, quietly irate Violet was believable as being close to the *real* Tomlin, just as Doralee obviously drew from Dolly.

In contrast, Fonda's klutzy, panicked Judy Bernly is decidedly un-Jane.

"I don't want to play liberated women, roles where people say, 'Oh, that's Jane Fonda, that's the way she perceives herself,'" Fonda said during a 1974 *New York Times* profile. "I would much rather play the antithesis of what I feel—a pro-war or apolitical kind of woman existing in a situation most average people live in, helping to clarify the situation for other women."

What worked for Sally Hyde and Kimberly Wells is not as effective for Judy Bernly, a mousy housewife hitting the workforce for the first time as she faces divorce.

Fonda fidgets comically from the moment she appears, fussing as she searches for the downtown address, waving an arm in the air a little helplessly and craning her neck to see the top of the skyscraper where she's newly employed. Judy is a flibbertigibbet, and in her blue pastel dress, owl eyeglasses, and wide-brimmed hat, she looks time-warped from the 1950s—a reversion to Fonda's naive, eye-batting 1960s ingenues.

"We're gonna need a special locker for the hat," Tomlin's Violet deadpans as she eyes the hapless new recruit.

Judy only gets to tell off the boss in a fantasy, one of the three virtuoso set pieces bonding the rebels against Hart's workplace tyranny. The women have gathered in a bar to hash over Hart's indignities. Judy is upset about Maria Delgado (Roxanna Bonilla-Giannini, effectively likable and defeated), a fellow secretary fired for talking about salaries

Violet Newstead (Lily Tomlin, right) and Judy Bernly (Fonda) face corporate spy Roz (Elizabeth Wilson) in *9 to 5*.

in the bathroom . . . where Roz, Hart's corporate spy, played with droll creepiness by Elizabeth Wilson, hides and eavesdrops.

Fonda's Judy frets about what to *do*. "Couldn't we all just get together and . . . and complain?" Judy suggests to Violet and Doralee, stammering as usual.

They relocate to Doralee's to smoke a joint, supplied earlier to a mildly stressed Violet by her helpful teenage son. Stoned, breathless with laughter, giddily flapping one arm and one leg on the floor, Fonda's Judy—who was appalled when she saw a mounted deer's head in Hart's office—imagines hunting Hart like big game. Her fantasy sequence, the first of the three, is glamorous, with Judy as composed as Ava Gardner on the prowl.

So it's Fonda who introduces the movie's celebrated catchphrase. Judy's wearing safari gear, with a wide-brimmed hat and a bandolier draped in an X across her chest; on Fonda, the getup looks maximally fashionable. She corners Hart. He pleads to know what he's done wrong.

Judy tells him: "You're a sexist, egotistical, lying, hypocritical bigot." The charge will be repeated in Doralee's fantasy, and in Violet's, and through the decades.

Still, the scene is barely Fonda's. She performs with frosty panache and is photographed splendidly in tones that are almost dialed down to black and white, but the laughs come from Coleman as he scampers through the office like prey. As he cowers in the ladies' room, Judy shoots the aptly named Hart. His head gets mounted trophy-style.

Parton gets the laughs in her own tables-turning sequence, with Doralee as the boss objectifying her cute male secretary. (Coleman again is in deft comic form, pert and shy as an unwilling sex object.) Ultimately Doralee ropes and hog-ties him in a rodeo fantasia; the script gives her quippy dialogue and lively action.

Tomlin, too, gets the laughs in Violet's fantasy, draped in Snow White's clothing and assisted by animated Disney-style creatures as she laces Hart's coffee with rat poison. Tomlin humming with the critters and twinkling as a mischievous do-gooder princess is a hoot. Fonda gets nothing that witty.

Judy's biggest *tell him off* moment is feminist, though not office related. It comes late in the picture, when Judy is supervising Hart, whom the women have imprisoned in his own spacious house—he's leashed to a garage door opener they rig in his bedroom—while they await invoices that will prove his embezzlement. (Sadly, the plot recognizes it will be easier to nail Hart for a *real* crime than for the vaguely understood notion of *systemic discrimination*—which the simply worded, three-sentence ERA would address.)* Judy's ex-husband, Dick (Lawrence Pressman)—another Dick for Jane—has been jilted by his young girlfriend. Dick wants Judy back. He stalks her to Hart's large mansion. He

* "ARTICLE—

"Section 1. Equality of rights under the law shall not be denied or abridged by the United States or by any State on account of sex.

"Section 2. The Congress shall have the power to enforce, by appropriate legislation, the provisions of this article.

"Section 3. This amendment shall take effect two years after the date of ratification."

discovers Hart gagged, handcuffed, and tethered in a bedroom upstairs. This being the end of the swinging '70s, Dick assumes it's a sexual relationship—S&M!

Judy, of course, does not know what S&M is.

"Don't you tell me what I can or can't do," she argues, chasing him out. "Those days are over. And if I want to have an affair, or play sex games, or do M&Ms, you can't stop me." She also declares to him, *a la* Sally Hyde: "I've changed."

The script, hungry for triumphs, gives her a defiant last word the audience can cheer, slamming the door on him in a wan echo of *A Doll's House*'s Nora: "Hit the road, buster! This is where you get off."

Fonda gets little else—losing a battle with a paper-spewing Xerox machine on her first day, a brief montage showing competence with the phone, the Rolodex, and that hulking copier, and a lot of lines blurting "Don't panic!" and twitching like a nervous bird through the long adventure with a cadaver in the car trunk once it looks like Violet really has poisoned the boss.

As an actress judging whether a role was worth her talent, it's hard to imagine that the mighty Jane Fonda of 1980 would have said yes to this. As activism, too, the breezy *9 to 5* left some observers feeling like there was a hole in the center.

It takes a mere (if entertaining) thirty minutes for Violet, Doralee, and Judy to fuse as a united front. Pay gaps, enforced salary nondisclosure, discriminatory hiring, sexual harassment, a demeaning workplace environment, even depressingly depersonalized workstations—the office grievances are all articulated, including pointing out when it's the comparatively privileged White ladies who are in the way. Violet introduces Judy to a young Black man named Eddie (Ray Vitte) during her initial office tour, and Eddie asks about Violet's pending promotion, since Violet and Eddie are comrades in arms against the stifling system.

But he is rightfully indignant to see inexperienced Judy getting the kind of shot he'd like. "How am I ever gonna get out of this mail room prison if they keep hiring people from the outside?" Eddie says. "Lady," he tells Judy, "you're gonna hate it here."

With the issues laid out and blissful revenge memorably fantasized as of the forty-seven-minute mark, what's left?

A caper, for almost an hour, as the trio mistakenly think they've killed the boss—and then as they kidnap the boss once Roz, eavesdropping again, arms Hart with info about what sounds to him like a botched murder attempt. None of this dramatizes workplace problems a bit.

It is slick and watchable comedy, though, as put together by Higgins. His movie debut came nine years earlier as writer of the cult hit *Harold and Maude*—Hal Ashby's second picture as director, which remains a black comic delight. It's the ultimate May-December romance, with macabre young Harold (Bud Cort) staging flamboyant mock suicides to shock his rich, prim, emotionally distant mother (Vivian Pickles) and mainstream society. Harold outgrows these death fantasies by meeting Maude (Ruth Gordon), a life-force octogenarian who gives him just enough lessons to carry on joyfully after her own demise. (Ashby's editorial knack can be seen in the climactic montage of two apparent suicides, Maude's and Harold's; the soundtrack of Cat Stevens songs showcases his flair for cinematic music.)

Curiously, Resnick's original *9 to 5* script was more like the dark *Harold and Maude*.* Resnick had the office women *really* try to kill Hart, and Higgins likely could have handled that. The *Harold and Maude* suicide sight gags are drolly executed (the pun is inevitable), and Cort, as Harold, even gives the camera one direct sly smile, making us partners in his latest wicked subversion.

Harold's sniffy mother, and all that she stands for in her opulent dark mansion, is the target of his pranks. Vietnam comes up: his mother refers him to his military uncle for reformation, and Uncle Victor proposes that Harold be drafted. Naturally, Harold and Maude arrange a gag. Strolling the ruins of the Sutro Baths at Lands End, Harold listens to his uncle's gung-ho speech, acts patriotically inspired, and goes apeshit on a little old lady encountered by chance (Maude, playing along splendidly) . . . until she drops through a trapdoor and into the Pacific.

Higgins would be swept to Paris for a successful French stage adaptation of *Harold and Maude*. That led to a job with a giant of European theater, director Peter Brook, helping adapt anthropologist Colin

* Also curiously, Resnick's replacement by a male writer on *9 to 5* echoes what happened to initial screenwriter Nancy Dowd on Fonda's *Coming Home*.

Turnbull's Ugandan-set *The Mountain People* into a play called *The Ik*. "A chilling, unsettling experience," *New York Times* theater critic Mel Gussow wrote of it.

The three movies Higgins directed subsequently are in a chirpier key, with *9 to 5* coming between the 1978 Goldie Hawn–Chevy Chase comedy-mystery-romance *Foul Play* and 1982's *The Best Little Whorehouse in Texas*, starring Parton. On the *9 to 5* DVD commentary, Tomlin can be heard murmuring in appreciation of Higgins's comic eye and tight plot twists. "He knew where every laugh was," Tomlin says.

The surety of Higgins's touch (and Fonda's, as she again guided the team against any "lecturing") is confirmed by the dreadfulness of another 1980 caper about three women skirting the law to battle the Man, *How to Beat the High Cost of Living*. Everyone's on the skids in a dud economy, so housewives Susan Saint James, Jane Curtin, and Jessica Lange plot to steal the cash from a jumbo raffle ball in the local mall. (Dabney Coleman, refining the conceited sexist authority figure that would propel him through *9 to 5* and 1982's *Tootsie*, is a dapper—and married—motorcycle cop putting his smoothest seductive moves on Curtin.) The movie is so poor that the *New York Times* barely deigned to notice it.

But *People* liked it, at Fonda's expense: "Jane Fonda's and George Segal's *Fun with Dick and Jane* took a similar approach to a similar problem, yet ended up sour and ponderous. This is light, bright and appropriately detached from reality, a perfect antidote to inflation blues."

Actually, it's practically unwatchable. The climax relies on Curtin's character to create a distraction as her pals pull off the heist. As a local history play is staged in the mall, she bares her breasts.

Even if the madcap *9 to 5* veers from its central mission, everyone keeps their shirts on, and decades later it still holds up as sturdy feminism. The three independent women work the problem *together*, distracted by romantic relationships only when Judy bids Dick adieu.

The labor activism, too, is exemplary—specific and realistic. With Hart tied up as a hostage for several weeks and not missed in the office (nobody wants to see this jerk, goes the joke), the rebels implement genuine reforms. In a montage cut together over Parton's "9 to 5" melody, we see memos about office decor, equal pay, an on-site day care center, part-time work, and job sharing. The unjustly fired Maria Delgado has been rehired. A wheelchair user is among the inclusive, intersectional workforce. Efficiency is up. So is morale. Everybody wins—until Hart manages to escape and cover up the evidence of his embezzlement.

But the women's victory is sealed with the arrival of the Consolidated chairman, played like Big Daddy by Sterling Hayden in a white suit and plantation hat (and steered by a top executive acted by Henry Jones, who excelled at corporate office types going back at least to *Will Success Spoil Rock Hunter?* in 1957 and *Cash McCall* in 1960). Hayden surveys the vibrant office. He congratulates Hart, who knows nothing about the progressive upgrades and is getting his first shocked glimpse. In the movie's ultimate revenge punch line, Hayden rewards Hart's "success" by shipping him to a new corporate outpost in remote Brazil.

It's true that this is all mere comic shorthand, not the kind of fulsome depiction of labor issues in blue-collar hits *Harlan County U.S.A.*, Barbara Kopple's 1976 Oscar-winning documentary about striking Kentucky coal workers, and the 1979 drama *Norma Rae*, for which Sally Field won an Oscar as a southern textile worker nervously leading a union charge. (Fonda turned that role down. Field, plucky and skeptical, was ideal.) Critics found *9 to 5*'s simplicity easy to grouse about.

"Concludes by waving the flag of feminism as earnestly as Russian farmers used to wave the hammer-and-sickle at the end of movies about collective farming," Vincent Canby grumbled in the *New York Times*, also using the word "militancy" to describe the lark. Canby's flag metaphor is apt: the final image arrays Tomlin dressed in red, Parton in white, and Fonda in blue from left to right, occupying Hart's desk. It's a patriotic tableau.* Pauline Kael nitpicked about Parton's "rooster to a hen" line ("capon" is the accurate term for a castrated rooster, Kael corrected, though the line as spoken sounds quite like Doralee), and she disliked the smug anti-male sexism.

Yet while the movie was still in theaters, the *New York Times* noted that it was plainly connecting with audiences, especially with working women—even those looking for something with more dramatic depth, like *Norma Rae*. A clerical worker, initially dubious, went twice,

* This all-American palette would be worked to the hilt a decade later in writer Callie Khouri's western-tinged feminist myth *Thelma & Louise*.

> searching the screen for signs of the issues and goals of Women Office Workers, a New York affiliate of the national organization, to which she belongs. "They're there," she conceded with a small smile. "For example, the low salaries. Women clerical workers earn only 59 cents for every dollar men make in similar jobs. The movie brought that out. Also, there was the secrecy thing. The person at the next desk must never know what you're making. This came across, too."

Decades later, the movie's relevance is constantly reaffirmed. "The plot of *9 to 5* feels nothing short of radical, even (and perhaps especially) today," *Rolling Stone* wrote in 2015.

"The 1980 Movie '9 to 5' Is Still Depressingly Relevant for Women at Work," *HuffPost* declared in 2019. "It uses those laughs to talk about a harder topic: the rage of not seeing your hard work recognized." The *HuffPost* article found that the issues persist—equal pay, flex work, and on-site day care. It cited the outdoor-wear company Patagonia as offering day care and boasting a 100 percent retention rate of mothers returning from maternity leave.

As of 2023, the Paycheck Fairness Act, first introduced in 1997, had passed the House four different times but stalled in the Senate. Its goal, according to the bill's language, is "To amend the Fair Labor Standards Act of 1938 to provide more effective remedies to victims of discrimination in the payment of wages on the basis of sex, and for other purposes." It was reintroduced in 2023 and 2025, but as of this writing it has failed to pass either house again.

As for glass ceilings, in 2016 who was Hillary Clinton but Violet Newstead, the super-qualified woman who knew the job inside out and still got passed over for a sexist, egotistical, lying, hypocritical bigot?* (That "highest, hardest glass ceiling," as Clinton called it, was no obstacle for Joe Biden in 2020. Kamala Harris couldn't break through it in 2024.)

* Fonda and Tomlin, with Parton standing alongside, both lobbed the phrase at the new president as the trio—greeted with a standing ovation—presented an award during the 2017 Emmys.

Then and now, is the public's bond with *9 to 5* despite the picture's light comedy, or because of it? "Perhaps we don't really care," Ebert wrote about the movie's zingy tone. "We learn right away that this is deliberately a lightweight film, despite its superstructure of social significance. And, making the necessary concessions, we simply enjoy it."

Fonda and her team had banked on that, breezily defining issues, showing solutions and recruiting viewers to its cause—for who in America can object to equality? The result attracted a massive constituency. *9 to 5* would end up making more money at the box office in 1980 than everything except *The Empire Strikes Back.*

"There are direct results when conglomerates take over movie companies," Pauline Kael wrote in 1980, after taking time off from her *New Yorker* reviewing to explore producing in Hollywood. Warren Beatty had coaxed her west, and though she obtained a leave of absence it was not a cinch that she would come back to a critic's job she only had for six months out of the year. (The *New Yorker* arrangement had Kael sharing reviewing duties with Penelope Gilliatt.) Beatty, arguably with ulterior motives, had challenged Kael to apply her celebrated critical taste to the making of movies, but nothing came of it but heartburn.* When Kael returned to the *New Yorker* she zapped a poison-pen letter back at a Hollywood process she found shockingly crude. The headline was WHY ARE MOVIES SO BAD? OR, THE NUMBERS.

Kael spilled about what she'd learned. Vapid producers now answered to the heads of the Engulf & Devours and Consolidateds that had acquired studios since the 1960s. They prepackaged projects, reduced risk, and guaranteed profits with presales to broadcast TV, cable, and international markets. At least, Kael wrote, the old bosses

* For a breakdown of what went wrong for the critic in La La Land—the politics, the missteps, the shattered confidence—see Brian Kellow's biography *Pauline Kael: A Life in the Dark* (2011) and Peter Biskind's *Star! How Warren Beatty Seduced America* (2010).

loved movies. The new bosses didn't *know* movies, and didn't care. They loved triumph and clout (another good name, potentially, for a Mel Brooks conglomerate).

Grousing about selling out is as old as Hollywood, but Kael's misadventure came at a notable turning point. New Hollywood was dead. The 1980s were coming. Corporatism ruled. "*Greed*, for lack of a better word," Michael Douglas would famously claim in 1987's decade-defining *Wall Street*, "is good."

Artists pushed back with mild anticorporate satires like *The Secret of My Success* and *Baby Boom* in 1987 and, in 1988, *Big Business*, a *Comedy of Errors* update with Tomlin and Bette Midler each playing sets of twins.* During a 2017 interview looking back at *9 to 5*, Patricia Resnick listed her top five office comedies; second on the list, after Billy Wilder's dark Jack Lemmon–Shirley MacLaine classic *The Apartment*, was the 1988 corporate fable *Working Girl*—a jumbled, split-personality picture that's half progressive, half reactionary.

As Mike Nichols's nuclear-industry-set *Silkwood* trailed Fonda's *China Syndrome* into theaters by several years, so his office-set *Working Girl* eventually followed *9 to 5*. And as *Silkwood* swapped *China Syndrome*'s political punch for a mellower lens, so does *Working Girl* distill *9 to 5*'s movement spirit into the tribulations of a single woman. Nichols, who initially found stardom with Elaine May in their acclaimed sketch comedy/improv act, emerges in Mark Harris's 2021 biography *Mike Nichols: A Life* as, above all, a gifted *character* artist—witty and insightful about human nature, which, as a director, he used to help shape top-notch performances.

The *Working Girl* plot, by writer Kevin Wade, echoes much of *9 to 5*. Tess McGill (Melanie Griffith) is a thirty-year-old Wall Street secretary who put herself through five years of night school to work in business. But the wheeler-dealers above Tess won't give her the time of day. She

* In 2019 Tomlin told a story illustrating the corporate mentality at work on set during *Big Business*: "This one guy, he was an executive producer or something, I had to tell him everything I wanted to do in a scene, making me audition what I wanted to do. I'd make a gesture, and this guy would say, 'Internalize it.' And I'm like: *Internalize* it? I'm doing a gag!"

thinks that will change when she gets a woman for a boss in Katharine Parker (Sigourney Weaver).

Katharine tells Tess she's open to ideas. But Katharine turns out to be a dead ringer for Franklin Hart. Just as Hart steals a winning notion from Violet, so Katharine steals an original merger proposal from Tess. Hart is kept out of the office so Violet, Doralee, and Judy can run the place better; likewise, Katharine is kept out of the office after she breaks her leg skiing in Vermont. In Katharine's absence, Tess engineers the profitable merger she'd envisioned.

Tess triumphs. *Working Girl* ends as she gets her own office way up in the Manhattan skyline.

Working Girl has enough feminist credibility that the website *Jezebel*—hardly alone in its enthusiasm—embraced it in a 2013 appraisal headlined EVERYTHING I KNOW ABOUT FEMINISM I LEARNED FROM *WORKING GIRL*. Tess is independent and cleverly navigates her way through a hostile system. She refuses to be reduced to a sexual object by a piggish colleague (Oliver Platt), or by a coke-addled, porn-watching Wall Street player (Kevin Spacey). She refuses a marriage proposal from her philandering partner (Alec Baldwin). She resists conventional peer pressure from her bestie (Joan Cusack; the movie is ridiculously well-cast, thanks to the lure of Nichols as director).

The movie became a pop hit and earned six Oscar nominations, including for picture, director, lead actress, and *two* nods—Weaver and Cusack—for supporting actress. Carly Simon won for her original theme song, "Let the River Run." (In 1981 Parton's "9 to 5" song had lost, as had Willie Nelson's "On the Road Again" from *Honeysuckle Rose*, to the title theme from *Fame.*) Years later scriptwriter Wade described meeting Fonda at the *Working Girl* studio screening: "Someone introduced me to Jane and she was very complimentary. She said, 'Do you know what happened in there?' I said that it seemed the audience liked it. She said, 'They *really liked it*, and that's the toughest audience in the world.'"

Yet feminist author Susan Faludi found *Working Girl* a backward step in her pivotal 1991 book *Backlash: The Undeclared War Against American Women*, analyzing the surging cultural and political undertow undermining the gains of the 1960s–70s movement for gender equality. Tess, Faludi writes, succeeds "by playing the daffy and dependent girl";

her chapter on 1980s Hollywood's abysmal depictions of women reads like a miffed sequel to Molly Haskell's groundbreaking 1976 survey *From Reverence to Rape*. Similarly, in 1997's *Screen Tastes*, Charlotte Brunsdon wrote, "Tess's quest obviously owes something to feminism, but this debt is the debt the film tries to erase." Making Katharine the villain is particularly problematic, suggesting that the main obstacle to women like Tess is another woman in power, since at best there will only be one slot for an executive who's female. That both women must compete for the same man compounds the problem. (Of course Tess wins this Prince Charming, played with fetching insecurity by Harrison Ford.)

Illustrating a shift as the 1980s settled in, *Working Girl* abandons any sense of solidarity. Tess is not part of a team, and she's not out to reform or improve anything. She is an individualist. Wade and Nichols saw the plot as an immigrant's story, with Tess arriving in Manhattan daily via the Staten Island Ferry, and the gap between Tess and Katharine is one of class: Katharine is an Ivy Leaguer, while Tess is an Everywoman from the working-class 'burbs. The movie opens with a spectacular, implicitly patriotic helicopter shot around the Statue of Liberty and closes with the reverse shot from Tess's office in Manhattan, receding back over the water to celebrate the fullness of her American Dream journey.

Her triumph: graduating into a gray suit. As Simon's anthemic "Let the River Run" rolls over the end credits, Tess has been emancipated to busy herself on Wall Street with what was also the quintessential Hollywood enterprise—making corporate media deals.

The singly titled *Working Girl* has no sense of collective action, despite the cheers from Cusack and the pals back in the typing pool (none of whom share Tess's ambition). Instead, it ratifies up-by-your-bootstraps, Reagan-age solo achievement. And how does Ford's character stand up for Griffith? By telling the corporate bigwig benevolently played by Philip Bosco, "She's your man."

9 to 5, on the other hand, was hostile to entrenched power, all about *group* effort, *class* progress. "To the beginning!" the change-agent trio toasts in the end, vowing continued action.

Fonda's film even staked a position in favor of equal pay, which is where Sterling Hayden's largely approving chairman character draws the line. As of 2025, though, women working full-time still earned only

83 percent of what men earn, and Equal Pay Day was March 25—the date representing how far into the new year women have to work to make what men made the year before. And as noted in chapter 8, Virginia's 2020 ratification of the Equal Rights Amendment did not get that legislation over the finish line, given the 1982 deadline established by Congress.

As if expressing a national yen to revisit the issue, in April 2020 Hulu released the nine-part miniseries *Mrs. America*, arriving in sync with the latest attempt to pass the ERA. The series marks the amendment's life and original apparent death, 1972–82, and the exuberant high tide and slow, messy erosion of 1970s second-wave feminism. Gloria Steinem (Rose Byrne), Betty Friedan (Tracey Ullman), Bella Abzug (Margo Martindale), and Shirley Chisholm (Uzo Aduba) are among the feminist figureheads jockeying for social progress, often at cross-purposes.

The focus of *Mrs. America* is the rise of Reaganite conservatism as driven by anti-ERA activist Phyllis Schlafly (Cate Blanchett, deeply starchy and with a grin of iron). The new strain of conservatism is clinched by the rise of Jerry Falwell's Moral Majority and the election of Reagan in 1980, when Reagan gets Republicans to knock the ERA off the party's platform.* Schlafly will be forced to take a lesson. In its novelistic sweep, the fractious, left-and-right-looking *Mrs. America* is a captivating anatomy of activism.

9 to 5, lite as it is, is activism itself.

During a 2007 interview with *Rolling Stone*, Fonda said of *9 to 5*:

> In many ways it was the most profound cultural experience that I've ever had. There's very little that I feel as proud of as that. Tens of thousands of women felt seen and heard and understood, and then they could move forward from there. I mean, it was just

* The Republican platform had been pro-ERA since the 1940s and in 1976 was so again, led by First Lady Betty Ford. The '76 platform language: "The Republican Party reaffirms its support for ratification of the Equal Rights Amendment. Our party was the first national party to endorse the E.R.A. in 1940. We continue to believe its ratification is essential to insure equal rights for all Americans." In 1981, Betty Ford and Maureen Reagan, the new president's eldest daughter, marched in Los Angeles as part of a national ERA fundraiser organized by the National Organization of Women.

> a perfect synthesis. Which means that it can happen—and it can happen again. I feel blessed that I was a successful enough actor at a particular time in our history, and I had the consciousness of these issues, that I could get these movies made, and they would say something very real about that moment in our history. I don't think anything quite like that has happened. It was like four or five years of these, you know, starting with *Coming Home* and all the way through. It was amazing.

Note the examples that Faludi, in *Backlash*, rounded up to illustrate "a critical aspect of the female quest in the [1970s] movies":

> The heroines did not withdraw into themselves: they struggled toward active engagement in affairs beyond the domestic circle. They raised their voices not simply for personal improvement but for humanitarian and political causes—human rights in *Julia*, workers' rights in *Norma Rae*, equal pay in *9 to 5*, and nuclear safety in *The China Syndrome*. They wished to transform not only themselves but the world around them. They were loud, belligerently loud, because speaking up was a social, as well as a private, responsibility. "Are you still as angry as you used to be?" Julia, the World War II resistance fighter, asked Lillian Hellman in the biographical *Julia*. "I like your anger . . . Don't let anyone talk you out of it."

"I have no time to waste as I once did, going down wrong paths," Fonda wrote in the 2011 self-help book *Prime Time*. The attitude applied equally to her activist filmmaking apex thirty years earlier. "If I want to make ripples, I better be sure I am throwing my pebbles into the right pond."

Tomlin and Parton recall Fonda whittling wood between scenes in preparation for her long-hoped-for role as a Kentucky farmer in *The Dollmaker*—but that project, first envisioned by Fonda in 1971, wouldn't be made for several more years. As the new decade progressed, Fonda began running out of wood for the activist fire, at least in terms of big-time mainstream moviemaking. *9 to 5*'s Judy Bernly, a minor figure in a major project, was a harbinger. Fonda was slipping out of the picture.

In the 1980s, her impact would be almost entirely on TV, though not before one last stab at making a powerful, American, consciousness-raising, star-driven Hollywood hit.

13

ON "THE MONEY"

On Golden Pond • Rollover

We are not just products of our insecure childhoods, or whatever. We are products of the social and historical forces of the era in which we live.

—Jane Fonda

On Golden Pond (1981)

Fonda's next IPC production was not activist. It drew on her privileged, troubled, insecure childhood. Its primary agenda was her father, Henry.

Ernest Thompson's play *On Golden Pond*, poorly reviewed but ultimately popular in its original 1979 Broadway run, fell like a gift into Jane's hands. The saccharine story of a cranky, ailing septuagenarian seemed tailor-made for Hank Fonda, at least in Jane's view. Even better, the story included a small but pivotal part for the mean old man's grown daughter, still wounded in her forties by his emotional distance and casual cruelties.

For Jane, that was as close to the bone as it could possibly get. The emotional damage with her father could be bared, and maybe repaired. And at last Jane and Henry—whose heart issues were slowing him substantially in his mid-seventies—could act together in a movie.

Henry's performance as Norman Thayer is laced with sarcasm, and it brims with mortal dread. He totters uncertainly through a cabin and around the pastoral woods of the New Hampshire lake where the film was shot. His Norman flirts charmingly with his wife, played by Katharine

Hepburn, whose imperiousness was all the more regal for powering through the palsy that bobbled the actress's head and wobbled her voice.

Norman mischievously jerks around his daughter's nervous dentist fiancé (Dabney Coleman, bearded and smiling nervously) and dispassionately sizes up the dentist's thirteen-year-old son (Doug McKeon), dropped off at the cabin so the adults can traipse to Europe. "You like that word, don't you?" Norman observes as Billy, the kid, repeatedly gripes about being left with the old folks: "bullshit." "It's a good word," the old man adds casually, disappearing up the stairs.

The daughter, Chelsea, calls her father "Norman" and her mother "Mommy," which tells you everything about this underwritten part ("a terrible role," Pauline Kael groused). Jane enters with a flinch as her father greets her with a smile and a hearty-sounding little knife in the ribs. "*Wellll*, look at you! Look at this little fat girl!" he says nonsensically, for she is played by arguably Hollywood's all-time fittest star. It's exactly the wound Henry inflicted on young Jane, who wrangled through bulimia and other complications for years.

Jane with father Henry Fonda and Katharine Hepburn in *On Golden Pond*. *Entertainment Pictures / Alamy*

Norman asks what kind of car Chelsea rented for her visit. Chelsea can't exactly say beyond "green." That microscopic failure is all it takes to tie her up in knots. Jane conveys it by nervously glancing left and right, twisting the straps of her purse.

"I'm in charge of Los Angeles and I come here, I feel like a little *fffat* girl," Fonda blurts later to Hepburn, slowly exploding the *f*s and puffing her cheeks with shame and disgust. "My father is a goddamn bastard."

They're sitting together outdoors. Fonda has her knees drawn up to her chin, like a turtle trying to hide.

Hepburn, who could not be bettered as the hardy, sensible soul of the picture (or, to shade it more critically, as the idealized maternal figure who must heal others' problems while having none of her own), soothes Chelsea without sugarcoating: "Here we go again, you had a miserable childhood. [. . .] Life marches by, Chels. I suggest you get on with it."

Jane's screen time is brief. Chelsea arrives thirty minutes in, exits at minute fifty-eight, and isn't back until the ninety-minute mark. Thompson's plot spends its time showing old Norman bonding with Billy the kid, as they banter and fish together on the lake.

Norman ages in front of us: he loses his way in the woods, then crumples to the floor during a heart incident. Tough Norman, suddenly disoriented: Henry Fonda's face droops with confusion. His eyes dart with fear. He's helpless, and he knows it. This is the stuff of the picture, which won Oscars for its screenplay and—joining *Coming Home* in the very rare club of movies accomplishing this—for both Best Actor (Henry Fonda) and Best Actress (Hepburn).

But Chelsea and Norman get one big moment together on the dock after her return. Chelsea finally asks if maybe she and her father can be better together.

With a weird, uncharacteristic jump cut to a close-up of Jane (director Mark Rydell's movie is otherwise a silky Hallmark card), Chelsea tells Norman, "I don't want anything . . . It just seems you and me have been mad at each other for so long." Jane's eyes are red and wet. In this moment, the grown woman we see is still fundamentally a fragile adolescent.

"I didn't know we were mad, I thought we just didn't like each other," Hank replies, offhand, almost flat.

Jane has told the story forever of surprising her father by touching his arm, unrehearsed, and drawing a spontaneous flicker of emotion from Norman/Henry, who looks away and brushes something (surely not a tear!) from his cheek. The picture makes this rapprochement very brief and very simple, a poignant breaking of the ice.

In real life it was not so simple. Jane found no new Henry available to her that night when she went to visit him and talk about the day. In *My Life So Far*, when she quotes Hepburn as calling Henry "Cold. Cold. Cold," Jane writes a one-word *Amen* paragraph: "Yup."

Jane has written that over the years men and women have told her how positively the portrayal affected them, but this would all appear to be more therapeutic than activist. Yet there is something specific in the impact of fathers on daughters that pushes things further, and that may help explain another, much more minor Jane Fonda appearance in a later film, 2016's *Fathers and Daughters*.

Fonda has five very brief scenes as the savvy, supportive, worried agent for the literary lion played by Russell Crowe. But as the second hour focuses on Amanda Seyfried, playing Crowe's grown daughter, you can see why Activist Jane wanted to support the project, even if there's nothing especially memorable for her to do.

Seyfried is Katie, who lost her mother when she was young (another point of connection for Jane) in a car crash that also injured Katie and her father. Katie is physically fine, but Jake, her dad, is subject to seizures that make it difficult for him to work. Unlike Fonda's/Chelsea's frosty father Henry/Norman, Jake is dogged, present, and intimate almost to a fault. He dotes on young Katie, especially when his rich-as-Croesus sister-in-law and her lawyer husband try to keep Katie after Jake's seven months in a mental hospital. Jake is a Pulitzer Prize winner, but his next book tanks, his money drains, and his seizures worsen with stress. (The director is Gabriele Muccino, and this is squarely in the mold of his potent 2006 weeper *The Pursuit of Happyness*, in which Will Smith toils epically through homelessness to support his young son.)

Brad Desch's screenplay varies the view between Crowe with young Katie (Kylie Rogers) and Seyfried's grown Kate as a promising young psychologist/social worker. As an adult, she struggles with intimacy issues and separation anxiety; her remedy is chronic anonymous sex. It's the kind of behavior that can lead to dismissive shaming, especially when she relapses into an especially degrading incident, sabotaging a promising relationship.

The story takes care, though, to show how psychologically rooted this compulsion is, and how hard it is to battle. It also shows how predatory men are ever present and ready to exploit her (a dynamic explored in writer-director Emerald Fennell's striking 2020 film *Promising Young Woman*, an Oscar winner for Fennell's mordant screenplay). It's a thoughtful, awareness-raising examination.

The same angle resonates in a 2016 conversation between Fonda and Lena Dunham, the creator, writer, and star of the HBO series *Girls*.

"Let's talk about body," Fonda directs as she interviews Dunham for *Paper*. "I grew up with *massive* body image [issues]—my father made me feel that I was fat and unattractive and I don't think he realized how destructive it was and then I watch you and your body is part of your brand and I would like you to talk about that. I feel like you made a conscious decision that you were going to make sexuality and your body part of your brand. Can you talk about that?"

"Well," Dunham replies, "firstly that's amazing to hear you say—you're someone who exudes so much confidence. I think it's so important for young women to hear you say that even you dealt with that sort of tyranny of body image, which is something we often think that celebrities or people who are physically fit or people who have all outward appearances of being healthy and powerful haven't dealt with. So to hear you say that is deeply powerful for people."

"That's why I talk about it," Fonda replies. "So tell me about the role that your body plays."

Dunham does, in illuminating detail. Then she adds: "But I think you can't underestimate how some of those characters that you played made it possible. Even if the 'Jane Fonda body' is a model of something that we'd all like to aspire to, you never, ever projected an image of unattainable perfection. That's not what you were going for. You have to know how powerful that is."

"Thank you," Fonda replies. "Thank you."

The imagery of *Golden Pond*, like the let's-look-at-Jane bikini scene in *California Suite*, belies Dunham's assertion. Fonda, then in her forties, is shot like a supermodel in her bikini on the lake dock. Her ultra-toned belly is practically concave.

Fonda has acknowledged that the way she looked in *Golden Pond* likely helped propel the *Workout* books and tapes that very shortly would become an international phenomenon. Inevitably, the movie's swimsuit bits read much less as "Chelsea" than as "Jane," even though the troubled subtext for both is the same:

You called me fat? I've got your "fat" right here.

Cultural imperatives played out on Fonda's body nearly all her life, from modeling and acting through fitness regimes, eating disorders, and plastic surgeries. Because Chelsea is embodied on-screen by Jane Fonda—trembling before her dad, preening on the dock—the fragile character goes through it too.

On Golden Pond was released at the beginning of December 1981. In contrast to the play's swift disappearance from Broadway two years earlier, the movie would be a big, very *fffat* hit, bested at the 1982 box office only by *E.T.*, *Raiders of the Lost Ark*, and *Rocky III*.

One week after *Golden Pond*'s release, Fonda's stock dropped.

Rollover (1981)

"In the '70s when I'd become an activist," Fonda told Dunham in 2016, "I thought, 'I just don't want to make the kind of films that are being offered me,' so I started making my own. That was when I was the happiest."

Maybe not with *Rollover*, though. It marked the end of Fonda's self-guided Hollywood activist run.

The hard flop at least was prescient about global economic fragility. But the misfire was dismal: bad title, porous plot, misguided casting. It was even a stylistic slip, despite Fonda reuniting again with director Alan J. Pakula—seemingly a perfect choice for a financial thriller to line up with his "paranoia trilogy."

"Easily the worst film he ever directed," declared Pakula biographer Jared Brown.

Like *The China Syndrome*, *Rollover* dramatized catastrophe. "You're playing with the end of the world, you know," says financier Maxwell Emery (Pakula favorite Hume Cronyn). This dark warning is addressed to a barely seen Saudi Arabian investor; this figure represents the invisible subversion of the US dollar. The oil-producing nations of OPEC are hoarding gold.

But whereas *The China Syndrome* exists to a) rigorously explain its subject and b) raise reasonable concerns, *Rollover* flinches from detail. It slouches toward romantic suspense while purporting to sound a very loud alarm about unregulated foreign investment.

"The issue," Fonda said as the movie came out, "is how come our national leaders have allowed this country to become a house of cards, to become so vulnerable." Her urgency was surprising: "I think it's the most important, the most important issue of our times. There's nothing as important as this."

Fonda and her IPC producing comrade Bruce Gilbert were hardly pulling the concern out of thin air. The 1973 oil crisis rattled Americans' sense of independence. Rich OPEC nations invested in US entities so aggressively that more than just eyebrows were raised. The Foreign Investment Study Act was passed in 1974. In 1975 the interagency Committee on Foreign Investment in the United States was established by President Gerald Ford's executive order.

Transparency was a problem, though. Congress investigated from 1978 to 1982, aiming to make public what had been allowed to remain secret. "Under four successive Administrations," the *New York Times* reported in September 1981, "the United States Government has been granting Arab oil-producing nations, notably Saudi Arabia and Kuwait, an extraordinary degree of favoritism, protected by a heavy veil of secrecy, in the operation of their multibillion-dollar financial investments and assets in this country." The article continued:

> Those in Congress who follow such matters closely are especially disturbed by the current "discrepancy" of more than $60 billion in the United States' balance of payments accounts, funds that

> have flowed to this country from abroad in recent years and that nobody seems capable of locating or identifying. . . .
>
> At the crux of the overall foreign-investment problem is the difficulty in determining its full scope. According to the Commerce Department, total foreign assets in the United States have jumped spectacularly in recent years—from $196 billion in 1974 (when the OPEC oil boom began) to $481 billion at the end of 1980. But these figures may, in reality, be much higher: Control and reporting systems are inadequate, statistical methods vary, and there are an endless number of hidden channels through which the funds flow to America. . . .
>
> While acknowledging that there is "no evidence that foreign investments are placed in such a way as to operate against the national interest," the G.A.O. study said that "the existence of a clear and present danger is not the issue. Instead, we question the ability of the executive branch to detect such a threat in a timely manner, should it occur."

Earlier in 1981, widely cited *Washington Post* reporting detailed that banks were finding themselves in a genuine squeeze:

> Citibank is on the hot seat. It has a choice between being an imprudent banker or losing its biggest investment account—Kuwait, the second-largest oil producer in the Organization of Petroleum Exporting Countries (OPEC). And the fallout could be a far more explosive and volatile stock market for the nation's nearly 30 million investors.
>
> Confidential documents obtained by the *Chicago Tribune* reveal that top officials in Kuwait—which has entrusted Citibank with the management of close to $7 billion worth of U.S. securities—are demanding a bold new investment strategy that would turn the bank into one of the most aggressive and biggest stock market traders in the United States. In brief, the OPEC producer—with $18.6 billion of petro-revenues last year—is insisting that sizable chunks of one of the largest pools of money in the world actively trade in and out of U.S. stocks as they go up and down.
>
> "We want more gains," Citibank is being told by Kuwait, which is unhappy with the bank's performance.

> An internal Citibank memo—covering meetings held last December between Kuwaiti and Citibank officials—indicates that the bank is ready to accede to Kuwait's demands, which are described by one market expert as "irrational."

The ingredients were firmly in place, then, for an international financial thriller with a cautionary activist bent. Fonda and Gilbert both readily acknowledged that *Rollover* was the most complicated subject they'd tackled to date, but Fonda took heart from the popular success of bestselling novelist Paul Erdman, who turned writer when he was jailed in Switzerland after the collapse of his bank, the United California Bank in Basel.

In prison Erdman penned *The Billion Dollar Sure Thing*, and followed that with *The Silver Bears*, a portrait of international banking as con artistry that became a 1977 movie with Michael Caine, Louis Jourdan, Tom Smothers, and Cybill Shepherd (plus a young, flip Jay Leno). Fonda said her awareness was shaped by Erdman's 1976 novel *The Crash of '79*, about a California banker who becomes head of Saudi Arabia's central bank. *Not a great writer*, she opined of Erdman, "but he knows whereof he speaks."

How can an activist raise awareness, though, if the central issue remains veiled?

Rollover consistently avoids its story's hot core, starting with its opening chaos of an edgy afternoon of Wall Street trading. Pakula serves up fast cuts and insider lingo laced with rapidly changing stock values. But the crisis is generic, with sweaty traders anxiously barking "The market's going against us" and "We can't buck the tide any longer."

"Gobbledygook," as Pakula said of the terminology he allowed to fly.

The scene simply establishes a specialized, adrenaline-fueled workplace, then stretches toward myth as Cronyn's cool, sage Max is shown outside it all, taking in information, photographed like a titan in his high, glassy corner office. He's framed with nothing but the Empire State Building behind him, making equals of man and monument.

Such are the picture's dominant interests, which the filmmaking brain trust agreed skewed away from Adam Smith and toward Alfred Hitchcock. An early nighttime shot of 2 World Trade Center is classic

Pakula, panning slowly upward, absorbing the vast, hulking darkness of the structure and its isolated pricks of light, finally closing in on a lone figure viewed through a window at his office desk. We see, and he does not, a silhouetted figure hidden behind the curtains.

Pakula's production designer, yet again investing his settings with menace, is George Jenkins; the glossy cinematography, at ease with darkness, is by Giuseppe Rotunno, a veteran of Federico Fellini and Lina Wertmüller films, Mike Nichols's camera eye on *Carnal Knowledge* (1971), and lately an Oscar nominee for Bob Fosse's *All That Jazz* (1979). Their imagery is alluring and, yes, a little paranoid. But the ensuing stabbing up in the World Trade Center will be all but forgotten, even though the victim is the petrochemical magnate married to Fonda's character, Lee Winters—who shows, throughout the picture, almost zero interest in solving her husband's murder. The movie gives us no cops, no detectives, no follow-up (the shrugging, hard-to-swallow explanation is that it must have been a burglary gone bad)—though, to be fair, Pakula didn't show tremendous interest in mystery logistics with *Klute* or *The Parallax View*, either.

"I guess I'm always surprised by evil," Pakula said as *Rollover* came out, and as he prepared for his next film, the Holocaust-shadowed *Sophie's Choice*.* "And that's a kind of American innocence."

In 1974's *The Parallax View*, Pakula, Jenkins, and cinematographer Gordon Willis had relocated their *Klute* look to the Pacific Northwest as Warren Beatty battles another hard-to-see nemesis. *Parallax* is filled with more negative space and brown tones as Beatty plays a journalist who witnesses an assassination near the top of Seattle's Space Needle. Over the next few years, a lot of the witnesses die mysteriously. The darkened newsroom run by Hume Cronyn is a creepy distillation: there's never anyone there except Cronyn, Beatty, and whoever delivers Cronyn's bagged dinner and coffee. (It's lit like the garment office after hours in *Klute*.) *Parallax*, like Sydney Pollack and Robert Redford's *Three Days of the Condor* the following year, basically whispers, *Threat is everywhere.*

* Pakula directed both Jane Fonda's and Meryl Streep's first Oscar wins for leading roles. Lucky, or good?

Pakula lets the mystery's details slide in *Klute* and *Parallax*, instead creating deep moody blots. The movies evoke the free-floating 1960s–70s angst of upheaval, assassination, wrongful war, and political cover-up.

The one time that Pakula cogently, doggedly follows the trail is in *All the President's Men* (1976), with Willis and Jenkins again providing dark caverns for skulking around as Redford's Bob Woodward wrenches evidence of the Nixon administration's corruption from the reticent Deep Throat (Hal Holbrook).

But that story is *real*. *Klute*, *Parallax*, and *Rollover* are not.

The big *Rollover* conflict is explained briefly in, of all places, a lecture hall, where Max is confronted by his protégé Hubbell Smith, played by Kris Kristofferson, the movie's leading man. Hubbell says he knows Max is buying gold, slowly, as Saudi investors pull out of the dollar. Cronyn plays the scene with the smug superiority of the amused, cynical elder statesman. "If we didn't handle it, they'd find a lot of other people who would," he purrs.

Hubbell righteously argues that Max ought to notify regulators, the treasury secretary, the president. "And start a real panic?" Max counters

Fonda and Kris Kristofferson amid the menacing shadows of *Rollover*. *© Orion / Courtesy Everett Collection*

in the picture's pivotal speech. "Then you'll see a worldwide depression that will make the 1930s look like a kindergarten. In two months, you'll have bread lines in Detroit, riots in Pittsburgh. In six months, you'll see grass right over Rodeo Drive, and Michigan Boulevard and Fifth Avenue."

Pakula tightens the camera as Max delivers his primer: "Money, capital, has a life of its own. It's a force of nature. Like gravity, like the oceans, it flows where it wants to flow. This whole thing with the Arabs and gold is inevitable. We're just going with the tide."

Fonda's purpose with *Rollover* was to dispute exactly that. But outside Max's bromides, the script—by the undistinguished team of David Shaber, Howard Kohn, and David Weir—is maddeningly foggy. (Journalists Weir and Kohn wrote no other Hollywood features.)

Instead, that tiny kernel of dialogue between Kristofferson and Cronyn, a rote scéne á faire between hero and villain in front of a chalkboard, is about as far as the movie delves. Rare for a Pakula film, *Rollover* gets too cute, obsessing over its attempt at a high Hitchcockian style (something Brian De Palma was already doing with delirious verve), meandering into a bland romance.

As Hubbell Smith, Kris Kristofferson looks stunned to be playing a banker and perplexed to be acting with Fonda. Wall Street adrenaline seems alien to Kristofferson, whose presence here is like a depressant, unlike the near-hormonal surge of pleasure Michael Douglas displays in Oliver Stone's *Wall Street* (1987).

"*Rollover* showed us what not to do," Stone would say.

Douglas's *Wall Street* takeover artist, Gordon Gecko, possesses one of Hollywood's most memorable character names, and the portrayal is effective because Douglas directs his ardor entirely toward *deals*. He flirts with interior designer Daryl Hannah, but that's an old conquest—something that adds to the glint in his eye and to his alligator leer.

Kristofferson brings nothing comparable. Clean-shaven and with his short hair neatly parted, he grins a lot at Fonda. It comes to nothing; it's as if his suits have leeched the life out of him. (Say this, too, for Douglas: with his slicked-back hair, jazzy collars, and snappy suspenders, he relished looking the part.)

Viewers were more accustomed to Kristofferson bearded, in denim, and sometimes—hell, often—bare chested. He was the grizzled rock heartthrob opposite Barbra Streisand in the 1976 iteration of *A Star Is Born*, and an equality-inclined rancher—the romantic prize at the end of the road for widowed mom Ellen Burstyn, winning her Best Actress Oscar—in Martin Scorsese's *Alice Doesn't Live Here Anymore* (1974). In Paul Mazursky's *Blume in Love* (1973), still new to movie acting, Kristofferson was spectacularly good as a hip, laid-back musician living in his truck, becoming the post-Blume love interest of the elusive social worker played by Susan Anspach. It's very funny to see George Segal's anxious, self-absorbed Blume grow a beard and try to turn himself into Kristofferson's carefree Elmo.

As Elmo leaves when things get complicated, the lawyer Blume asks, "How will you live?"

"Nothin' to it," shaggy Kristofferson says, sauntering away down the hall.

Offhand is where Kristofferson excels. He's intelligent but near frozen in the role of a Wall Street "glamour boy"; he doesn't make the script's leaden finance details dance.

Though Fonda is more dynamic, the picture uses her less as a conduit of information than as a *very big star*. "I liked playing somebody who didn't see the light at the end," Fonda said of Lee Winters as interviewers laughed. "I just thought it was good at this point that I played somebody who was not on the side of the angels."

The problem is how vacant Lee is. She's an ex–film star, which means she's comfortable with power and independence, as she explains to Hubbell on a flight back from wooing investors in the Middle East. At a power lunch on a swanky eightieth floor after her husband's murder (which seems to be plum forgotten), Lee, with the mighty Manhattan skyline behind her, leans in hungrily and makes a sure-handed proposal. Implied: she wants to chair the board.

Fonda looks chic in a businesslike chocolate-and-black outfit. She slings the technical lingo confidently. But the plot lacks spring as it follows her notion to acquire a company in Spain. Progressive though it was to show a woman on the cusp of helming a major petrochemical company, the stakes are foggy. As with Judy Bernly in *9 to 5*: fine idea, weak follow-through.

When Hubbell tracks down Lee at home, she's posed like Jean Harlow in a silky getup and a strand of pearls, draped on a couch by the fireplace. The palatial manse smacks of 1930s MGM.* Banter and cocktails ensue.

Archly, Lee says, "We're playing the classic scene, aren't we? The banker and the widow."

They play it, but it doesn't take. There's no crackle. That's fatal: the movie poster showed the stars embracing, Fonda's head thrown back in ecstasy.

Fonda looks hungrily at Kristofferson as they parley, but what can she do with a paralyzed partner? Or with Lee, a character she confessed she didn't like?

Or with abysmal dialogue? "I've never been afraid of risks," Fonda's Lee murmurs, eyes twinkling, growing breathy as they get close.

The subsequent *Gone with the Wind* kiss as Fonda and Kristofferson spiral up a grand staircase is forced, to say the least.

Oddly, the most Fonda has to do is react in scenes again repeated from Pakula's *Klute* playbook. As Bree Daniels listened, frozen, to a tape recording of a murder, so Lee Winters stumbles onto a microcassette in her late husband's desk and listens for *two solid minutes* to a discussion of a bribe deal. Fonda looks smashing in another slinky gown by the prodigious Hollywood and Broadway designer Ann Roth, who also did *Klute*, *Coming Home*, and *9 to 5*. In straight-on close-ups, Fonda frets persuasively, the black Manhattan night behind her, vertically striped by the folds of white drapes. (Hubbell gets photographed through vertical shades when he's in an office too—the same subtle cage effect.) Fonda listens intently, glancing around, touching her chin in wonder, finally pulling the fur around her shoulders protectively when the tape is done. Pakula knows he can keep his camera on Fonda for two minutes and she'll find things to do.

He does it again when Hubbell, now under her suspicion, calls. The camera stares at her in medium close-up, again straight on, for another minute. Her coral lipstick is near the center of the frame. Her chestnut

* The actual house was owned by the government of the Philippines, occasionally occupied by First Lady Imelda Marcos.

hair is pinned up in elegant twists. Her dark gown is well off her shoulders. Silver earrings gleam. At all times Fonda's Lee looks like money.

Talking on the phone to Hubbell, she murmurs trite lines, feigning trust: "Listen, you're tired. Why don't you just finesse it? It's only a benefit . . . I'll call you tomorrow . . . Call me, OK?"

That's her last dialogue—monologue?—until they dance together at the gala, each thinking the other is a double-crosser.

"I went to the Saudis. I'm cutting my own deal," she tells him with quiet urgency. The kicker is ridiculously glib: "Sorry, partner, I guess I just lost confidence."

Of course Fonda, the nation's top female box office star, appearing in the thirty-second big-screen role of her career,* was capable of occupying the same Hollywood terrain as brassy Barbara Stanwyck and ritzy Grace Kelly. But Lee Winters never gets anywhere near to helping make the movie's point. She blunders into the mysterious account number of the Arab-North American Bank–Riyadh. Foolishly, she tries to leverage her would-be Saudi partners with it. That misstep detonates the pullout from American banks, and an ensuing montage of CNN coverage depicts financial panic and worldwide riots. But the sequence practically comes out of the blue.

"With 'Rollover,' I wanted people to be deeply disturbed," Fonda said after the movie came out. "It's a cautionary movie. I would hope it would stagger and grip the throat of everyone in this country that cherishes the concept of democracy."

Democracy seems like a peculiar word. But it jibes with the fact that her activist organization with Tom Hayden, post–Indochina Peace Campaign, was the Campaign for Economic Democracy. Largely headed by Hayden and substantially funded by Fonda, the CED regarded corporate accountability as a front-burner issue. "Economic democracy" meant making sure that stakeholders of all stripes, from labor to neighbors to activists, had meaningful voices inside companies doing business that significantly impacted the public.

* This count doesn't include an hour-long NBC film noted briefly by the *New York Times* in a December 12, 1960, snippet headlined JANE FONDA WILL MAKE TV DEBUT JAN. 3 IN "A STRING OF BEADS."

If *Rollover*'s final cataclysm seems alarming now, it's because the fragility of the American economy was driven home by the 2008 financial collapse and the shockingly swift Depression-level conditions of the 2020 COVID lockdown. At the time, however, *Rollover* was too scattered to be disturbing.

"Is the Arab Euro-dollar really a good subject for movie banter?" Janet Maslin opened in her *New York Times* review. "The dramatic possibilities of the material are weak at best. . . . If the worldwide monetary situation is indeed as bad as the screenplay makes it out to be, movies this extravagantly silly only make it worse."

It wasn't entirely sloppy, as a review in the *American Banker* noted. "Jane Fonda and her company, IPC Films, have done their research," Paul Nadler judged. "It is extremely realistic about the problems of one bank trying to survive in a world of liability management against other bankers' loss of confidence in that institution. Yet it is completely garbage when it talks about a loss of confidence in all banks and a collapse that hurts everyone. It was intended to show the power of bankers to control our lives and bankrupt all of us—a power bankers just do not have and a possibility that does not exist."

The 2008 collapse gave the lie to that, and revived the problem of how to make compelling movies out of economic complexity. "It can't be easy to create a financial thriller," reporter Michael Kinsley began in his lukewarm *New York Times* review of HBO's 2011 film *Too Big to Fail*, a brink-of-catastrophe picture about that 2008 economic calamity directed by Curtis Hanson (*L.A. Confidential*).

Too Big to Fail is movie-as-journalism, a kind of *All the President's Men* based on the tick-tock chronicle by reporter Andrew Ross Sorkin, meticulously following the money as it spirals down the drain. The characters are real, and the cast is appropriately big league: Treasury Secretary Henry Paulson (William Hurt), Federal Reserve chairman Ben Bernanke (Paul Giamatti), Lehman Brothers CEO Richard Fuld (James Woods), Federal Reserve Bank of New York chair Timothy Geithner (Billy Crudup), Warren Buffett (Ed Asner), Morgan Stanley CEO John Mack (Tony Shalhoub), JPMorgan Chase CEO Jamie Dimon (Bill Pullman), French finance minister Christine Lagarde (Laila Robins), and more. The pistol fires and the racehorse sprints for one hundred minutes. Hanson cuts restlessly. Sinister music works our nerves.

To bail, or not to bail? That is the question. The tight story confines itself to the period from the imminent failure of Lehman Brothers through the passage of the massive federal bailout, gingerly called the Troubled Asset Relief Program. Hurt's uneasy, empathetic Paulson listens to a Chinese diplomat tell him quietly that Russia approached China about dumping Fannie Mae and Freddie Mac holdings, which would crumble the economy. Paulson is depicted as heroic. He draws a firm line, insisting on "moral hazard"—making companies pay the price when they risk too much.

But he can't control the collapse. The housing market is a swelling black hole, which gets explained as Paulson's inner circle helps Treasury's head of public affairs (Cynthia Nixon) figure out how to explain the mess to the press.

Paulson also explains the toppling dominoes to his wife on a bench in their front yard, predawn. He paints her a picture of panic. "Couple of weeks," he murmurs, sounding the same alarm as Cronyn's Max, "there's no milk in the store."*

This is reliable, insightful, and valuable, if not the hitmaking stuff of the simple moral fable *Wall Street*—which, while giving Douglas a wide berth to play the devil, is a blunt fictional melodrama of good and evil, based on headline-making 1980s inside traders that included Ivan Boesky (inspiration for the movie's *greed is good* speech) and Michael Milken.

In *Wall Street*, the young acolyte played by Charlie Sheen breaks into an anxious sweat the second he crosses an ethical line, because it's *just that clear*. Oliver Stone's dad was a banker, and underlining a sense of filial affinity, Sheen's virtuous dad here is played by his real father, Martin Sheen, as a blue-collar airline machinist and union leader. Stone's OK with finance. His movie is out to get bad *players*, not to throw the whole *system* under the bus.

* In the spring of 2020, in fact, at times there was no milk or other staples in American stores as pandemic stay-at-home orders lasted for weeks and into months, with unemployment soaring, supply chains fraying, and the government sending businesses and workers emergency bailout money.

Too Big to Fail, like *Rollover*, took bigger aim, gunning for the big, fat, labyrinthine capitalist system. Unlike the Hitchcockian dud *Rollover*, the single-minded *Too Big to Fail* has the advantage of lively reporting. We know it's all true, even if we didn't (don't) understand it. (Finance? Forget it, America. It's Chinatown.)

Reporting similarly lifts the far more flamboyant *The Big Short* (2015), which also deals with real-life people involved in the 2008 mortgage crisis (often with names changed) and draws from the book of the same name by Wall Street reporter Michael Lewis. *Short* is a zippy gas, amped up to entertain as it hacks through the thickets of the crisis. Adam McKay's movie winks at us with a lot of direct address, guiding viewers through the diabolical language and the devilishly inventive, prismatic structures of financial products.

"It's pretty confusing, right?" says the swaggering investor played by Ryan Gosling in an early voice-over. "Does it make you feel bored, or stupid? Well, it's supposed to. Wall Street loves to use confusing terms to make you feel like only they can do what they do. Or even better—for you to just leave them the fuck alone."

With that, McKay—who cut his teeth on satire with the Upright Citizens Brigade comedy troupe and as head writer on *Saturday Night Live*, and whose frivolous ventures with Will Ferrell include everything from *Anchorman* and *Talladega Nights* to the Broadway run of Ferrell's sharp George W. Bush solo act *You're Welcome America*—cuts to Margot Robbie. She's in a bubble bath, as herself. She sips champagne.

She unpacks mortgage terminology. It's frisky, funny, and direct. "By the way," Robbie says, letting dense sentences trip impishly off her tongue, "these risky mortgages are called *subprime*. So whenever you hear *subprime*, think *shit*."

The insider terms keep coming, enticing viewers to keep up. "What if we bet against the double-A tranches?" goes a heady play call. Cue a fizzy Vegas montage of investment bros cutting the off-angle deals and knowing they're scoring *huge*.

Brad Pitt, as market visionary and social recluse Ben Rickert (based on trader Ben Hockett), wears a face mask and sanitizes his hands when he goes out in public. He cools down the bros' giddy celebration with an arresting rebuke: "You just bet against the American economy."

The picture also features Steve Carell as a fund manager seething with righteousness and blessed/cursed with an ungovernable tongue, and Christian Bale as the misfit visionary who first spots the exploitable flaw in the nation's mortgage boom and invests heavily against it—the big short.

The movie's spicy style demystifies Wall Street's obfuscations. *The Big Short* became a moderate hit. Unless you want to count Mel Brooks's *The Producers*, it's the only screenplay about finance to win an Oscar.*

In the same way that Pakula bracketed *Rollover* with long, slow pans around its trading floor, lighting up at the beginning of the picture and going dark at the end, *The Big Short* ends in an eerily emptied-out office: Lehman Brothers. It's as hollow as the foreclosure-riddled housing development that an astonished investor, earlier in the movie, compares to Chernobyl.

Steven Soderbergh's mischievous 2019 dramedy *The Laundromat* followed the *Big Short* formula by adapting yet another nonfiction book, this by Pulitzer winner Jake Bernstein, tracing the Panama Papers scandal of 2016 that unmasked massive asset manipulation via offshore banking.

Soderbergh is a veteran muckraker, having provided a heroic frame for Julia Roberts during her Fonda-worthy Oscar turn as a small-time crusading lawyer in *Erin Brockovich* (based on a true story), then vamped through all ten episodes of HBO's DC lobbyist satire *K Street* (created with DC political insiders), and injected visual and narrative jazz into the anticorporate comedy *The Informant!*, with Matt Damon as a wonky agrobusiness executive (based on a true story). *The Laundromat* dives into the con artist complexity of the Panama Papers by toying around, with Antonio Banderas and Gary Oldman playing real-life lawyers Ramón Fonseca and Jürgen Mossack as a pair of cocktail-sipping dandies walking us through the scandal. In 2019 Fonseca and Mossack sued the film's distributor, Netflix, for defamation; the movie was advertised as "based on some real shit." Fonseca and Mossack lost.

* *The Producers*, Brooks's lark about two lovable Broadway scammers, won for original screenplay over *The Battle of Algiers* and *2001: A Space Odyssey*.

Meryl Streep plays a fictional lower-middle-class Midwesterner who discovers the shell game of offshore companies when she tries to collect on an insurance policy. The dashingly theatrical finale is sheer agitprop, with Streep revealing her *own* shell game. Having doubled as a secretary in the con men's office, she strips off wigs and costume layers and directly asserts that US laws need to be changed—especially regarding *campaign finance.*

"'The Laundromat' aims to provoke a sense of spirited outrage, the sort of righteous disgust that might express itself through reform-minded citizen action," critic A. O. Scott wrote in the *New York Times.* "There's no reason to be cynical about that."

"The so-called experts mystify things," Fonda said of finance during the *Rollover* release. "They can be understood. . . . I'm somebody who firmly believes that an active, activated, alerted citizenry can control the flow of money. . . . When it comes to something as fundamentally as important as our economy and how it's run, we need regulations. . . . That's the point that I think we're trying to make in this movie: Hey, we better take a close look at this, because we have no idea what's going on in our names."

Rollover was not that close look. Broadly targeting "the Arabs" and foreign investment seems off-base for global citizen Fonda (and Hayden), until you realize that it bolstered a key CED agenda of energy independence and clean, renewable fuel sources—nothing to do with *Rollover*'s executive-suite melodrama.

The movie's few prophetic breezes: its now-tragic imagery of 2 World Trade Center as Wall Street waltzes with secretive Saudis, and its attention—rare in movies—to the ever-baffling American economy. The capitalist engine roars; it implodes. Its masters of the universe discourage public understanding. They shelter inside their own gold-mining gobbledygook.

It is heartening that Hollywood has grown more than marginally better at grappling with the economy and its discontents. Fonda was right, at least, to stick her neck out and invest in that.

14

"THE WORLD WE'RE WORKING FOR"

CONSERVATIVE TALK RADIO HOST CLIFF CASTLETON (MIGUEL FERRER): Chucky and I go back to campus politics. You know the American Students' League?
PRIVATE INVESTIGATOR DANNY O'BRIEN (DANNY HUSTON): The information tables at the airport? Something about nuking Jane Fonda?
CASTLETON (after a beat): God, we miss her.

—From John Sayles's 2004 campaign satire / murder mystery *Silver City*

"JANE FONDA LEFT," ROSANNA ARQUETTE frets at the beginning of her 2002 women-in-Hollywood documentary *Searching for Debra Winger*. "Debra Winger left."

Fonda didn't leave "the business" until the end of the 1980s, following *Rollover* with one more IPC project—*The Dollmaker*, a 1984 TV movie for ABC based on Harriette Arnow's 1954 novel. With a screenplay by Susan Cooper and Hume Cronyn, the project gave Fonda a hardworking, multidimensional woman to embody. She delivered a long, tremulous performance, in hillbilly dialect ("kilt" for "killed," "littl'uns," etc.), of Kentucky woman Gertie Nevels, ripped up by her farm roots, along with her five children, when her husband takes an auto factory job in Detroit during World War II. Gertie has the soul of an artist, and ultimately the crafty figures she whittles from wood lead to the family's salvation. Gertie's heroic strength begins with lifting a stranger's car out of a ditch so she can have her choking son driven to a hospital, and then deciding to perform a roadside tracheotomy herself when it's clear the child is running out of time. The ordeals keep Fonda's brow furrowed and her lips pinched as she becomes a Tom Joad–like migrant adapting to a Motor City tenement.

The medium (broadcast television), the rural/blue-collar story, and the heartland demographic were a departure for actress Jane, for activist Jane—but maybe not for workout Jane, by then a fixture in VCRs across America. As it turned out, 1984 was a watershed year for major Hollywood actresses making movies about heartland/rural/farm women: Jessica Lange in *Country*, Sally Field in *Places in the Heart*, Sissy Spacek in *The River*, with each performer nominated for an Oscar. (The Academy liked Field.)

Fonda only had four more big-screen movies in her before taking a fifteen-year break. She played a chain-smoking lapsed-Catholic psychiatrist involved in figuring out how a convent nun unexpectedly gave birth in *Agnes of God* (1985), an adaptation of the popular stage drama but a flat picture from *In the Heat of the Night* and *Fiddler on the Roof* director Norman Jewison (the chilly gray compositions of the Montreal-set movie are by Ingmar Bergman cinematographer Sven Nykvist). She played a blackout drunk who wakes up one morning with a corpse in her bed in Sidney Lumet's thriller *The Morning After* (1986), opposite Jeff Bridges, earning her final Best Actress nomination.

She was an American schoolteacher in Mexico encountering expat journalist Ambrose Bierce (Gregory Peck) and falling in love with a revolutionary played by Jimmy Smits in *Old Gringo* (1989). The adaptation of Carlos Fuentes's novel was produced by Fonda Films and directed by Argentinian Luis Puenzo (*The Official Story*). Fonda and Puenzo saw *Old Gringo* as a counternarrative to exclusionist 1980s American attitudes: "I wanted to show that something positive can come out of contact with those who are different," Puenzo told the *New York Times*, "in contrast to the ideology reigning in the policy of the United States and in American films of recent years, which characterizes those who are different as enemies, or worse. I'm referring not only to obvious things like 'Rambo,' but also to more ingenuous things like 'Gremlins' and 'Ghostbusters,' not to mention Reagan's policies." The movie was booed at Cannes.

Ending the string, she played a widowed mother teaching an illiterate cook—Robert De Niro—to read in *Stanley & Iris* (1990), the last film from director Martin Ritt (*Hud*, *Sounder*, *Norma Rae*). The drama raised awareness about adult illiteracy; both stars are wonderfully settled in their blue-collar roles, and it's a particularly overlooked turn in De Niro's oeuvre.

Did Fonda then quit acting because she was asked to by new beau and soon-to-be third husband Ted Turner? Or because she was just plain *done*? Both; in her 2011 book *Prime Time*, she confessed to losing interest in movies, and to detecting a blankness in herself as an actress as she revisited *Old Gringo* and *Stanley & Iris*.

Her 2005 comeback movie was *Monster-in-Law*, playing a former high-flying TV journalist imperiously protecting her precious son from a supposedly inferior bride (Jennifer Lopez). It functioned like *Fun with Dick and Jane*: a mainstream comedy aimed mainly at getting her back on the Hollywood map.

Additional roles came slowly at first, but through 2024 she made over a dozen more movies. She's played walk-on parts (Nancy Reagan in Lee Daniels's *The Butler*), ensemble pieces (the French film *All Together*, as an irrepressible life force in a small circle of aging friends), and finally another string of starring roles. She was the unconventional matriarch in the 2014 dysfunctional-family comedy *This Is Where I Leave You* (daughter Tina Fey comforting herself on Mamma Fonda's pillowy fake bosom is a particular hoot), the lonely, practical widow in 2017's *Our Souls at Night* with Robert Redford, and a successful Fonda-like businesswoman with undimmed sexual appetite in the 2018 hit *Book Club*, with Diane Keaton, Candice Bergen, and Mary Steenburgen as her friends and reading group.

Pop culture liked her as Leona Lansing in Aaron Sorkin's *The Newsroom* on HBO, *loved* her with Lily Tomlin on the Netflix hit *Grace and Frankie*, and then came that three-picture burst to start 2023—*Book*

Club: The Next Chapter and, in the boundless partnership with Tomlin, *80 for Brady* and *Moving On*. End of the line? As of September 29, 2025, Fonda didn't know, telling CNN's Christiane Amanpour, "I haven't worked since then. And I want to work, I need to work. I miss . . . I miss . . . I miss the craft. It's a noble profession that we're in, getting into the skin of another human being. That's why we tend to be very empathic, actors do." Still, the screen reemergence has evolved into a perpetual presence—a reaffirmation of her brand as a maverick, increasingly treasured as political and artistic notches accumulate on her belt.

"People need to be able to envision what the world we're working for will look like," she told a producing partner after watching the bleak Armageddon of the sensation-heavy *Mad Max* movies. That American optimism has been characteristic of Fonda, both as an activist and as a movie artist—a belief that things *have to be better*. The 1970s were marked by paranoid movies—*The Parallax View, Three Days of the Condor, Chinatown*, menace everywhere. The battle-scarred Fonda aimed to say something else creatively, every time: *The menace is* ***specific****. We can* ***fix*** *it.*

Her 2025 acceptance of the Screen Actors Guild Life Achievement Award, one harrowing month into the second Trump administration's shotgun roar of executive orders and reckless slashing of federal agencies by Elon Musk's DOGE, underscored it all. "A whole lot of people are going to be hurt by what is happening, by what is coming our way," Fonda warned.

> This is a good time for a little Norma Rae, or Karen Silkwood, or Tom Joad. We must not isolate. We must stay in community. We must help the vulnerable. We must find ways to project an inspiring vision of the future—one that is beckoning, welcoming, that will help people believe that, to quote the novelist [and playwright] Pearl Cleage, "on the other side of the conflagration there will still be love, there will still be beauty, and there will be an ocean of truth for us to swim in."

Five years earlier, in February 2020, Fonda took the stage at L.A.'s Dolby Theatre to present the Oscar night's big prize, Best Picture. Her short hair was newly frosted silver. She sported a formfitting scarlet

Fonda presents the Oscar for Best Picture at the 2020 Academy Awards. *ZUMA Press Inc. / Alamy*

gown—it looked flame-licked—and a crimson cape, banners of the Fire Drill Fridays effort that migrated with her from Capitol Hill to the west as she started filming the final season of *Grace and Frankie*. As she peeked coyly from behind the envelope, the Hollywood crowd greeted her with whoops and a standing ovation.

Call it fate: Jane Fonda handed the trophy to the most radically political of the night's nine nominees, a missive about class from South Korea. Bong Joon Ho's mischievous *Parasite* showed struggling lower-class workers "infesting" a wealthy household. The parable was strikingly in tune with the widening income gap in America.

Taking the stage, Fonda surveyed the crowd, smiled, and shared her credo:

"Nothing is more important than raising awareness, right?"

Soul of an activist.

NOTES

1. She Used to Be a Movie Star, or It's the Pictures That Got Small

"She's a genuine American icon": Bosworth, *Jane Fonda*, 4.

"The most politically outspoken star": Hoberman, "G.I. Jane."

rainy November afternoon in 2019: I was on the scene myself and heard what was said.

"You'll never catch me now": Fonda, *My Life So Far*, 439.

"This is a stupid fucking actress": Bosworth, *Jane Fonda*, 378.

"Good night, Jane Fonda!": Carol Burke, "Why They Love to Hate Her," *Nation*, March 4, 2004.

"No one voted for you": Laura Ingraham, *The Ingraham Angle*, Fox News, aired February 15, 2018.

"You're in no position": 77th Golden Globe Awards, NBC, aired January 5, 2020.

"The people on that stage are already": Megan McArdle, "Ricky Gervais Teaches Hollywood What Speaking Truth to Power Really Means," *Washington Post*, January 7, 2020.

"Actors, you see, are not": David Thomson, *The Whole Equation: A History of Hollywood* (New York: Knopf, 2004), 161.

"I love looking at Angelina Jolie": Tina Brown, "Beyond Rummy, the Stars," *Washington Post*, June 30, 2005.

"By playing to celebrity": Ross, *Hollywood Left and Right*, 415.

"It's as though we want": Francis Davis, *Afterglow: A Last Conversation with Pauline Kael* (Cambridge: Da Capo Press, 2002), 99–100.

"Whether we like it or not": Fonda, *What Can I Do?*, 45.

"the actress, philanthropist, feminist": Als, "Queen Jane, Approximately."

"a wildly contradictory part": Mlotek, "Jane Fonda's Extreme Bravery," https://www.vulture.com/2018/05/jane-fondas-extreme-bravery-then-and-now.html.

"Even at the height of my career": Keegan, "Jane Fonda on Cancer Battle."

"Rocks red lipstick and sparkling jumpsuit": Samantha Sutton, "Jane Fonda, 86, Rocks Red Lipstick and Sparkling Jumpsuit on the Cannes Red Carpet." *Page Six*, May 15, 2024, https://pagesix.com/2024/05/15/style/jane-fonda-86-rocks-red-lipstick-and-sparkling-jumpsuit-on-the-cannes-film-festival-2024-red-carpet/.

"Most Americans over the age of fifty" through *"In 1973, after she went"*: Hershberger, *Jane Fonda's War*, 1–3.

"Jane Fonda stands a good chance": Kael, *Deeper into Movies*, 89.

"Since 1977, IPC" and *"She will star in 'The Dollmaker'"*: Aljean Harmetz. "Jane Fonda: She Makes Ideas Pay at Box Office," *New York Times*, March 25, 1982.

heaped attention on Fonda: Richard Dyer, *Stars* (London: British Film Institute, 1979).

"What does this mean to you?" and *"I, on the other hand"*: Fonda, *My Life So Far*, 430.

her daughter Vanessa suggested: Fonda, 532.

"I and the people I was working with": Hershberger, *Jane Fonda's Words*, 9.

"Fonda's work as an actor deserves": Nell Minow, review of *Jane Fonda in Five Acts*, RogerEbert.com, September 18, 2018, https://www.rogerebert.com/reviews/jane-fonda-in-five-acts-2018.

2. A New Star in Old Hollywood

"Fonda is a different type": Dyer, *Stars*, 61.

"For all its privilege": Ann Patchett, "Famous, Infamous Jane—Confusing Life a Real Workout," *Guardian*, April 18, 2005.

"performed" bulimia in an Actors Studio class: Bosworth, *Jane Fonda*, 150.

gives the earlier date: Fonda, *My Life So Far*, 196.

one of 116 Hollywood signees: Tim Gray, "'Trumbo' and Five Facts You Didn't Know About the Hollywood Blacklist," *Variety*, September 12, 2015.

Henry Fonda didn't appear: Bosworth, *Jane Fonda*, 57.

"I couldn't get a job": Harmetz, "Jane Fonda: She Makes Ideas Pay."

Actor's Daughter Gets Lead: Sam Zolotow, "Jane Fonda Is Signed to Star on Broadway with 'Fun Couple,'" *New York Times*, March 13, 1962.

"She resisted his suggestion": Charles McGrath, "A Radical Vixen Retakes the Stage," *New York Times*, February 19, 2009.

"Her acting style is her own": Brooks Atkinson, "Theatre: A Tawdry Tale," *New York Times*, March 1, 1960.

"Kafkaesque nightmare": Fonda, *My Life So Far*, 128.

"A tall ear of comedy corn": Howard Thompson, "Basketball and Education at the Palace," *New York Times*, April 7, 1960.

"I had to play the part": Delphine Seyrig, dir., *Be Pretty and Shut Up* (*Sois belle et tais-toi!*), 1981.

"merely titillating and frequently salacious": Daniel Talbot, "In a Swamp of Erotica," *New York Times*, May 29, 1960.

"Cukor loves to watch his actors": Dan Callahan, "Great Directors: George Cukor," *Senses of Cinema*, October 2004, https://www.sensesofcinema.com/2004/great-directors/cukor/.

"a comedy, set in Memphis": Arthur Gelb, "Williams and Kazan and the Big Walk-Out," *New York Times*, May 1, 1960.

"It is a relatively recent convention": Haskell, *From Reverence to Rape*, 99.

Christine's remarkable but misguided look: John Houseman, *Final Dress* (New York: Touchstone, 1983), 227–229.

"Fonda was asked which picture": "After Show: Jane Fonda and Lily Tomlin's Most Annoying Habits," *Watch What Happens Live with Andy Cohen*, YouTube, January 19, 2018, https://www.youtube.com/watch?v=niLN5QW0e_s.

Fonda "hates that movie": Michael Riedel, "Very Few Fonda Memories," *New York Post*, November 7, 2008.

rate only a sentence: Fonda, *My Life So Far*, 135.

"The fact that we had": Keith Beattie, *D. A. Pennebaker* (Urbana: University of Illinois Press, 2011), 135.

3. On the Ground

"What in the world is the matter": Richard Nixon, White House recording, September 19, 1971, excerpted in Lacy, *Jane Fonda in Five Acts*.

"They arrested Jane Fonda": Donald Trump, rally in Louisiana, November 6, 2019, quoted in "Donald Trump Reacts to Jane Fonda's Arrests: 'Nothing Changes'" by Tyler McCarthy, Fox News, November 7, 2019, https://www.foxnews.com/entertainment/donald-trump-reacts-jane-fonda-arrested.

"too much baggage": Associated Press, "Fonda has 'Too Much Baggage' to Protest War," TODAY.com, April 17, 2006, https://www.today.com/popculture/fonda-has-too-much-baggage-protest-war-1c9493386.

first time she has raised: Michael Ruane and Fredrick Kunkle, "Thousands Protest Bush Policy as Senate Prepares to Debate Troop Increase, Demonstrators Demand War's End." *Washington Post*, January 28, 2007.

"How do you ask a man": "Excerpts of Kerry's 1971 Vietnam Testimony," *Washington Post*, February 20, 2004.

"I can't explain the chaos": John Kerry, "Diplomacy Was Working Until Trump Abandoned It," *New York Times*, January 9, 2020.

"It's the most dangerous thing": *The Last Word with Lawrence O'Donnell*, MSNBC, aired January 8, 2020.

"It did not take the jury long": John Kifner, "For the U.S., It's the Gainesville 0," *New York Times*, September 2, 1973.

"Preparing for the Winter Soldier investigation": Fonda, "Terror and Trauma."

"Its distributors say that the war": David Halbfinger, "Film Echoes the Present in Atrocities of the Past," *New York Times*, August 9, 2005.

"People are realizing today": Hershberger, *Jane Fonda's Words*, 57.

"I believe Jane Fonda believes": *The Big Story with John Gibson*, Fox News, aired January 29, 2007.

"Meaning-making paradigms": Diana Taylor, *The Archive and the Repertoire: Performing Cultural Memory in the Americas* (Durham, NC: Duke University Press, 2003), 26.

"So bright it looked": Frederick Kunkle, "Jane Fonda Is Arrested Leading Environmental Protest at the Capitol," *Washington Post*, October 11, 2019.

stylish two-minute video: "'The World Is at Stake': Jane Fonda Moves to D.C. to Fight Climate Change," *Washington Post*, October 10, 2019, https://www.washingtonpost.com/video/politics/the-world-is-at-stake-jane-fonda-moves-to-dc-to-fight-climate-change/2019/10/10/d22bef0d-1bde-4888-8d9b-eb809a92dd74_video.html.

Soderbergh continued his years-long lament: Ann Hornaday, "Steven Soderbergh Says the Cinema Is Still in a Crisis. (But He's Making Movies Anyway.)," *Washington Post*, October 11, 2019.

a headline gushes: Lauren Geall, "Jane Fonda Just Accepted a BAFTA Award While Being Arrested, and the Internet Is Impressed," *Stylist*, October 27, 2019, https://www.stylist.co.uk/people/jane-fonda-arrested-accepting-bafta-award-ted-danson-climate-protest-internet-reactions-twitter/317328.

"Jane Fonda is possibly the coolest octogenarian": Tait McGregor, "The Indisputably Badass Jane Fonda Accepted an Award While Being Arrested," MTV Australia, October 27, 2019, https://www.mtv.com.au/climate-change/news/the-indisputably-badass-jane-fonda-accepted-an-award-while-being-arrested (site discontinued).

writes about the "star power": Barbara Demick, "The Star Power of Jane Fonda's Climate-Change Arrests," *New Yorker*, December 27, 2019.

"Fueled by the power": Sarah Kaplan, "'We're Building an Army': Jane Fonda Caps Off Weeks of Climate Protests in D.C.," *Washington Post*, January 10, 2020.

"She is well fortified now": Molly Haskell, "Introduction to Jane and the Enemy," *Village Voice*, November 7, 1974.

4. Kiss Kiss Bang Bang: Lessons from the '60s, Part I

"Movie making is like fighting a war": Kirk Honeycutt, "The Five-Year Struggle to Make 'Coming Home,'" *New York Times*, February 19, 1978.

"Four door Ford": Michael Caine, *The Elephant to Hollywood* (New York: Henry Holt, 2010), 97–98.

"one of the longest": Richard Brody, "DVD of the Week: 'Hurry Sundown,'" *New Yorker*, May 4, 2011.

"one of the finest and most influential": Peter Bogdanovich, *Movie of the Week: 52 Classic Films for One Full Year* (New York: Ballantine, 1999), 172–173.

"an offense to intelligence": Bosley Crowther, "Weak Preminger Film Stars Michael Caine," *New York Times*, March 24, 1967.

"I had written what I": Fred Gardner, "An Interview with Lillian Hellman," in *Conversations with Lillian Hellman*, ed. Jackson R. Bryer (Jackson: University Press of Mississippi, 1986), 112.

"his unsigned first draft": Nat Segaloff, *Arthur Penn, American Director* (Lexington: University of Kentucky Press, 2011), 129–130.

"It was not a happy experience": Gardner, "Interview with Lillian Hellman," 112.

"Penn's first indisputable": Robin Wood with Richard Lippe, *Arthur Penn*, new ed. (Detroit: Wayne State University Press, 2014), 39.

the 1966 audience laughed: Kael, *Kiss Kiss Bang Bang*, 187.

"indigenous American berserk": Philip Roth, *American Pastoral* (New York: Vintage, 1997), 86.

"Bubber makes the movie's point": Callan, *Robert Redford*, 115.

"Seated at a desk, she sighed": Vadim, *Bardot, Deneuve, Fonda*, 245–246.

"three of Mr. Brando's subtlest": A. O. Scott, "Critic's Notebook: Marshaling His Talent to Battle His Fame," *New York Times*, July 3, 2004.

"Bubber, for me": Callan, Robert Redford, 115.

"What a package, right?": Fonda, *My Life So Far*, 163.

5. *Vive la Différence*: Lessons from the '60s, Part II

"'There was a time'": Martin Kasindorf, "Fonda: A Person of Many Parts," *New York Times*, February 3, 1974.

"One night I'd come home": Jack Kroll with Martin Kasindorf and Katrine Ames, "Hollywood's New Heroines," *Newsweek*, October 10, 1977.

"I lived all over Paris,": Olivier Joyard, "A Conversation with Jane Fonda," *Numéro*, September 8, 2020.

headline as Fonda sued: "Drawing of Jane Fonda Is Draped with Canvas," *New York Times*, March 16, 1965.

"Barbarella has no sense": Gerald Jonas, "Here's What Happened to Baby Jane," *New York Times*, January 22, 1967.

"the very first to play characters": Williams, *Screening Sex*, 164–169.

"For a while, the audience": Renata Adler, "Screen: Science + Sex = 'Barbarella,'" *New York Times*, October 12, 1968.

"I mean, that's a big swing": Josh Horowitz, "Sydney Sweeney Talks *Immaculate*, *Euphoria*, *Anyone but You*, *Madame Web*," *Happy Sad Confused*, YouTube, March 22, 2024, https://www.youtube.com/watch?v=-V-HMCiCDts.

6. Wild in the Streets: Lessons from the '60s, Part III

"I still believe that there": Thomson, *Whole Equation*, 323.

"The film is really": Elizabeth Campbell, "*Rolling Stone* Raps with Peter Fonda," reprinted in *Easy Rider: The Complete Screenplay*, ed. Nancy Hardin and Marilyn Schlossberg (New York: Signet, 1969), 32.

actually was penned by Southern: Lee Hill. *A Grand Guy: The Life and Art of Terry Southern* (New York: HarperCollins, 2001), 292.

"cinema verité in allegory": Campbell, "*Rolling Stone* Raps."

"[Hopper] knew he could not": Robert Christgau, "Rock & Roll: The Music of 'Easy Rider,'" *Village Voice*, July 24, 1969.

"about Vietnam. Not literally": Callan, *Robert Redford*, 149.

"One must talk about": Kael, *Going Steady*, 118.

"Hoppe always quoted Jean Cocteau": Peter Fonda, *Don't Tell Dad* (New York: Hyperion, 1998), 257.

"the automatic handwriting": Biskind, *Easy Riders*, 75.

"the only film I know": Christgau, "Rock & Roll."

"A cinematic accident": Mark Rozzo, *Everybody Thought We Were Crazy: Dennis Hopper, Brooke Hayward and 1960s Los Angeles* (New York: Ecco, 2022), 306.

"The Democratic Party fell": Haskell Wexler, commentary track, *Medium Cool*, directed by Haskell Wexler (1969; Paramount, 2001), DVD.

"students invited him to film": Brody, *Everything Is Cinema*, 324.

"dense assemblage of social commentary": Oliver Gruner, "'About as Brutal, Relevant and Exploitable as They Come': *Medium Cool* (1969) and Political Filmmaking," in *The Hollywood Renaissance: Revisiting Cinema's Most Celebrated Era*, ed. Peter Krämer and Yannis Tzioumakis (New York: Bloomsbury Academic, 2018), 98.

"It was conceived as both a filmic": Gruner, 106.

"personifying American tensions": Kael, *Deeper into Movies*, 89.

"If you think of 'They Shoot Horses'": A. O. Scott, "Sydney Pollack, Filmmaker New and Old," *New York Times*, May 28, 2008.

"regimented as soldiers": Hershberger, *Jane Fonda's War*, 18.

"About the Depression, it could": Hayden, *Reunion*, 443.

headline surveying that long history: Bernard Weinraub, "Play a Hooker and Win an Oscar," *New York Times*, February 20, 1996.

"Operating on alternating currents": Anderson, "Jane Fonda in the '70s," https://4columns.org/anderson-melissa/jane-fonda-in-the-70s.

"From a woman's point of view": Haskell, *From Reverence to Rape*, 323.

shot scads of footage: Jared Brown, *Alan J. Pakula: His Films and His Life* (New York: Back Stage, 2005), 107–108.

"It was the first time": Ross, *Hollywood Left and Right*, 232.

"our national theater": Kael, *Deeper into Movies*, xvii.

"special kind of smartness": Kael, 355–356.

7. Fighting for It

"killing machines": Phil McCausland, "Trump Announces 'Review' of Green Beret Murder Case: 'We Train Our Boys to Be Killing Machines,'" NBC News, October 12, 2019, https://www.nbcnews.com/politics/donald-trump/trump-announces-review-green-beret-murder-case-we-train-our-n1065421.

"A shocking and unprecedented intervention": Richard Spencer, "I Was Fired as Navy Secretary. Here's What I've Learned Because of It," *Washington Post*, November 27, 2019.

"Can't overcome the dullness": Mike Hale, "From George Clooney and Hulu, 'Catch-22,' with a Catch," *New York Times*, May 17, 2019.

beaten to the punch: Mark Harris, *Mike Nichols: A Life* (New York: Penguin, 2021), 258.

"Don't fuck with me": Mike Nichols and Steven Soderbergh, commentary track, *Catch-22*, directed by Mike Nichols (1970; Paramount, 2001), DVD.

"A whore with a heart of gold": Julia Phillips, *You'll Never Eat Lunch in This Town Again* (New York: Random House, 1991), 99.

"I like its earnestness": Vincent Canby, "'Steelyard Blues' Arrives," *New York Times*, February 1, 1973.

"Clearly no one involved": Richard Jameson, review of *Steelyard Blues*, *Movietone News*, April 22, 1973.

"static and unfunny": Phillips, *You'll Never Eat Lunch*, 108.

"It may be because": Canby, "'Steelyard Blues' Arrives."

"remarkable—light, offhand, witty": Quoted in Hoberman, "G.I. Jane."

"There was something shrill": Hayden, *Reunion*, 266.

"The only film made": David Zeiger, dir., *Sir! No Sir!* (Balcony Releasing, 2005).

"You must pay them": James Conaway, "Said Jean-Pierre Gorin: 'We Have No Answers.' Said Friend Jean-Luc Godard: 'Only Questions,'" *New York Times*, December 24, 1972.

"We didn't want the vulgarity": Brody, *Everything Is Cinema*, 351.

"By imagining that they": Bertolt Brecht, *Brecht on Theatre*, ed. and trans. John Willett (New York: Hill and Wang, 1964), 34.

Gorin largely handled: Brody, *Everything Is Cinema*, 360–361.

"being interested in the grammar": "Jean-Pierre Gorin on Jean-Luc Godard," Criterion Channel, 2004, https://www.criterionchannel.com/videos/jean-pierre-gorin-2004.

"I remember cautioning her": Hayden, *Reunion*. 267.

"The effect can be numbing": Conaway, "Said Jean-Pierre Gorin."

In 1968, Godard: Brody, *Everything Is Cinema*, 342.

"No other country had ever": Mary Hershberger, *Traveling to Vietnam: American Peace Activists and the War* (Syracuse, NY: Syracuse University Press), xviii.

"I was amazed, and still am": Hayden, *Reunion*, 276.

"Why should American atrocities": Tom Hayden, *Writings for a Democratic Society: The Tom Hayden Reader* (San Francisco: City Lights, 2008), 445.

the movie's "ambitions" as "modest": Haskell, "Introduction to Jane."

"We feel like it's becoming": Paul McIsaac, "An Introduction to the Enemy: An Interview with Jane Fonda." Pacifica Radio, 1974, via Internet Archive, https://archive.org/details/pra-BC2167.

"I had made all kinds": McIsaac, https://archive.org/details/pra-BC2167.

8. Fun with *Jane* and *Julia*

"We're not interested in being": Ross, *Hollywood Left and Right*, 249.

"My 'she's back' film": Fonda, *My Life So Far*, 369.

Fonda's blockbuster workout business: Robert Lindsey, "Jane Fonda's Exercise Salons Aiding Her Husband's Candidacy," *New York Times*, May 2, 1982.

"a deceptively sunny": Vincent Canby, "Dick and Jane in Screen Romp." *New York Times*, February 20, 1977.

"Jane Fonda looks radiant": Kael, *When the Lights Go Down*, 269.

the government admitted wrongdoing: Hershberger, *Jane Fonda's War*, 171; and Fonda, *My Life So Far*, 354.

"torn from the headlines" and *"I knew it would be"*: *Fun with Dick and Jane* production notes, Columbia Pictures, 2005, via Jim Carrey Online, https://www.jimcarreyonline.com/movies/dickandjane.html?p=3.

"It's nonsense to expect": Manohla Dargis, "The Flip Side of the American Dream," *New York Times*, December 21, 2005.

cited nine scribes: John Horn and Rachel Abramowitz, "Credit Ascribed, Denied," *Los Angeles Times*, December 4, 2005.

"Currently, there is an unprecedented": Joanne Laurier, "Not So Much Fun for Dick and Jane," *World Socialist Web Site*, January 21, 2006, https://www.wsws.org/en/articles/2006/01/dick-j21.html.

Schumer, among others, rerouted money: Stephanie Strom, "Funds Aid Ex-Workers of Enron and WorldCom," *New York Times*, January 18, 2003.

"That's a cheap shot": James Hohmann with Mariana Alfaro, "The Daily 202: The Democratic Debate Descends into Class Warfare, as the Billionaire and Socialist Play Off Each Other," *Washington Post*, February 20, 2020.

"I'd done A Doll's House": Fonda, *My Life So Far*, 367.

"They're both rebels": Howard Thompson, "Claire Bloom to Appear in Ibsen Plays," *New York Times*, August 21, 1970.

"I had, as has become unfairly": Michel Ciment, *Conversations with Losey* (London: Methuen, 1985), 329.

"She's an absolutely electric person": Ciment, 333.

"I am not willing": Lillian Hellman to HUAC, May 19, 1952, quoted in "The 1950's and the Cold War: An Online Professional Development Seminar" by Ellen Schrecker, America in Class, March 12, 2013, https://americainclass.org/wp-content/uploads/2013/03/WEB-1950s-CW-Presentation.pdf, 28.

"Shut up! Stop talking drivel": Bosworth, *Jane Fonda*, 416.

"served the larger political purpose": Victor Navasky, "The Antagonist: On Lillian Hellman," *Nation*, August 29, 2012.

"I always find questions": Joanne Rapf, "Mythic Figures: Women and Co-being in Three Films by Fred Zinnemann," in *The Films of Fred Zinnemann*, ed. Arthur Noletti (Albany: State University of New York Press, 1999), 236.

"theater of thought": "Fred Zinnemann: Cinema of Resistance (Julia)," Getty Research Institute, April 24, 2012, via YouTube, https://www.youtube.com/watch?v=Te1C1r2YqmQ.

"The picture depended on that": Fred Zinnemann, *Fred Zinnemann: A Life in the Movies* (New York: Charles Scribner's Sons, 1992), 227.

"I said once in some interview": Marcia Chambers, "Lillian Hellman Wins Round in Suit," *New York Times*, May 11, 1984.

"I cannot prove that": Stephanie Mansfield, "Muriel Gardiner, Echoes of 'Julia,'" *Washington Post*, July 6, 1983.

"It's beginning to appear": William Wright, "Why Lillian Hellman Remains Fascinating," *New York Times*, November 3, 1996.

"Preconceived ideas were out": Zinnemann, *Fred Zinnemann*, 59.

Vanessa Vadim got her name: Fonda, *My Life So Far*, 203; Vanessa Redgrave, *Vanessa Redgrave: An Autobiography* (New York: Random House, 1994), 177.

"not named after Redgrave": Kroll with Kasindorf and Ames, "Hollywood's New Heroines."

"What had happened at Tal al-Zaatar": Redgrave, *Vanessa Redgrave*, 222.

"Vanessa Redgrave is stalking": Judith Weinraub, "Two Feisty Feminists Filming Hellman's 'Pentimento,'" *New York Times*, October 31, 1976.

"Jane is technically superb": Noletti, *Films of Fred Zinnemann*, 17.

"I am angry and I own it": Gregory Krieg and Eric Bradner, "Elizabeth Warren Responds to 'Angry' Charge: 'I Am Angry and I Own It,'" CNN.com, November 9, 2019, https://www.cnn.com/2019/11/08/politics/elizabeth-warren-joe-biden-sexism-charges.

New York Times headline decided: Bruce Fretts, "The Most Political Ceremony in Academy History," *New York Times*, January 11, 2019.
"I often feel that only drama": Redgrave, *Vanessa Redgrave*, 242.
"What makes Julia such a satisfying": Carl Rollyson, *Lillian Hellman: Her Legend and Her Legacy* (New York: St. Martin's Press, 1988), 504–505.
Beverly Hills theater was bombed: Aljean Harmetz, "Theater for Redgrave Film Bombed," *New York Times*, June 16, 1978.
"She is likely to be the most": Kroll, "Vietnam Hero Worship."
"She pares away her life": Rollyson, *Lillian Hellman*, 7.
"She was hard on herself": Vadim, *Bardot, Deneuve, Fonda*, 275.
"It is very important to make": Weinraub, "Two Feisty Feminists."

9. A Farewell to Arms

"Even though I'm Jane Fonda": Zheutlin and Talbot, *Creative Differences*, 133.
script from Nancy Dowd: Aljean Harmetz, "2 Vietnam Films Cast Aside Ghosts on Way to Oscars," *New York Times*, April 11, 1979.
Dowd went with Fonda: Bosworth, *Jane Fonda*, 384.
calling Fonda an "ex-friend": Janet Maslin, "Four-Letter Screenwriter," *Newsweek*, March 7, 1977.
"Am I too bossy?": Bruce Dern, Jon Voight, and Haskell Wexler, commentary track, *Coming Home*, directed by Hal Ashby (MGM, 2002), DVD.
"Coming Home was made": Dern, Voight, and Wexler, commentary track, *Coming Home*.
"The first important movie": Kroll, "Vietnam Hero Worship."
"ten individual roles with the potential": Aaron Hunter, *Authoring Hal Ashby: The Myth of the New Hollywood Auteur* (New York: Bloomsbury, 2016), 123.
"This propensity for making": Hunter, *Authoring Hal Ashby*, 23.
"It's filled with woozy": Kael, *When the Lights Go Down*, 230.
"heroic resources as a mime": Kael, *When the Lights Go Down*, 518.
"Our story has a Marine": Fonda, *My Life So Far*, 360.
urging Fonda to "ride him": Williams, *Screening Sex*, 176.
"Dr. Joshua Golden, director": Honeycutt, "Five-Year Struggle."
The rate has been substantially worse: Jeffrey Allen Smith, Michael Doidge, and Ryan Hanoa, "A Historical Examination of Military Records of US Army Suicide, 1819 to 2017," *JAMA Network Open*, December 13, 2019, https://jamanetwork.com/journals/jamanetworkopen/fullarticle/2757484.
"As romantic as John Wayne": Kroll, "Vietnam Hero Worship."

"Jane Fonda isn't playing": Kael, *When the Lights Go Down*, 402.

"Nice try": Bosworth, *Jane Fonda*, 429.

"It was like the day": Ron Kovic, *Born on the Fourth of July* (New York: Simon & Schuster, 1976), 141.

"Something I will never forget": Kovic, 148–149.

"Cimino is big on hubbub": Kael, *Taking It All In*, 113.

"More about the mind": Vincent Canby, "The Vietnam War in Stone's 'Platoon.'" *New York Times*, December 19, 1986.

"The war is really incidental": Production notes bonus feature, *The Deer Hunter*, directed by Michael Cimino (Universal 2008), DVD.

observe that the picture played: Kael, *When the Lights Go Down*, 516.

"biliously ironic" and *"cinematic heroes and martyrs"*: Richard Brody, "Postscript: Michael Cimino, 1939–2016," *New Yorker*, July 12, 2016.

"Slips into the wildest sort": Vincent Canby, "Blue-Collar Epic," *New York Times*, December 15, 1978.

"Precisely when film ceased": Michael Anderegg, ed., *Inventing Vietnam: The War in Film and Television* (Philadelphia: Temple University Press, 1991), 3.

"The U.S. genre of Vietnam": Pamela Blafer Lack, letter to the editor, *New York Times*, September 9, 1979.

"In addition to liking": Janet Maslin, "Screen: Norris in 'Missing in Action,'" *New York Times*, November 17, 1984.

"'Were we right to fight'": Gaylyn Studlar and David Desser, "Never Having to Say You're Sorry: *Rambo*'s Rewriting of the Vietnam War," in *From Hanoi to Hollywood: The Vietnam War in American Film*, ed. Linda Dittmar and Gene Michaud (New Brunswick, NJ: Rutgers University Press), 104.

"What had been virtually forgotten": Anderegg, *Inventing Vietnam*, 29.

"This is a tale of extraordinarily": Vincent Canby, "A Woman's View of Vietnam Horrors," *New York Times*, December 24, 1993.

"What 'Platoon' does—better": Pat H. Broesky, "After Seeing 'Platoon,' Fonda Wept," *Los Angeles Times*, January 25, 1987.

10. Star, Power

"Why aren't we prepared?": Gillian Steinberg, "Quarantined but Not Alone," *Washington Post Magazine*, March 29, 2020.

"Inside the reactor": B. Drummond Ayres Jr., "Three Mile Island: Notes from a Nightmare," *New York Times*, April 16, 1979.

"Jane was one of the first": Aljean Harmetz, "Fallout from 'China Syndrome' Has Already Begun," *New York Times*, March 11, 1979.

friend and colleague Don Widener: William K. Knoedelseder Jr. and Ellen Farley. "When Fate Follows Fiction," *Washington Post*, March 29, 1979.

"feeling this was an unforgiving": "The China Syndrome: A Fusion of Talent" (featurette), *The China Syndrome*, directed by James Bridges (Columbia Tristar, 2004), DVD.

"The best role he [Lemmon]": Vincent Canby, "Nuclear Plant Is Villain in 'China Syndrome': A Question of Ethics," *New York Times*, March 16, 1979.

"These were personal issues": Fonda, *My Life So Far*, 376.

"Not the least bit fair-minded": Richard Schickel, "An Atom-Powered Thriller," *Time*, March 26, 1979.

"Basically, the movie's intended": Harmetz, "Fallout from 'China Syndrome.'"

"The China Syndrome is less": Canby, "Nuclear Plant Is Villain."

"So tensely eager to act": Kael, *When the Lights Go Down*, 530.

"I had to get into shape": Fonda, *My Life So Far*, 387.

"I've learned how hard" and *"I will only be"*: Zheutlin and Talbot, *Creative Differences*, 131.

"The three stars are splendid": Canby, "Nuclear Plant Is Villain."

"the political drama is outrageously": David Ansen, "Nuclear Politics," *Newsweek*, March 19, 1979.

Streep was quickly stereotyped: Molly Haskell, "Meryl Streep: Hiding in the Spotlight," *Ms.*, December 1988, reprinted in *Holding My Own in No Man's Land* (New York: Oxford University Press, 1997), 43–50.

"growing political opposition": David Burnham, "Nuclear Experts Debate 'The China Syndrome,'" *New York Times*, March 18, 1979.

a vivid case of life": Pete Hamill, "The Life and Death of an Idealist," *New York Times*, December 13, 1981.

"It's often said that": Steven Pinker, *Enlightenment Now: The Case for Reason, Science, Humanism and Progress* (New York: Penguin, 2018), 148.

"But," they concluded: Steven J. Dubner and Steven D. Levitt, "The Jane Fonda Effect," *New York Times*, September 16, 2007.

"In 60 years of nuclear power": Joshua S. Goldstein, Staffan A. Qvist, and Steven Pinker, "Nuclear Power Can Save the World," *New York Times*, April 6, 2019.

"As Eric Schlosser, a journalist": Carolyn Kormann, "Is Nuclear Power Worth the Risk?," *New Yorker*, December 22, 2019.

"I don't feel confident": Steinberg, "Quarantined but Not Alone."

"Even today, the Big Speech": Terry Christensen, *Reel Politics: American Political Movies from "Birth of a Nation" to "Platoon"* (New York: Blackwell, 1987), 25.

11. Side Tracks: Horses for Courses

"*The public doesn't want*": Barbara Zheutlin and Jim Richardson, "Hollywood's Progressive Producer: An Interview with Bruce Gilbert," *Cinéaste* 9, no. 4 (Fall 1979): 4, quoted in Christensen, *Reel Politics*, 216.

"*joined the big leagues*": Callan, *Robert Redford*, 263.

"*Stardom is defined by intuition*": Callan, 267.

12. On Target

"*Jane can do some really remarkable work*": Wood with Lippe, *Arthur Penn*, 228–229.

Women's participation rate: Mitra Toosi and Teresa L. Morisi, "Women in the Workforce Before, During and After the Great Recession," US Bureau of Labor Statistics, July 2017, https://www.bls.gov/spotlight/2017/women-in-the-workforce-before-during-and-after-the-great-recession/home.htm.

raved mainly about Parton: Roger Ebert, review of *9 to 5*, *Chicago Sun-Times*, December 19, 1980, via RogerEbert.com, https://www.rogerebert.com/reviews/nine-to-five-1980.

"*I don't want to play liberated*": Kasindorf, "Restless Yawing."

"*A chilling, unsettling experience*": Mel Gussow, "'Ik,' a Dramatization of 'Mountain People,' Portrays Tribe Lacking Human Emotions," *New York Times*, October 18, 1976.

against any "lecturing": Joan Goodman, "Fonda: Seeking Acceptance," *Times* (London), February 6, 1981.

"*Jane Fonda's and George Segal's*": "Picks and Pans Review: How to Beat the High Cost of Living," *People*, July 28, 1980.

"*Concludes by waving the flag*": Vincent Canby, "'Nine to Five,' Office Comedy," *New York Times*, December 19, 1980.

"capon" is the accurate term: Kael, *Taking It All In*, 164.

"*searching the screen for signs*": Georgia Dullea, "Secretaries See Parallels in 'Nine to Five,'" *New York Times*, January 2, 1981.

"*The plot of 9 to 5 feels*": Tara Murtha, "'9 to 5' Turns 35, and It's Still Radical Today," *Rolling Stone*, December 18, 2015.

"*The 1980 Movie '9 to 5' Is Still*": Monica Torres, "The 1980 Movie '9 to 5' Is Still Depressingly Relevant for Women at Work," *HuffPost*, November 4, 2019, https://www.huffpost.com/entry/movie-9-to-5-film-dolly-parton_l_5db6fa34e4b079eb95a7299a.

"*Perhaps we don't really care*": Ebert, review of *9 to 5*, https://www.rogerebert.com/reviews/nine-to-five-1980.

"There are direct results": Kael, *Taking It All In*, 9.

zapped a poison-pen letter: Kael, 8–20.

Resnick listed her top five: Oliver Staley, "The Screenwriter of the 1980 Hit Film '9 to 5' Says We're Finally Facing Reality," Quartz, December 10, 2017, https://qz.com/work/1150399/a-lot-has-changed-for-working-women-since-1980s-9-to-5-even-more-hasnt.

"This one guy": David Marchese, "It's a Tough World. Lily Tomlin Has Always Tried to Make It More Tender," *New York Times*, December 30, 2019.

embraced it in a 2013 appraisal: Rosemary Counter, "Everything I Know About Feminism I Learned from 'Working Girl,'" *Jezebel*, October 25, 2013, https://www.jezebel.com/everything-i-know-about-feminism-i-learned-from-working-1452145089.

"Someone introduced me to Jane": Chris Gardner, "'Working Girl' Turns 30: On-Set Romances and Secrets of the Staten Island Ferry Revealed in Juicy Oral History," *Hollywood Reporter*, December 3, 2018.

"by playing the daffy": Susan Faludi, *Backlash: The Undeclared War Against American Women* (New York: Crown, 1991), 128.

"Tess's quest obviously owes": Charlotte Brunsdon, *Screen Tastes: Soap Opera to Satellite Dishes* (London: Routledge, 1997), 88.

still earned only 83 percent: American Association of University Women, Equal Pay Day Calendar, March 5, 2025, https://www.aauw.org/resources/article/equal-pay-day-calendar/.

"In many ways it was": "Talking with Jane Fonda," *Rolling Stone*, https://www.rollingstone.com/politics/politics-news/talking-with-jane-fonda-for-rolling-stones-40th-anniversary-237564/.

"The Republican Party reaffirms": Warren Weaver Jr., "Full G.O.P Platform Panel Votes to Abandon Rights Amendment," *New York Times*, July 10, 1980.

"The heroines did not withdraw": Faludi, *Backlash*, 138.

"I have no time to waste": Fonda, *Prime Time*, 10.

13. On "the Money"

"We are not just products": Kasindorf, "Restless Yawing."

"a terrible role": Kael, *Taking It All In*, 271.

calling Henry "Cold": Fonda, *My Life So Far*, 437.

"Let's talk about body": Fonda, "Lights, Camera, Lena!"

"In the '70s": Fonda, "Lights, Camera, Lena!"

"Easily the worst film": Brown, *Alan J. Pakula*, 218.

"The issue," Fonda said: John C. Tibbetts, "*Rollover*: Conversations About the Film" (audio recordings), 1981, John C. Tibbetts Archive of Conversations in the Arts and Humanities, KU ScholarWorks, https://kuscholarworks.ku.edu/entities/publication/e51ba912-b44c-4ff3-b904-283f4a1b1793.

"Under four successive Administrations": Tad Szulc, "Recycling Petrodollars," *New York Times*, September 20, 1981.

"Citibank is on the hot seat": Dan Dorfman, "Kuwait Puts Citibank on Investment Hot Seat," *Washington Post*, June 7, 1981.

"but he knows whereof": Tibbetts, "*Rollover*: Conversations," https://kuscholarworks.ku.edu/entities/publication/e51ba912-b44c-4ff3-b904-283f4a1b1793.

"Gobbledygook," as Pakula said: Tibbetts, "*Rollover*."

"I guess I'm always surprised": Tibbetts, "*Rollover*."

"Rollover showed us what not to do": Charles L. P. Silet, ed., *Oliver Stone Interviews* (Jackson: University Press of Mississippi, 2001), 58.

"I liked playing somebody": Tibbetts, "*Rollover*," https://kuscholarworks.ku.edu/entities/publication/e51ba912-b44c-4ff3-b904-283f4a1b1793.

"With 'Rollover,' I wanted": Fred Yager, "Actress, Protestor, Author . . . Daughter," Associated Press, January 31, 1982.

"Is the Arab Euro-dollar": Janet Maslin, "Kris Kristofferson and Jane Fonda in 'Rollover,'" *New York Times*, December 11, 1981.

"Jane Fonda and her company": Paul J. Nadler, "Rollover Is Must-See Film for Bankers," *American Banker*, January 4, 1982.

"It can't be easy": Michael Kinsley, "Economic Crisis Unfurls in Hushed Suspense," *New York Times*, May 22, 2011.

"'The Laundromat' aims to provoke": A. O. Scott, "'The Laundromat' Review: Meryl Streep in a Cycle of Spin," *New York Times*, September 25, 2019.

"The so-called experts": Tibbetts, "*Rollover*," https://kuscholarworks.ku.edu/entities/publication/e51ba912-b44c-4ff3-b904-283f4a1b1793.

14. "The World We're Working For"

"I wanted to show": Larry Rohter, "Why the Road Turned Rocky for 'Old Gringo,'" *New York Times*, October 22, 1989.

losing interest in movies: Fonda, *Prime Time*, 59.

"I haven't worked since": "Jane Fonda Gets Candid About Acting in Her 80s," *Amanpour*, CNN, aired September 29, 2025, https://www.cnn.com/2025/09/29/us/video/jane-fonda-acting-amanpour-vrtc.

"People need to be able to envision": Fonda, *My Life So Far*, 475.

SELECTED BIBLIOGRAPHY

Als, Hilton. "Queen Jane, Approximately." *New Yorker*, May 2, 2011.

Anderson, Melissa. "Jane Fonda in the '70s." *4Columns*, June 6, 2018, https://4columns.org/anderson-melissa/jane-fonda-in-the-70s.

Biskind, Peter. *Easy Riders, Raging Bulls: How the Sex-Drugs-and-Rock 'n' Roll Generation Saved Hollywood*. New York: Touchstone, 1998.

Bosworth, Patricia. *Jane Fonda: The Private Life of a Public Woman*. New York: Houghton Mifflin Harcourt, 2011.

Brody, Richard. *Everything Is Cinema: The Working Life of Jean-Luc Godard*. New York: Henry Holt, 2008.

Brough, James. *The Fabulous Fondas*. New York: David McKay, 1973.

Burke, Carol. *Camp All-American, Hanoi Jane, and the High-and-Tight: Gender, Folklore, and Changing Military Culture*. Boston: Beacon Press, 2004.

Callan, Michael Feeney. *Robert Redford: The Biography*. New York: Knopf, 2011.

Fonda, Jane. "Lights, Camera, Lena!" *Paper*, February 16, 2016.

Fonda, Jane. "My Convoluted Journey to Feminism." *Lenny Letter*, March 23, 2016, https://www.lennyletter.com/politics/news/a311/my-convoluted-journey-to-feminism/ (site discontinued).

Fonda, Jane. *My Life So Far*. New York: Random House, 2005.

Fonda, Jane. *Prime Time*. New York: Random House, 2011.

Fonda, Jane. "Terror and Trauma." *Guardian*, November 17, 2005.

Fonda, Jane. "We Have to Live Like We're in a Climate Emergency. Because We Are." *New York Times*, December 5, 2019.

Fonda, Jane. *What Can I Do? My Path from Climate Despair to Action*. New York: Penguin, 2020.

Haskell, Molly. *From Reverence to Rape: The Treatment of Women in the Movies.* 2nd ed. Chicago: University of Chicago Press, 1987.

Hayden, Tom. *Reunion.* New York: Random House, 1988.

Hershberger, Mary. *Jane Fonda's War: A Political Biography of an Antiwar Icon.* New York: New Press, 2005.

Hershberger, Mary, ed. *Jane Fonda's Words of Politics and Passion.* New York: New Press, 2006.

Hoberman, J. "G.I. Jane." *Village Voice*, May 1, 2001.

Kael, Pauline. *Deeper into Movies.* New York: Little, Brown, 1973.

Kael, Pauline. *Going Steady.* New York: Little, Brown, 1970.

Kael, Pauline. *Kiss Kiss Bang Bang.* New York: Little, Brown, 1968.

Kael, Pauline. *Reeling.* Boston and Toronto: Little, Brown, 1976.

Kael, Pauline. *Taking It All In.* New York: Holt, Rinehart and Winston, 1984.

Kael, Pauline. *When the Lights Go Down.* Henry Holt, 1980.

Kasindorf, Martin. "A Restless Yawing Between Extremes." *New York Times*, February 3, 1974.

Keegan, Rebecca. "Jane Fonda on Cancer Battle, Privilege and Coming into Her Own at 85." *Hollywood Reporter*, January 27, 2023.

Kroll, Jack. "Vietnam Hero Worship." *Newsweek*, February 20, 1978.

Lacy, Susan, dir. *Jane Fonda in Five Acts.* HBO, 2018.

Lembcke, Jerry. *Hanoi Jane: War, Sex and Fantasies of Betrayal.* Boston: University of Massachusetts Press, 2010.

Mlotek, Haley. "Jane Fonda's Extreme Bravery, Then and Now." *Vulture*, May 31, 2018, https://www.vulture.com/2018/05/jane-fondas-extreme-bravery-then-and-now.html.

Rolling Stone. "Talking with Jane Fonda for Rolling Stone's 40th Anniversary." May 8, 2007, https://www.rollingstone.com/politics/politics-news/talking-with-jane-fonda-for-rolling-stones-40th-anniversary-237564/.

Ross, Steven J. *Hollywood Left and Right: How Movie Stars Shaped American Politics.* New York: Oxford University Press, 2011.

Seidman, Barbara. "'The Lady Doth Protest Too Much, Methinks': Jane Fonda, Feminism, and Hollywood." In *Women and Film*, edited by Janet Todd, 186–230. New York: Holmes & Meier, 1988.

Shorto, Russell. *Jane Fonda: Political Activism.* Brookfield, CT: Millbrook Press, 1991.

Vadim, Roger. *Bardot, Deneuve, Fonda: My Life with the Three Most Beautiful Women in the World.* New York: Simon & Schuster, 1986.

Williams, Linda. *Screening Sex*. Durham, NC: Duke University Press, 2008.

Zeidler, Jeanne. "Speaking Out, Selling Out, Working Out: The Changing Politics of Jane Fonda." In *Women and American Foreign Policy: Lobbyists, Critics and Insiders*, edited by Edward P. Crapol. Wilmington, DE: Scholarly Resources, 1992.

Zheutlin, Barbara, and David Talbot. *Creative Differences: Profiles of Hollywood Dissidents*. Boston: South End Press, 1978.

INDEX

Page numbers in italics indicate photographs

ABOUT THE AUTHOR

Jennifer Corbett

Nelson Pressley was a longtime *Washington Post* theater critic / arts contributor and a staff critic from 2013 to 2019. He is the author of the 2014 book *American Playwriting and the Anti-political Prejudice* and the David Mamet chapter for *Modern American Drama: Playwriting in the 1980s*, and has written for *American Theatre*, the *Sondheim Review*, the *Eugene O'Neill Review*, and *Irish Theatre Magazine.* His undergrad degree included a concentration in film studies, and he subsidized part of his graduate work by managing video stores in the heyday of home movie rentals. He lives in Delaware.